HEALTH WORKFORCE GOVERNANCE

Law, Ethics and Governance Series

Series Editor: Charles Sampford, Director, Key Centre for Ethics, Law, Justice and Governance, Griffith University, Australia

Recent history has emphasised the potentially devastating effects of governance failures in governments, government agencies, corporations and the institutions of civil society. 'Good governance' is seen as necessary, if not crucial, for economic success and human development. Although the disciplines of law, ethics, politics, economics and management theory can provide insights into the governance of organisations, governance issues can only be dealt with by interdisciplinary studies, combining several (and sometimes all) of those disciplines. This series aims to provide such interdisciplinary studies for students, researchers and relevant practitioners.

Recent titles in the series

Ethics and Socially Responsible Investment
A Philosophical Approach
William Ransome and Charles Sampford
ISBN 978-0-7546-7581-5

Improving Health Care Safety and Quality
Reluctant Regulators
Judith Healy
ISBN 978-0-7546-7644-7

Idealism and the Abuse of Power
Lessons from China's Cultural Revolution
Zhuang Hui-yun
ISBN 978-0-7546-7208-1

Integrity Systems for Occupations
Andrew Alexandra and Seumas Miller
ISBN 978-0-7546-7749-9

Promoting Integrity
Evaluating and Improving Public Institutions
Edited by Brian W. Head, A.J. Brown and Carmel Connors
ISBN 978-0-7546-4986-1

Health Workforce Governance

Improved Access, Good Regulatory Practice, Safer Patients

Edited by

STEPHANIE D. SHORT
The University of Sydney, Australia

FIONA MCDONALD
Queensland University of Technology, Australia

Routledge
Taylor & Francis Group
LONDON AND NEW YORK

First published 2012 by Ashgate Publishing

2 Park Square, Milton Park, Abingdon, Oxon OX14 4RN
711 Third Avenue, New York, NY 10017, USA

Routledge is an imprint of the Taylor & Francis Group, an informa business

First issued in paperback 2016

British Library Cataloguing in Publication Data
Health workforce governance : improved access, good
regulatory practice, safer patients. -- (Law, ethics and
governance)
1. Health services administration. 2. Medical personnel--
Supply and demand. 3. Health services accessibility.
4. Medical personnel--Discipline. 5. Medical errors--
Prevention. 6. Medical laws and legislation.
I. Series II. Short, Stephanie D., 1956- III. McDonald,
Fiona, LLB.
362.1'068-dc23

Library of Congress Cataloging-in-Publication Data
Short, Stephanie D., 1956-
Health workforce governance: improved access, good regulatory practice,
safer patients / by Stephanie D. Short and Fiona McDonald.
p. cm. -- (Law, ethics and governance)
Includes bibliographical references and index.
ISBN 978-1-4094-2921-0 (hardback)
1. Medical laws and legislation. 2. Medical personnel--Government
policy. 3. Medical care--Law and legislation. 4. Medical personnel--Supply
and demand--Government policy. 5. Medical personnel--Recruiting--Law and
legislation. 6. Medical policy--Social aspects. 7. Occupational
mobility--Social aspects. 8. Labor laws and legislation, International. I.
McDonald, Fiona. II. Title.
K4365.S56 2012
362.1068'3--dc23

2011052194

ISBN 978-1-4094-2921-0 (hbk)
ISBN 978-1-138-27370-2 (pbk)

Contents

List of Figures

List of Tables

List of Abbreviations

ACCC	Australian Competition and Consumer Commission
ACGME	Accreditation Council for Graduate Medical Education (US)
AGA	Agenda for Global Action
AHMAC	Australian Health Ministers' Advisory Council
AHMC	Australian Health Ministers' Conference
AHPRA	Australian Health Practitioner Regulation Agency
AHWAC	Australian Health Workforce Advisory Council
AIDS	Acquired immune deficiency syndrome
AIHW	Australian Institute for Health and Welfare
AIIMS	All India Institute of Medical Sciences
AMA	Australian Medical Association
AMWAC	Australian Medical Workforce Advisory Committee
ANHWT	Australian National Health Workforce Taskforce
APEC	Asia-Pacific Economic Cooperation
ASEAN	Association of South East Asian Nations
AusAID	Australian Agency for International Development
CHPRE	Council on Health Professions Regulatory Excellence (proposed Canada)
CHRE	Council for Healthcare Regulatory Excellence (UK)
CIDA	Canadian International Development Agency
CIHC	Canadian Interprofessional Health Collaborative
CJC	Criminal Justice Commission (Queensland, Australia)
COAG	Council of Australian Governments
CPSM	College of Physicians and Surgeons of Manitoba (Canada)
CPSO	College of Physicians and Surgeons of Ontario (Canada)
CSL	Critical Skills List
DFID	Department for International Development (UK)
EARC	Electoral and Administrative Review Commission
EU	European Union
FNAB	Fine needle aspiration biopsy
GATS	General Agreement on Trade in Services
GP	General Practitioner

GMC	General Medical Council
GDP	Gross Domestic Product
G-20	The Group of Twenty
HIV	Human immunodeficiency virus
HMO	Health Maintenance Organization (US)
HPRAC	Health Professions Regulatory Advisory Council (Canada)
HRH	Human Resources for Health
HRST	Human Resources for Science and Technology
HSC	Hospital for Sick Children (Toronto, Canada)
IAMRA	International Association of Medical Regulatory Authorities
ICR-GHW	International Consortium for Research on Governance of the Health Workforce
IGA	Intergovernmental Agreement
ILO	International Labour Organization
Inpres	*Instruction of the President* (Indonesia)
IOM	International Organization for Migration
JCAHO	Joint Commission on Accreditation of Healthcare Organizations (US)
MDGs	Millennium Development Goals
MGTF	Medical Governance Task Force (proposed for Indonesia)
MIDA	Migration for Development in Africa
MRI	Medical resonance imaging
M&M	Mortality and morbidity
NAFTA	North American Free Trade Agreement
NGO	Non-government organization
NHS	National Health Service (UK)
NPM	New Public Management
NS	Nova Scotia (Canada)
OECD	Organisation for Economic Cooperation and Development
PNS	Permanent civil service employment (Indonesia)
PTT	Contract civil service employment (Indonesia)
RHPA	*Regulated Health Professions Act* (Canada)
RLCH	Royal Liverpool Children's Hospital (UK)
SAMP	Southern African Migration Project
SSA	Sub-Saharan Africa

SSCSAT	Senate Standing Committee on Social Affairs, Science and Technology (Canada)
The Alliance	The Global Health Workforce Alliance
TI	Transparency International
TSAPP	Taskforce on Sexual Abuse of Patients by Physicians (Canada)
UK	United Kingdom
UN	United Nations
URT	United Republic of Tanzania
USA	United States of America
USD	United States dollars
WHO	World Health Organization
WHSC	Winnipeg Health Sciences Centre (Canada)
WTO	World Trade Organization

Contributors

Charles Sampford (BA, LLB, DPhil) was appointed Foundation Dean of Law at Griffith University in March 1991, Foundation Director of the Key Centre for Ethics, Law, Justice and Governance in 1999 and Foundation Director of the Institute for Ethics, Governance and Law (a joint initiative of the United Nations University, Griffith, Queensland University of Technology and Australian National University) in 2004. Professor Sampford has written over 90 articles and chapters in Australian and foreign journals and collections ranging through constitutional law, legal philosophy, legal education, politics, applied ethics and economics and has completed twenty-one books and edited collections for international publishers including OUP, Blackwell, Routledge, Cavendish and Ashgate. Foreign fellowships include the Visiting Senior Research Fellow at St John's College Oxford (1997) and a Fulbright Senior Award to Harvard University (2000) following which he was appointed a member of a task force co-chaired by Secretary Albright and Ambassador Geremek on Threats to Democracy.

Craig Veitch (BA Hons, DipAppSc Rad Ther, PhD) is Professor and Chair in Community Based Health Care in the Faculty of Health Sciences at the University of Sydney, and heads the jointly-funded Community Based Health Care Research Unit at the Royal Rehabilitation Centre Sydney. He is an epidemiologist and health services researcher, with a clinical background in radiation therapy and nuclear medicine. His key research interests include community based health care, community health services development, rural health, primary health care and health services evaluation.

Daniel Klass (MD.CM, FRCP(C), FACP) is Adjunct Professor and Senior Scholar in the Department of Medical Education, University of Manitoba Faculty of Medicine, Canada, and Adjunct Professor in the Department of Medicine, University of Toronto. He recently retired from the post of Associate Registrar, College of Physicians and Surgeons of Ontario, where he was the Director of the Quality Management and Registration Divisions from 2001 to 2009. He graduated from McGill University in 1967 with the degree of doctor of medicine, and obtained his specialty certifications in Internal Medicine and Respiratory Disease in 1973 from the Royal College of Physicians and Surgeons of Canada. Over his 45 year career in medicine, Daniel Klass has been an active researcher in medical education and respiratory physiology, a teacher and administrator in medical education, performance assessment and regulation, and has practised and taught in the field of respiratory medicine. He currently is a consultant in the field of medical education.

Fiona McDonald (BA, LLB, LLM, JSD) is a Senior Lecturer at the School of Law at Queensland University of Technology in Australia and is a member of QUT's Health Law Research Group. Fiona's research focus is health governance, particularly the governance of health professionals, health institutions and health systems. Her recent book, with Ben White and Lindy Willmott (eds.), is *Health Law in Australia* (Thomson, 2010).

Fiona Pacey (BA (Soc Sci) Hons, Grad.Dip.Lab.St, MPP) is a PhD student in the Faculty of Health Sciences at The University of Sydney and a member of the Healthgov network. She was awarded a Master of Politics and Public Policy from Macquarie University in 2007, and has worked in management and policy roles in the field of medical education for over a decade.

Firman Lubis (MD, MPH) is a Professor in the Department of Community Medicine, Faculty of Medicine, University of Indonesia. His core specialisations are epidemiology, biostatistics, socio-anthropology and family medicine. Dr Lubis has collaborated with and served as consultant to key international organizations, including USAID, AusAID, UNFPA, Population Council, Family Health International, WHO, World Bank and ADB.

Hasbullah Thabrany (MD, Dr.PH) is Professor at the School of Public Health, University of Indonesia, Jakarta. He coordinates research and training, and advocates to the Ministry of Health and the Parliament on health policy. He served as the Secretary General of the Indonesian Medical Association and established the Indonesian Association of Health Insurance Managers, aiming at capacity building in health insurance fields. He has worked as a general practitioner and completed his graduate and doctoral studies in health policy and administration at the University of California at Berkeley USA.

Helen Turnbull (BA, LLB) was admitted to legal practice in New Zealand in 1983, in England in 1992 and in New South Wales, Australia in 1997. She is Special Counsel – Professional Conduct for Avant Mutual Group Limited, the largest indemnity organisation for medical practitioners in Australia. Her area of particular expertise and interest is professional regulatory law. She has multi-jurisdictional experience in litigation, health, insurance, disciplinary and medical indemnity law. She advocates on behalf of medical and allied health practitioners in professional conduct matters and appears before parliamentary and government inquiries. She is closely involved in the new National Registration and Accreditation Scheme in Australia.

Judith Healy (BA, MSW, PhD) is an Associate Professor in the Regulatory Institutions Network, Australian National University. She has worked in Australia, the United States and Europe for universities, policy think tanks and the European Observatory on Health Systems and Policies and currently with the Asia Pacific Observatory on Health Systems and Policies. Her research interests include health sector regulation and the comparative analysis of health systems. Her books include, with Martin McKee (eds.) *Hospitals in a Changing Europe* (Open University Press, 2002), also with Martin McKee (eds.) *Health Care: Responding to Diversity* (Oxford University Press, 2004), with Paul Dugdale (eds.) *Patient Safety First: Responsive Regulation in Health Care* (Allen & Unwin, 2009), and her recent sole-authored book is *Improving Health Care Safety and Quality: Reluctant Regulators* (Ashgate 2011).

Kirsten Harley (BSc, BA(Hons), PhD) is a Postdoctoral Research Associate in the Faculty of Health Sciences and Honorary Associate in the Department of Sociology and Social Policy at the University of Sydney, Australia. She is a sociologist whose research interests include public and private health care systems and health care choice, and is a member of the HealthGov network. She received the University of Sydney's inaugural Rita and John Cornforth Medal for PhD Achievement in 2011.

Paul Dugdale (BMBS, MA, MPH, PhD, FAFPHM) is Director of Chronic Disease Management at Canberra Hospital and Health Services and Director of the Australian Centre for Health Stewardship at the Australian National University. He is a public health physician with first-hand governance experience in the health sector, including as ACT Chief Health Officer, Director of General Practice Finance in the Commonwealth Department of Health (Australia) and Medical Superintendent of Liverpool Hospital (NSW). He is the author of *Doing Health Policy in Australia* (Allen & Unwin, 2008) and editor (with Judith Healy) of *Patient Safety First: Responsive Regulation in Health Care* (Allen & Unwin, 2009).

Robyn R. Iredale (BA Hons, MA, Phd) is an Adjunct Associate Professor at the Australian Demographic and Social Research Institute at the Australian National University. She has undertaken a wide range of projects on labour migration (especially skilled migration), skills recognition, women migrants, refugees and related issues. She has wide experience in Asia and the Pacific. She has undertaken projects for a wide range of Australian and international agencies, including the International Labour Organization, the Association of South East Asian Nations, UNCTAD and the International Organization for Migration.

Stephanie D. Short (DipPthy, BA (Hons), MSc (Economics), PhD) is Professor and Associate Dean Postgraduate in the Faculty of Health Sciences at the University of Sydney, Australia. She is Convenor of the HealthGov Network of researchers, regulators and professionals. She is the author, with George Palmer, of *Health Care and Public Policy: An Australian Analysis* (Palgrave Macmillan, 4th edition, 2010).

Suchaya Thongyoo (BAppSci, MPubHealth) has qualifications in Health Information Management and Public Health. She has worked as a research assistant in the Faculty of Health Sciences at the University of Sydney.

Toni Schofield (BA Hons, Dip.Ed., PhD) is Associate Professor in the Faculty of Health Sciences at the University of Sydney. Her research and teaching focus on sociology and public policy mainly in relation to health and health care. Specific areas of interest are gender and health, workplace health, the health workforce and alcohol use and harm minimization. Professor Schofield has served as a health policy and research consultant for numerous Australian and international organizations, most recently the Canadian Department of Health (2011) and the Swedish Secretariat for Gender Equality (2012)

Valentin D. Hadjiev (LLB, Dip H Ed) is a Senior Research Assistant in international law at the Law and Justice Research Centre, Queensland University of Technology, and Adjunct Research Fellow, Institute of Ethics, Governance and Law, Griffith University in Brisbane, Australia. He is a member of the HealthGov network. He has worked as an academic in international law at the Universities of Sofia and Sydney and been a Senior Fulbright Fellow to the University of Virginia Law School.

William Lahey (BA, BA (Jurisprudence), LLM) is an Associate Professor, Schulich School of Law, Dalhousie University, Canada. He has qualifications in Arts, Jurisprudence and Law from Mount Allison, Oxford and Toronto. He teaches Public Law, Administrative Law and Health Systems Law and Policy. His research interests include law and health systems, administrative law, legal history, and regulatory governance in a range of sectors, including health and environment. He has served as Nova Scotia's Assistant Deputy Minister of Health and Deputy Minister of Environment and Labour and is past Director of the Dalhousie Health Law Institute.

William Ransome (BA Hons, PhD) is a research fellow in philosophical ethics at the Law and Justice Research Centre, Queensland University of Technology, and adjunct research fellow and program director for corporate governance and social responsibility at the Key Centre for Ethics, Law, Justice and Governance, Griffith University. His research interests include moral psychology, ancient Greek and Kantian ethics, virtue ethics, theories of wellbeing, the ethics of governance and corporate social responsibility. His recent books include *Moral Reflection* (2009) and *Ethics and Socially Responsible Investment: A Philosophical Approach* (2011, co-authored with Charles Sampford).

Yaslis Ilyas is a Senior Lecturer in the Graduate Program, School of Public Health, University of Indonesia. His health workforce and health services research has attracted support from the Ministry of Health, Indonesia; the Health Office of Provinces in Indonesia; Office of Human Resources Development, Province of Papua, Indonesia; the World Health Organization (WHO); the World Bank; the Asia Development Bank; and UNICEF.

Acknowledgements

Many colleagues have assisted with the production of this edited collection. We thank all our authors for their valuable contributions and forbearance in meeting tight deadlines. We are grateful to our publisher at Ashgate, Alison Kirk, for her advice and support, and we thank Professor Charles Sampford, the series editor for Law, Ethics and Governance, for his strategic advice at crucial stages of the project. Carmel Connors, Publications Manager in the Institute for Ethics, Governance and Law at Griffith University, provided wise counsel and advice on numerous occasions for which we are grateful. We thank also Professor Bill Duncan, former Director of the Law and Justice Research Centre at the Queensland University of Technology and Valentin Hadjiev for their ongoing support of HealthGov and this project. We thank also Professor Gwynnyth Llewellyn, Dean of the Faculty of Health Sciences, and the University of Sydney which has provided a congenial base for HealthGov and this project. We acknowledge support received from the Australian Research Council which funded the establishment of HealthGov as a division of the Governance Research Network, GovNet. Many of the ideas and evidence presented herein derive from work generated by members of HealthGov, a network of regulators, professionals and academics established in 2007 as a division of the Australian Research Council-funded Governance Network.

From the Faculty of Health Sciences at the University of Sydney, Dr Kirsten Harley provided invaluable intellectual and practical input to the project and manuscript. We are also grateful to Kanchan Marcus for her expert assistance with the manuscript. We thank our colleagues in HealthGov at the University of Sydney and nationally, the International Association of Medical Regulatory Authorities, and the International Consortium for Research on Governance of the Health Workforce, most notably Howard Adelman, Emeritus Professor of Philosophy at York University and Adjunct Professor Daniel Klass, former associate registrar of the College of Physicians and Surgeons of Ontario. Indeed we dedicate this book to Howard Adelman and Daniel Klass for their pioneering work on the transnational regulation of the medical profession.

Stephanie Short and Fiona McDonald,
Sydney and Brisbane, April 2012

INTRODUCTION

Chapter 1

The Health Workforce Governance Continuum: Improved Access, Good Regulatory Practice, Safer Patients

Stephanie D. Short and Fiona McDonald

Governance of the health workforce is an important and topical issue internationally as demonstrated by substantial reports from the World Health Organization (WHO), the Organisation for Economic and Cooperative Development (OECD) and the European Union (EU), amongst others. This book, *Health Workforce Governance: Improved Access, Good Regulatory Practice, Safer Patients*, provides a critical analysis of the complex arena of health workforce governance at local, national, and international levels.

Traditionally, the governance of the health workforce has been addressed at provincial and national levels in what Moran (1999) has described as a 'closed regulatory world'. In an increasingly globalized world, the governance of the health workforce is moving from a national pursuit to a global endeavour, with increasing recognition of the international market in health professionals and the impact of globalism on regulation. There is an increasing appreciation that although the governance of the health workforce raises some specialist issues, it does not sit apart and aloof from broader governance related trends and broader workforce related developments. It is also moving from a process that was controlled by the health professions to processes with greater public engagement, increased transparency, and a focus on the public interest.

Improved Access, Good Regulatory Practice and Safer Patients

We submit that these evolutions create a governance continuum where challenges to ensure access to health services and health professionals (improved access) merge with concerns about reforming existent governance structures to ensure that they are participatory, accountable, transparent, fair and just (good regulatory practice) and how to ensure the quality of health services and the safety of patients (safer patients).The challenge faced by policy makers, planners and regulators is to create integrated governance strategies that balance these three sets of concerns and which take into account the impact of an increasingly globalized world. The effectiveness of our health systems depends to a large degree upon the workforce that provides health services but this raises some important questions. Where does health workforce regulation fit in relation to government ambitions as a whole? How can we most effectively integrate the consequences of globalization into health workforce governance? Do our systems have the coherence they need to ensure improved access, good regulatory and governance practices and safer patients? How can existing models of governance be modified and developed to more adequately serve the health professions and the public? While many chapters focus on developments in Australia and the Asia and Pacific region, the challenges discussed and the conceptual framework employed are of international applicability and contain valuable lessons for policy makers, planners, regulators, and professions internationally.

Health Workforce Governance contributes to the literature on managing the health workforce in three significant ways.

First, it acknowledges that the central reality of public problem-solving is collaborative in nature (Braithwaite, Healy and Dwan 2005) and as such this book includes contributors who represent a range of perspectives and experiences to inform and enrich the debate in this area – the regulators and regulated, academics, lawyers and health managers – as opposed to only presenting an academic perspective.

Secondly, the scope of the book is global. Much of the subject matter of *Health Workforce Governance* covers issues that recur in many jurisdictions and which cross international borders and, as indicated at the beginning of this chapter, the issue is attracting the focus of global and regional, as well as national and provincial actors.

And thirdly, *Health Workforce Governance* brings together concerns about access, regulatory practices and quality and safety within the heuristic framework of the health workforce governance continuum. *Health Workforce Governance* advocates an integrated approach to governance of the health workforce suggesting three primary fields of concern – improved access, good regulatory practice, and patient safety – that must be addressed by health workforce policy makers, planners and regulators. The inter-connectedness of these facets of health workforce governance must be acknowledged in the debates about how best to manage the health workforce.

The Health Workforce Governance Continuum

This book describes and analyses the health workforce governance continuum in three interrelated parts. In Part I we focus on improved access, in the second part we focus on good practice, and then in the third part we address patient safety. We of course acknowledge that as this is an integrated continuum, while the chapters in each part may focus on one of these themes they also touch upon or encompass the other elements of the continuum. This notion of the health workforce continuum is unique to this book. Whilst it is not unusual to combine the twin challenges of health professional regulation (protection of the public) with the quality of care (safer patients) it is rare to combine these twin challenges with the most fundamental challenge: the right to health (access to health care). In an increasingly globalized world, with global health challenges and a highly mobile global workforce, the reality is that improvements in one jurisdiction's health workforce may have detrimental effects in another jurisdiction. Concerns about brain drain, brain gain and brain circulation are local, national and international.

Moreover, whilst there may be improvements in one domain, such as quality of care, through improved regulatory standards, this can very well present new challenges for policy makers and planners who are responsible for providing quality health care to meet local health needs, as the care may very well become less accessible financially, geographically and/or culturally. The complexity and interconnectedness of the challenges faced by regulators and others working in this area is illustrated by this continuum. This is the first book to present and analyse these contemporary health workforce governance challenges within this integrated conceptual framework.

Improved Access

The first chapter in Part I of this book sets the scene with analysis of the major issues relating to access to health services and health professionals. Ensuring access to health services is a significant concern and a challenge in developed and developing countries. This is a complex issue involving an examination of global patterns of migration, policies in respect of recruitment and integration and the organisation of work. The first chapter focuses on the global mobility of health professionals. Robyn Iredale, a labour migration specialist as an academic and a consultant, examines the historic context and the major players: the sending countries and their health systems; the receiving countries with their workforce shortages; and the migrants themselves with their desire for better pay, professional opportunities and improved life chances. The viability of health systems in poorer countries is of grave international concern. The migration of health professionals from these countries places a major strain on their health systems and raises questions about sustainability. She looks at national, regional and international initiatives that attempt to balance the three sets of interests; most especially the World Health Organization's (WHO) Global Code of Practice on International Recruitment of Health Personnel (2010).

We then turn to examine, from a philosophical point of view, the endeavours of the World Health Organization and other agencies to create more ethical and sustainable health professional recruitment practices. In Chapter 3 ethicists William (Bill) Ransome and Charles Sampford introduce and explain the 'integrity systems' approach to ethical and sustainable governance, and outline its relevance for global health professional recruitment. The starting point, in their view, involves 'integrity mapping' of current systems of practice which aims to bring to light areas of existing and potential ethical tension for individuals and institutions in contemporary recruitment regimes.

In the fourth chapter, sociologist Toni Schofield advances a gender and organizations approach to conceptualize the global health workforce 'crisis' and inequities in access to health care. The chapter focuses on the impending health workforce shortages in wealthy countries that occur mainly among rural and remote communities, and in the more socially and economically marginalized communities in urban areas. The chapter analyses the *Working Together for Health Report*, produced by the World Health Organization in 2006, which identified an imminent global health workforce crisis. Whilst the Report supported the transformation of prevailing hierarchical clinical relations, this has not been realized to any great extent. Yes, independent management structures for the allied and nursing professions have been established in public hospitals and other public health settings. However, this has typically been accompanied by the appointment of the team's medical practitioner, usually with specialist qualifications, as the director. Much research and evidence suggests the gendered organizational subordination of the allied and nursing professions is primarily accountable for problems with morale and retention, and hence workforce shortages. Schofield concludes '… being a man or a woman does matter – not only in terms of who does what work but also in relation to who is likely to *stay* doing it'.

Chapter 5 reveals and analyses attempts to address health workforce governance challenges in Indonesia, the fourth most populous country in the world (and the most populous Moslem country in the world). Stephanie Short, Hasbullah Thabrany and colleagues report the results of a collaborative bilateral multidisciplinary study of medical governance in Indonesia. The key challenges in Indonesia are the interrelated problems of maldistribution of health professionals, which raises issues of access, the quality of the medical workforce, and patient safety. They outline the processes undertaken by key stakeholders: government decision-makers, public officials, health professionals, consumers and academics, to develop an integrated governance continuum to address these challenges.

Good Regulatory Practice

The chapters in Part II of *Health Workforce Governance* explore the many challenges around how to regulate the health professions to ensure good practice. Regulation is generally a process of applying rules to ensure order. It is generally accepted that a robust regulatory framework is required to address workforce issues and that such a framework is particularly important when considering the health workforce, given the levels of risk associated with the provision of health services. But what should or could this framework look like? What evidence, if any, informs it? What policy imperatives drive it? And crucially what impact does a regulatory framework have on practice and what influence does practice have on policy and regulation? We begin with legal academic Fiona McDonald's overview and analysis of international trends in health professional regulation, most especially in Britain, Canada, Australia and New Zealand. Traditional regulation relied on the trinity of regulatory tools that pre-dated modern health systems: civil litigation, criminal law and government-sanctioned self-regulation. Over the last 25 years these regulatory instruments have been challenged and reformed. This contemporary period is characterized by less deference to the professions, increased accountability of the professions to the public, and increased pressure on regulators to focus on protection of the public (rather than the regulated) as evidenced in new forms of responsive regulation (see also Chapter 11). Whereas traditional regulation protected professional and clinical autonomy, the contemporary regulatory regime is characterized by a broader and more complex mosaic of governance actors and strategies.

Chapter 7, by William Lahey, a legal academic and former provincial policy maker, traces the evolution of an emergent paradigm in Canadian health workforce governance: collaborative self-regulation. This means collaboration among health professional regulatory bodies, that is colleges or associations which are responsible for self-regulation of the professions in the provinces of Canada, most especially Ontario and Nova Scotia, to ensure effective, fair and just processes for regulating health professionals. In Ontario the Health Professions Regulatory Advisory Council is mandated by legislation to facilitate collaboration, and the Nova Scotia approach sees inter-professional collaboration voluntarily nurtured from below by its 22 regulated health professions. These two provinces have distinctive approaches to professional self-regulation, based on institutional consolidation and coordinated effort respectively. In Lahey's view this natural experiment provides ideal material for analysis by regulators, policy makers and researchers.

The next chapter, Chapter 8, is written from the perspective of an experienced physician, academic and former medical regulator in Ontario, Canada. Klass contends that professional self-regulation can and should continue to play a role in regulation, even within the staggeringly complex environment of contemporary health care. Klass reflects on the limitations of professional self-regulation which derive from the widespread perception of medicine as a self-serving profession, and concerns about negligence, over-servicing and related problems. He reflects on the approach taken in Australia, New Zealand, the UK and Ireland, in which separate agencies have been created under government mandate, with lay management, to conduct disciplinary investigation and management, with physicians acting in advisory or consultative roles. Klass then provides a rationale for the continuing role for self-regulation and argues in support of a particular innovation: evidence-based regulation. With this innovation each of the models of professional regulation can be scrutinized and evaluated at provincial, national and international levels in the interests of improving health workforce governance processes.

This brings us to the case of Australia, discussed in Chapter 9 by Fiona Pacey and colleagues, and the establishment in 2010 of a national scheme for health practitioner registration and accreditation. This world-leading development, underpinned by legislation, provides consistency across six states and two territories for ten of the largest health professions: including medicine, nursing and midwifery, and dental practitioners (see Table 9.3). Pacey and colleagues discuss the evolution of this scheme which saw 80 governance bodies brought into one national regulatory and accreditation scheme. The chapter identifies the problems, policy solutions and politics that opened a window of opportunity onto this healthcare policy landscape. Crucial was the decision-making role of the Coalition of Australian Governments, and the role of the Productivity Commission which effectively articulated the need for reform of health workforce governance in Australia to enable workforce mobility, as well as in the interests of ensuring consistency amongst the regulated – fairness. Pacey and colleagues bring to light the significance of the Jayant Patel scandal at Bundaberg Hospital, which focused the minds of governments, professionals and the community on the failure by a number of actors to adequately regulate the practices of this overseas-trained surgeon (later convicted of the manslaughter of three patients).

We turn then to attend to governance of primary health care, in Chapter 10. Paul Dugdale's analysis focuses on the styles of thought and rationality that pervade contemporary primary care governance drawing on his experience as a physician, health manager and academic. This chapter draws on the ideas of responsive regulation and networked governance developed by John Braithwaite and others (see Chapter 11). This approach sees regulatory agencies working together in a network of interdependent strategies that variously clash, overlap or align. The chapter focuses on meeting the primary care governance challenges created by chronic diseases, particularly cardiovascular disease, diabetes and lung disease that will increasingly affect the baby boomer generation. The creation in 2011 of new healthcare governance arrangements for secondary (local hospital networks) and primary care (Medicare locals) in Australia represents a new level of formal cooperation between the state/territory and federal governments in health care governance. Medicare locals represent also, according to Dugdale, opportunities for formal renegotiations to take place between patients, carers and health professionals in order to place patients at the helm of primary health care governance.

Patient Safety

Part III comprises three chapters that foreground patient safety. While ensuring access to health services is important, it is also important to ensure, as much as it is possible to do so, the safety of patients receiving those services. Incidents in which patients have been harmed and research confirming significant rates of adverse events in hospitalised patients has highlighted the risks associated with the provision of health services. This increased perception of risks (by all actors and especially the public), coupled with changing societal norms that demand greater accountability, have focused attention on prioritising safety and quality in the health sector. These chapters, from a social scientist (Judith Healy) a legal academic (Fiona McDonald) and a practising lawyer (Helen Turnbull), provide valuable and distinctive insights into this vexed component of the health workforce governance continuum.

Judith Healy's chapter (Chapter 11) addresses one of the core questions posed in this book: does health professional regulation protect the profession or the public? This chapter traces answers to this question back to the origins of government sanctioned self-regulation in England in the nineteenth century. Since the 1980s, however, we have seen an international trend away from government sanctioned self-regulation towards a network of actors and strategies designed to protect the safety of the public. This trend is analysed with reference to the 'regulatory pyramid' (Braithwaite et al. 2005) that offers a framework for classifying and understanding responsive regulation, that is responsive to context, culture and conduct. As part of this transformation the public perception of the medical profession has moved between a 'good guys interpretation' on one hand and a 'greedy guys interpretation' on the other. This shift towards pluralist or co-regulation involves a greater number of actors and regulatory strategies in order to produce safer health care (Allsop and Jones 2006). In Healy's view transparency has become a key instrument for increasing accountability of the profession to the public and of safety, and in this regard Australia has lagged behind North American and European countries.

This theme of increasing transparency and accountability in the interests of ensuring the safety of patients pervades the penultimate chapter, by Fiona McDonald, as well. This chapter focuses on the role of investigatory inquiries conducted in Canada and Britain since 1980 in response to scandals that may be seen to represent perceived failures in health professional regulation. The most notable of these include the inquiry into mortality rates associated with paediatric cardiac surgery at the Bristol Royal Infirmary, and the inquiries sparked by the behaviour of general practitioner Harold Shipman (also known as Dr Death), later convicted of the murder of 15 patients, in the north of England. In this chapter McDonald argues that these scandals have tended to undermine public trust in the profession, and thus create a demand for greater controls to be placed upon the health professions by the state or the profession to ensure patient safety. Of particular note is the conclusion that the scandals in Britain were larger in both scale and consequence as compared with Canada. This goes some way towards explaining why government-sanctioned self-regulation continues to be the primary mode of regulation in Canada, while Britain has seen the introduction of government oversight of health professional regulators.

Health Workforce Governance draws to a close with a moving account of a case in which a highly-respected surgeon performed a mastectomy on the wrong breast, with serious consequences for the patient and the professional. This chapter illustrates how major clinical errors can and do occur. Helen Turnbull, a senior medical defence lawyer, then outlines how such major clinical errors should be identified and prevented in the future. This requires a combination of forms of self-regulation by health professionals, including the development and application of checklists, reliance on the values, behaviours and relationships that underpin professionalism (including courtesy, kindness, understanding, humility, honesty and confidentiality) and systemic support at the organizational level.

The health workforce governance continuum illuminates the complexity and interconnectedness of the challenges faced by regulators and others working in this area, a complexity only enhanced by increasing globalization. We anticipate that questions about how to achieve more effective health workforce governance will continue to be a subject of debate, discussion and innovation and we hope that the ideas and evidence discussed in this book will enhance the quality of these deliberations.

References

Allsop, J. and Jones, K. 2006. *Quality Assurance in Medical Regulation in an International Context. Report for the Department of Health.* Lincoln: University of Lincoln.

Allsop, J. and Saks, M., eds 2002. *Regulating the Health Professions.* London: Sage.

Braithwaite, J., Healy, J. and Dwan, K. 2005. *The Governance of Health Safety and Quality.* Commonwealth of Australia.

Braithwaite, J., Makkai, T. and Braithwaite, V.A. 2007. *Regulating Aged Care: Ritualism and the New Pyramid.* Cheltenham: Edward Elgar.

Commission of the European Communities. 2008. *Green Paper on the European Workforce for Health.* [Online]. COM(2008) 725 final. Brussels: European Union. Available at: http://ec.europa.eu/health/archive/ph_systems/docs/workforce_gp_en.pdf [Accessed: September 2011].

Davies, M. 2007. *Medical Self Regulation: Crisis and Change.* Hampshire: Ashgate.

Freckelton, I., ed. 2006. Regulating Health Practitioners. *Law in Context,* 23(2).

Healy, J. 2011. *Improving Health Care Safety and Quality: Reluctant Regulators.* Farnham: Ashgate.

Healy, J. and Dugdale, P., eds 2009. *Patient Safety First: Responsive Regulation in Health Care.* Sydney: Allen & Unwin.

Healy, J. and McKee, M., eds 2004. *Accessing Health Care: Responding to Diversity.* Oxford: Oxford University Press.

Kuhlmann, E. and Saks, M., eds 2008. *Rethinking Professional Governance: International Directions in Healthcare.* Bristol: The Policy Press.

Moran, M. 1999. *Governing the Health Care State: A Comparative Study of the United Kingdom, the United States, and Germany.* Manchester: Manchester University Press.

OECD (Organisation for Economic Cooperation and Development). 2008. *The Looming Crisis in the Health Workforce: How Can OECD Countries Respond?*, OECD Health Policy Studies. Paris: OECD.

WHO (World Health Organization). 2006. *Working Together for Health*. Geneva: WHO.

WHO (World Health Organization). 2010. *Global Code of Practice on International Recruitment of Health Personnel*. Geneva: WHO.

PART I
Improved Access

Chapter 2
Major Issues in the Global Mobility of Health Professionals

Robyn R. Iredale

Background

The international mobility of health professionals has increased markedly in recent years and has come to include very different and complicated patterns. One would be hard pressed to find a country that was not impacted by mobility, somehow, in its efforts to provide accessible, quality health services.

The movement of health workers, especially doctors, began in the colonial era when doctors and other health professionals from Europe provided services to the colonies.[1] Later this movement reversed as doctors moved from the former colonies to the former colonial powers in the quest for higher education and better opportunities. From the 1960s this movement grew, as part of what Connell (2010: 40–44) describes as the second phase of migration and the globalization of health care. Migration also commenced to other countries, such as Australia, Canada and the USA, with the end of their discriminatory immigration policies. Mejia et al. (1979: 399–400) state that by the early 1970s 'about 6 per cent of the world's physicians (140,000) were located in countries other than those of which they were nationals'.

In Connell's third phase, globalization, movements have escalated and expanded to include large numbers of doctors, nurses and nursing aides (Connell 2010: 48). The patterns have become increasingly more global and more complex. In Asia, India, Sri Lanka, Pakistan, Nepal and Bangladesh have been joined by a range of other countries, notably the Philippines, China, Vietnam, Indonesia and Malaysia, as major sources of health workers. In Africa, Egypt, Zimbabwe, Botswana, South Africa and others have become sources of doctors and nurses and the Caribbean has become a notable supplier of skilled health workers. Flows have also escalated from more developed countries, such as Australia, New Zealand and Finland.

Some of the sending countries lack adequate resources to pay higher wages, upgrade facilities, provide promotional opportunities or hire enough staff to meet their real needs. Thus many health workers are under pressure and look for opportunities to leave. At the same time, some governments see overseas

1 Connell's (2010) first phase in the globalization of health care.

labour deployment as a means of siphoning off surplus labour or as a way of earning valuable foreign exchange (for example, Myanmar, Philippines, India). In countries such as India, Pakistan and the Philippines there are more health professionals trained than are required and/or existing health workers retrain for international labour markets (for example, doctors retraining as nurses).

English-speaking countries are the major destinations for skilled health workers, though the Middle East, other parts of Asia and elsewhere have also become significant destinations. Once particular flows of migrants emerge, they tend to spawn further movements as people learn more easily about overseas opportunities and have friends and family who can smooth their adjustment in the destination country. Migration can, therefore, be supply-driven when skilled workers migrate to find their own jobs. At the same time, destination countries have a growing range of policies, visas and programmes to enable the entry of health workers in growing demand – due to aging, increased expectations, the rise of private facilities, inadequate training and high attrition rates. The role of recruiters, which include governments and private companies, has become extremely important as they advertise widely, interview offshore and provide assistance with migration applications and relocation costs. This makes migration much easier.

At the same time as developed country demand has been increasing, so has demand in developing countries. More rapidly growing populations, the rise of HIV/AIDS and other non-communicable diseases, aging, changing family structures, rising expectations as a result of education and access to television have all had an impact on the demand for health workers. Supply has simultaneously been affected by a shortage of finance for training programmes, high attrition rates (especially in countries with high rates of HIV/AIDS), out-migration and preference for other occupations.

Movements are both permanent and temporary. Temporary movement includes the General Agreement on Trade in Services (GATS) Mode 4 movements whereby the movement of natural persons as service providers is promoted under the World Trade Organization's (WTO) trade arrangements. GATS Mode 4 movement is for a definite period and cannot transform into permanent residency, whereas some temporary movement ultimately becomes permanent.

There are three main sets of forces at work in all mobility: the sending countries and their interests; the receiving countries and their shortages, conditions and treatment of overseas trained workers; and migrants' desires for better pay, self-improvement and a chance to upgrade their skills. Key stakeholders are involved in all three. The challenge is how to retain the right to free movement of all individuals while at the same time ensuring that all people, especially those in sending countries, have access to an adequate and appropriate health care system. Mobility may lead to shortages at home but it is not the only factor: insufficient training opportunities, lack of interest in the occupation and high mortality (due, for example, to HIV/AIDS) are other possible explanations. Mobility, however, can compound an existing shortage. Connell (2010: 47) argues that:

> Health workers were the forerunners in the gradual globalisation of skilled migration and, then as now, their migration was of greater concern than other skilled international migration flows, just as the idea of a brain drain was largely centred on the mobility of health workers.

It is debatable whether they were the forerunners but the impact of these migration flows on the health systems of both sending and receiving countries, and on the workers themselves, has raised growing concern at a variety of levels – national, regional and international. This chapter will examine the emergence of these concerns and identify the major issues that are impacting on the delivery of quality services. The focus will be on developing countries as they are in the most dire need and they are at risk of not meeting their obligations to provide universal access to even basic services. The possible options for national governments to alleviate shortages and concerns about the quality of their health workforces will be discussed.

However, the paucity of service providers in some of the poorer countries and the threat that this poses to the viability of their health systems is of grave international concern. International actions will be critically examined and the vital importance of receiving countries becoming more self-sufficient will be proposed as the most important policy step that needs to be undertaken.

Rising Concern and Research into the Mobility of Health Professionals

The National Level

Concern about health workforce issues is widespread and has long been the subject of enquiries, research and government reports in some of the more industrialized countries. The issues vary from place to place but mainly stem from the political pressure that is brought to bear in the absence of the provision of adequate and appropriate health care services. These issues need to be understood as they are what is driving the global increase in skilled health worker flows.

In more developed countries this often relates to actual or relative shortages, shortages of particular types of skilled health workers (for example, specialists, General Practitioners (GPs), nurses, aged care workers, and so on) or shortages in particular areas. Countries such as Australia, Canada, the US and the UK have long histories of shortages of health workers and of bringing in overseas trained workers – either by direct recruitment or by dint of their wider immigration policies. The USA with the largest number of doctors and little loss to international migration is expected to have a projected shortage of 200,000 doctors by 2020 (Cooper and Aiken 2006) and this has been the focus of their attention.[2]

2 It has high doctor:patient ratios and calculates its needs accordingly.

Australia has experienced geographical and particular specialty shortages for a long time but, since the late 1990s, the situation has become more serious. A major change occurred after 1996, driven by the severe shortage of doctors in disadvantaged and rural and remote areas and subsequent employer demand. There was a marked policy shift and a rapid rise in temporary arrivals on 422 visas (medical practitioner temporary – ended in June 2010), 442 visas (occupational trainee) and 457 (temporary business long-stay) visas. The diversity of sources grew and by 2001 temporary recruit doctors were arriving from over 27 countries, with the major sources being UK/Ireland, India, Malaysia, Sri Lanka, China and Germany (Hawthorne 2007). At this time Australia was unusual, as the Organization for Economic Cooperation and Development (OECD) (2007a: 191–192) points out.

> Very few countries have specific migration policies for health professionals. Australia is one major exception. The medical practitioner visa (subclass 422) allows foreign nationals, who are medical practitioners, to work in Australia for a sponsoring employer for a maximum of four years. Since April 2005, however, medical practitioners can also apply to the general program for *Temporary Business Long Stay* (*subclass 457*).

Australia and New Zealand have tinkered with their migration selections points systems to better target permanent migrants who are in occupations that are in shortage. For example, the Australian government introduced changes to its priority processing arrangements and revised its shortage occupation list. A new 'Critical Skills List (CSL) was announced, comprising 58 occupations identified as remaining in shortage … ' (OECD 2010: 57–58). 'Since the introduction of the CSL, the number of nurses, general practitioners, mechanical engineers and secondary school teachers increased by 50 per cent compared to the previous year' (OECD 2010: 187).

Other OECD countries have introduced points systems for their permanent skilled migration programmes, similar to Australia and New Zealand, and they can now target occupations in which they have a shortage. This includes the United Kingdom (October 2008), Denmark (July 2008) and the Netherlands (January 2009) (OECD 2010: 58). In the United Kingdom, for example, the points-based system operates under 'Tier 2', for highly skilled workers who are on a shortage occupation list, are recruited after a resident labour market test or are intra-company transferees. Elsewhere, countries are implementing new policies to attract highly-qualified people or modifying existing policies. Japan, Malaysia, Singapore South Korea and Thailand are relatively new to identifying shortages and to using immigration as a means of increasing supply. They mostly admit health workers on temporary work visas, though Singapore is moving in the direction of more permanent migration for selected highly skilled workers.

In less developed countries, the issues have also been the focus of research and/or policy attention. The Philippines Department of Labor *Report on the Problem of the Brain Drain in the Philippines*, partly focusing on nurses, was produced in 1966. The 'apparent validity of the concept [brain drain] was quickly recognised in health contexts elsewhere, from Latin America to India' after this report was produced, according to Connell (2010: 43).[3] India has a long history of medical migration and the All India Institute of Medical Sciences (AIIMS) estimated that 56 per cent of its medical graduates in the period 1956–1980 left the country (Khadria 2004: 35). Khadria argues that India is currently almost at the top of the list of countries as far as emigration of the 'brain drain' category of Human Resources for Science and Technology (HRST) is concerned and these movements include significant numbers of medical practitioners. Khadria (2006) has also examined current trends in nurse education and migration and has explored the possible consequences of these trends for stakeholders in India.

Other regions became increasingly concerned about the outflow of their health workers. Government officials and researchers in Africa (Osunkoya 1974), the Caribbean (Gish 1971), Latin America (Horn 1977) and Pacific states (Bartsch 1974) registered their concerns about 'brain drain' as early as the 1970s. Such concern has continued to be voiced by a growing number of researchers from these regions: for example, Nyonatar and Dovlo (2005) discuss Ghana in 'The Health of the Nation and the Brain Drain in the Health Sector'. South Africa, Ghana and Nigeria were the major African sources in the 1970s but structural adjustment policies that were introduced in many Sub-Saharan Africa (SSA) countries in the 1980s led to a drop in real wage levels (due to inflation) and salary compression (McCoy et al. 2008). The outcome was more rapid out-migration from SSA countries and movement towards a regional health workforce crisis. A recent paper by Clemens and Pettersson (2008) on African health professionals abroad provides valuable data which show that between 60 and 80 per cent of doctors born in Mozambique, Guinea-Bissau, Angola, Liberia, Equatorial Guinea and Sao Tome and Principe were working abroad in 2000. Similar data are available for nurses.

Thomas-Hope (2002: 9) has consistently focused on this issue in relation to the Caribbean and has documented how the processes work, often in the absence of official data. Her 2002 report for the International Labour Organization (ILO) relied largely on newspaper articles and key informant interviews. Almost two-thirds of nurses trained in Jamaica from 1980 to 2000 emigrated, mainly to the United States, and few returned. Thomas-Hope (2002: 9) maintains that notices for teachers and nurses appear frequently in the Jamaican daily newspaper, as in the following case:

> REGISTERED NURSES – FLORIDA U.S.
> Salary from US$36k – $50k annum, no state taxes. Permanent visa processing at no cost for nurse who passes an interview with our Florida Hospital clients. … Call for schedule of local interviews soon (*The Gleaner*, November, 2000, 13F).

3 The term 'brain drain' was first used in the 1960s to describe skilled worker migration between developed countries.

The absence of official or reliable data on the out-migration of health workers has been a considerable hindrance to researchers in less developed regions. It is one reason why country studies have been limited and the impact of the out-migration of health workers has gone relatively unreported in many areas. One possible exception is South Africa. The apartheid era in South Africa increased the exodus of mostly highly skilled South African workers (Mattes et al. 2000) and most emigrated to other countries of the Commonwealth where their health training was usually readily accepted. This trend continued and escalated from 1991, as shown in Figure 2.1. On the other hand, the immigration of health professionals fell sharply over this period.

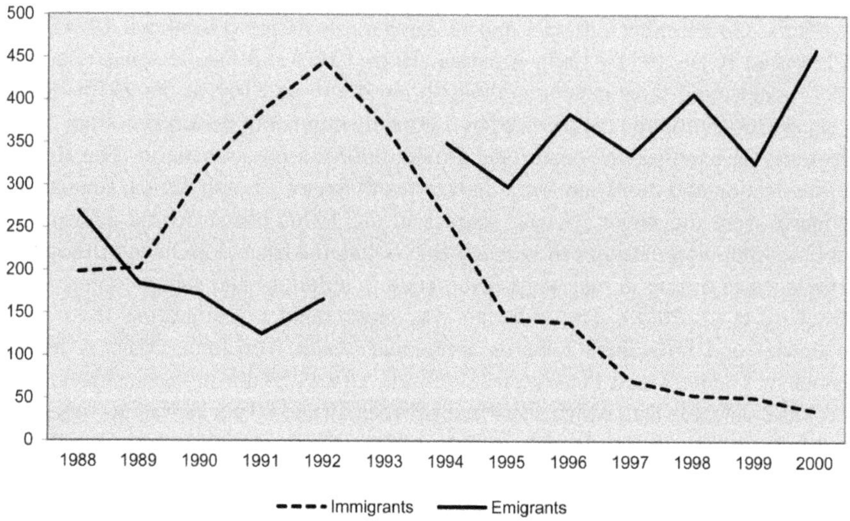

Figure 2.1 Migration flows of health professionals in South Africa, 1988–2000 (official data)

Source: Adapted from Dumont and Meyer 2004

Unlike elsewhere in Africa, South Africa's data collection systems have enabled this type of detailed analysis, though underestimation of emigration by a factor of three or four has been observed.[4] The above data are broken down by occupation and the two major occupations are doctors and nurses, with the latter becoming by far the most important. Besides the availability of data, another important factor that has enabled such research to be conducted in South Africa was the establishment in 1996 of the Southern African Migration Project (SAMP),

4 See OECD (2003: 119).

an international network of organizations.[5] It has been conducting applied research on migration and development issues, as well as providing training and education, since that time. Its Migration Policy Series has included reports on *Gender and the Brain Drain from South Africa* (Dodson 2002) and *The Brain Gain: Skilled Migrants and Immigration Policy in Post-apartheid South Africa* (Mattes et al. 2000). Some of this research was commissioned by the UK Department for International Development (DFID) and the European Commission (see Martineau and Martinez 1997, Martinez and Martineau 2002) thereby indicating their growing interest in the topic of mobile health workforces.[6] Clearly, the availability of funds has been a major factor, as well as SAMP's connection with Canadian academic colleagues in Ontario, in facilitating research.

The Regional Level

Interest in Europe in what is happening in Africa, especially South Africa, is manifested in the major piece of work from the OECD in its flagship publication on mobility, the 2003 Edition of *Trends in International Migration.* It included a chapter on the international mobility of health professionals, using South Africa as a case study. This chapter was the first attempt by a regional body to analyse the growing phenomenon of health worker mobility.

By the late 1990s, the OECD began collecting data from destination countries under its umbrella, and estimating the expatriate rate of doctors and nurses from various source countries to OECD countries. Obviously these data are limited as they exclude all non-OECD destinations. Nevertheless, the chapter on 'Immigrant Health Workers in OECD Countries in the Broader Context of Highly Skilled Migration' in the 2007 Edition of *Trends in International Migration* represents a breakthrough in terms of data collection and availability.[7] The data show that in OECD countries in 2000, 18 per cent of employed doctors and 11 per cent of employed nurses were foreign-born. Nurses from the Philippines (110,000) and doctors from India (56,000) accounted for the largest share of the migrant health workforces in these occupations (OECD 2007a: 163). Asia non-OECD (Asia excluding Japan and South Korea) provided the most doctors to OECD countries (163,600 in 2000). Latin America non-OECD (Latin America excluding Mexico) was the second most important source region and had provided 42,500 doctors:

5 It was funded until 2005 by the Canadian International Development Agency (CIDA) and is currently funded by the UK Department for International Development (DFID).

6 Most research within the UK has focused on nurse and doctor migration and much of this research has adopted a human resources perspective, focusing on issues of ethical recruitment and brain drain from the global south (Buchan and Dovlo 2004, Buchan et al. 2005).

7 The project was financed in part by a grant from the European Commission and by the Swiss authorities.

especially to the US and Spain where 55 per cent of foreign-born doctors were from Latin America. North Africa (28,300) was an important source of doctors for France. Other Africa had provided 30,700, Europe non-OECD had provided 22,200 and Oceania non-OECD (Oceania excluding Australia and New Zealand) had provided 800 doctors.

The study found that the most significant indicator of 'loss' is the percentage of trained doctors who have left a country, or the emigration rate. Using World Health Organization (WHO) Global Health Atlas data on the number of doctors at home and the number working in OECD countries, the OECD calculated emigration rates. The 23 most seriously affected countries are shown in Figure 2.2 where it is seen that all have rates above 40 per cent. Those with above 50 per cent emigration rates have more doctors working in OECD countries than at home. They could, of course, have doctors working elsewhere as well but they do not show up in the OECD data. For example, most Filipino doctors and nurses and Sudanese doctors work outside of OECD countries, in the Middle East (OECD 2007a: 177). Thus, the OECD data underestimate the emigration rate.

Clearly some Caribbean and Pacific Islands and parts of SSA are most affected by the loss of medical practitioners to OECD countries. The most severely affected, Antigua and Barbuda, Grenada and Guyana, had 89.3 per cent, 72.7 per cent and 72.2 per cent, respectively, of their medical workforces overseas in OECD countries in 2000. Fiji (58 per cent) and the Cook Islands (54 per cent) from the Pacific feature in the graph. Five African countries, Mozambique, Angola, Sierra Leone, United Republic of Tanzania (URT) and Liberia, had rates above 50 per cent. All of these, except for URT, have experienced conflict in recent decades and are amongst the poorest countries in the world. South Africa had a rate of 17.4 per cent in 2000, which is not high on the world scale but nevertheless has a serious impact on the population and health of the country. The impact of the shortage on the delivery of HIV/AIDS programmes has been highlighted recently.

Countries that have high emigration rates and low doctor density ratios (number of doctors per 1,000 population) are particularly badly affected: French-speaking African countries, such as Senegal and Malawi, fall into this category. On the other hand, some countries with high emigration rates may be less impacted as they have 'not-too-low' density ratios: Cuba, Barbados, Bahamas and some other Caribbean countries fall into this category.

Subsequently the OECD in collaboration with the WHO undertook a review of health care workers in OECD countries, covering skills shortages and source country for overseas recruitment. Detailed case study country reports were produced for the United States, Italy, France, New Zealand and others. The final report, *The Looming Crisis in the Health Workforce: How Can OECD Countries Respond?* (OECD 2008), was produced as a result of concern about how the demand for health workers would be met in OECD countries in the next 20 years. The challenge 'arises in a world which is already characterized by significant international migration of health workers, both across OECD countries and between some developing countries and the OECD area' (OECD 2008: 9). Growing

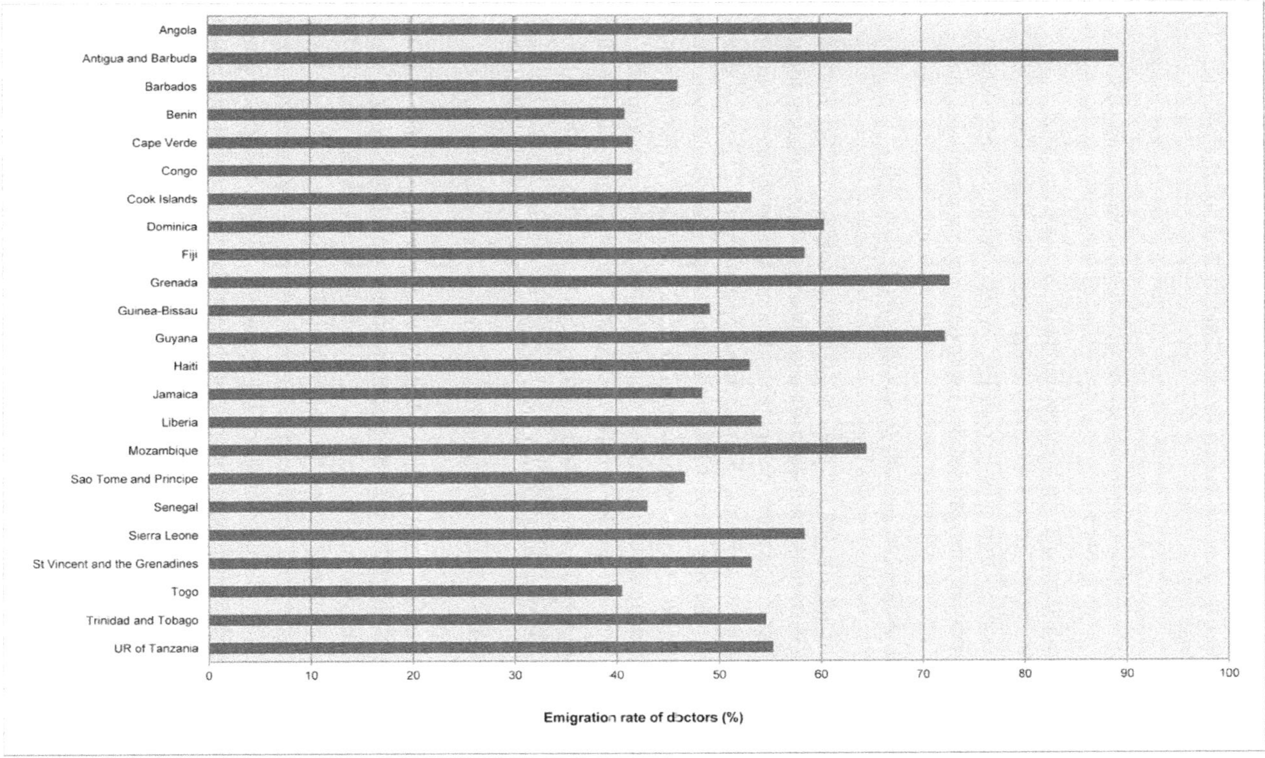

Figure 2.2 Rate of emigration of doctors for the 23 most seriously affected countries, 2000
Source: OECD 2007b

concern was evident in the OECD about the impact on sending countries and this report canvassed various avenues for increasing supply, besides international recruitment. Additional training, encouraging retention and delaying retirement, and raising productivity were all posed as alternate or additional strategies. The report concluded that:

> Reducing reliance on migration by addressing structural imbalances in OECD countries, improving health human resource planning, as well as improving workforce distribution and deployment certainly go hand in hand with confronting some of the ethical concerns about international recruitment of health human resources from poorer countries ... Unless public health systems in origin countries are strengthened, by improving working conditions, thus ensuring better retention within the profession and the country, practices which attempt to block outflows are unlikely to succeed (OECD 2008: 78).

The OECD report urged better international communication on health workforce policy and planning between countries to manage shortages and surpluses, together with the need for better and more comparable data collection systems. No other regional bloc (such as Asia-Pacific Economic Cooperation (APEC), Association of South East Asian Nations (ASEAN), North American Free Trade Agreement (NAFTA) or the Southern Common Market (MERCOSUR)) has collected similar data, conducted the same level of analysis or manifested similar concern. ASEAN commissioned one project on the mobility of health professionals but the study was designed to find ways to increase intra-regional mobility within ASEAN (ASEAN-ANU Research Team 2005).

The International Level

The WHO is the premier body with concern in this area. It has estimated that there are currently about 60.5 million health workers worldwide, and a global shortage of about 4 million health workers (Connell 2010: xi). In the early 1970s, the WHO became concerned about the international migration of skilled health workers and its impacts and sponsored a major study of 40 countries (13 were covered in more detail). The project report by Mejia et al. (1979) found that poorer countries experienced greater losses, income differentials were a major motivating factor, migrants often ended up in junior or other positions that were inappropriate to their level of training, and return migration was limited. The WHO now has a separate policy programme, titled Health Workforce Migration and Retention, and has an ongoing research brief through its many offices around the world. The most recent *Migration of Health Workers* Fact Sheet (No. 301) provides recent data and summarizes the issues for both sending and receiving countries.

The ILO was established in 1919 and became a United Nations (UN) specialized agency in 1946. It has ongoing responsibility for monitoring global workforce trends, conditions and issues. It has a specific focus on labour mobility and the rights of migrant workers, and within this context it has carried out a number of major studies on health workforces. In particular, the *International Migration of Health Workers: Labour and Social Issues* (Bach 2003) came about as a result of a Joint Meeting on Social Dialogue in the Health Services: Institutions, Capacity and Effectiveness that was held at the ILO in Geneva in 2002. The study provides an overview of existing information on the migration of health workers with an emphasis on related labour and social issues; it considers migration policies and practices, working conditions and the role of international standards and trade agreements. It was meant as a preliminary document: to contribute to a 'discussion on policies and practices for socially acceptable management of health worker migration, allowing for decent working conditions for migrant health workers as well as for health workers remaining in their countries, with the aim of ensuring the equal access to quality health services for all' (Bach 2003: 1–2).

The International Organization for Migration (IOM), an intergovernmental body with 118 member and 20 observer states, is committed to the principle that humane and orderly migration benefits migrants and society. To this end it works to meet the operational challenges of migration; advance understanding about migration; encourage development through migration, and respect the dignity and well-being of migrants. The mobility of health workers has come into its focus in the last decade and it has stressed the need for:

> a global approach that considers both the health care systems providers and consumers. Strategies and policies need to be developed and implemented, to ensure better management of the mobility of health care workers. … The shortage of human resources for health has been identified as the most critical public health constraint in achieving the UN Millennium Development Goals, as well as the WHO/UNAIDS '3 by 5 Initiative'.
>
> The management of the mobility of health care workers involves a migration, health and labour perspective. Thus, a multidisciplinary approach is needed to move the agenda from awareness to action (IOM 2006a).

IOM is particularly involved in projects to upgrade the skills of migrant health workers in some contexts and to encourage the temporary or permanent return of skilled health workers to their countries of origin. Some examples are:

- Canadian Live-In Caregivers Orientation (Manila).
- Polish Nurses in the Netherlands: Monitoring and Evaluation of Recruitment, Employment and Return-Reintegration (IOM Hague with IOM. Warsaw/Vienna).
- Establishment of an Information Website for Pakistani Nurses seeking employment abroad (Islamabad).

- Migration for Development in Africa (MIDA) Ghana Health II: A Brain Gain in the Health Sector of Ghana Involving Ghanaians from the Netherlands and Other European Countries.
- IOM MIDA Pilot Project: Return of Qualified Ethiopian Health Care Professionals from Sweden to Ethiopia (IOM 2006a).

A fourth global body is unique in that it can best be described as a global network. The Global Health Workforce Alliance (The Alliance) was created in 2006 as a common platform for action to address the shortage of health workers. The Alliance is hosted by the WHO but it is a partnership of national governments, civil society, international agencies, finance institutions, researchers, educators and professional associations dedicated to identifying, implementing and advocating for solutions. It is unique in that it includes such a broad church.

The Alliance aims to exert pressure and improve coordination through its global fora. The First Global Forum on Human Resources for Health was held in Kampala in March 2008. The event brought together over 1,500 participants to discuss the way forward for the 'global health workforce crisis' (Global Health Workforce Alliance 2011a). The Kampala Declaration and Agenda for Global Action (AGA) were agreed upon and formed the basis for The Alliance. The Second Global Forum on Human Resources for Health (HRH) was held in Bangkok in 2011 and reviewed progress to date. It renewed the commitment to strengthening the global health workforce, restating that a robust health workforce is a core element of health systems in all countries, and is critical to achieving the Millennium Development Goals (MDGs) and Universal Health Coverage. Its vision is that 'All people, everywhere, shall have access to a skilled, motivated and supported health worker within a robust health system' (Global Health Workforce Alliance 2011a: 7).

In preparation for the second forum, the Alliance prepared a report on progress since Kampala. This report devotes Chapter 5 to 'Managing the pressures of the international health workforce market and its impact on migration'. This chapter acknowledges that health workers tend to migrate to countries where working conditions and remuneration are better. 'Such dynamics lead to a breakdown of public health systems in poorer countries that have already used their meagre resources to train health workers' (Global Health Workforce Alliance 2011a: 37). The following priority actions were proposed in the report to manage the pressures of the international health workforce market and the impact of these pressures on migration:

- Governments must monitor the flows of their health work force to inform policy decisions.
- Governments should implement the WHO Global Code of Practice on the International Recruitment of Health Personnel, which provides guidance on the international recruitment of health workers.

- All countries must work collectively to address current and anticipated shortfalls in global health workforces, with richer countries giving high priority to training and recruiting health workers within their own countries.
- Governments should be supported to develop coherent policies and build capacity to analyse the implications of trade agreements on health workforces.
- Innovative approaches to assist health worker retention should be tested (Global Health Workforce Alliance 2011a: 37).

The Alliance acknowledges the juxtaposition of the individual right to freedom of movement but also the right of a community to access health care. 'With regard to international migration (AGA 5), both source and destination countries should work collaboratively to develop laws, systems and administrative procedures to effectively implement and measure the impact of the WHO Code of Practice on International Recruitment of Health Personnel' (Global Health Workforce Alliance 2011a: 9). Major gaps that The Alliance identified in 2011 as needing to be addressed include the issue of distribution and retention:

> Suitable policies and strategies should be adopted to attract and retain health workers with appropriate skills mix in rural and other under-served areas, including the deployment of community-based and mid-level health providers. As relevant to country context, strategies may include tailoring education to practice in rural areas, financial and non-financial incentives, regulation, personal and professional support, career development, improvements in rural infrastructure, and partnerships between the public and private sectors (Global Health Workforce Alliance 2011b: 2).

Profession-specific Studies at the Global and Regional Level

Along with the major national, regional body and international concerns, there has been increased research and debate at the level of individual professions. Nursing seems to have attracted the greatest interest. For example, *The Global Shortage of Registered Nurses: An Overview of Issues and Actions* (Buchan and Calman 2004) which was undertaken for the International Council of Nurses identified migration as one of the critically important issues for source countries. Brush (2010) writes that after independence in 1946:

> nurse education in the Philippines was driven largely by US market demand in tandem with local messages linking work and nationalism and explicit policies to send nurses abroad. As these ideologies and practices became firmly entrenched, nurse production not only exceeded the country's numerical requirements but focused largely on preparing practitioners for the health care needs of developed nations rather than the public health needs of the indigenous population. This historical trend has important present-day ramifications for the Philippines, whose continued exodus of nurses threatens its public health.

On the other hand, *Tackling Nurse Shortages in OECD Countries* (Simoens et al. 2005) focused on the variety of policies that could be used to enable the provision of an adequate nursing workforce in more developed countries: such as, innovative approaches to nurse education and training, strong incentives to recruit domestic and foreign nurses, raising productivity and improving pay and conditions to retain nurses. This study was one-sided and was only interested in the perspective of developed countries.

The medical profession has also attracted attention at the global level, from a variety of perspectives. Adelman and Klass (2006: 1) state that the international mobility of physicians is 'valuable and inevitable' but it sets up a tension between medical regulators and individual practitioners. They are mostly interested in the issue of governance and say that ensuring 'just ground rules for the enforcement of professional standards' is a key element in the global governance of medical practitioners and international mobility. Competence must be assessed according to *universal* standards but at the moment it is done at the national or state/provincial level (Klass 2005). Other papers (Iredale 2009, Labonté et al. 2006) discuss international mobility as a means of alleviating national or regional shortages in developed countries and others address the impacts of medical mobility on sending countries.

Key Impacts of the International Mobility of Skilled Health Workers

Based on the global assumption that countries need 2.3 skilled health workers for every 1,000 people, WHO (2006) has estimated that 57 countries are below this threshold and have critical shortages. Such shortages are due to a combination of factors that include poor working conditions, lack of promotional opportunities, shortage of finance, high attrition rates, inadequate training and emigration.

> Of the 57 priority countries, 39 (68 per cent) are in Africa, 12 (21 per cent) in Asia, 4 (7 per cent) in Central America, 1 (2 per cent) in South America and 1 (2 per cent) in Oceania. There are no priority countries in Europe or North America. The 57 countries have 2.74 billion (40 per cent) of the world's estimated 6.75 billion people. India has the largest population among these countries, with 1.18 billion people, while Equatorial Guinea is the least populous country, with a population of 659 000.
>
> According to the World Bank country classification, 36 (63 per cent) countries are low-income, 19 (33 per cent) are lower-middle-income, 1 (2 per cent) is upper-middle-income and 1 (2 per cent) is a high-income country (The Global Health Workforce Alliance 2011a: 13).

If absolute numbers are considered, the shortfall is greatest in Asia because of highly populous countries such as Bangladesh, India, Indonesia and Pakistan.

But the greatest discrepancy related to the burden of disease occurs in SSA, which accounts for 24 per cent of the global burden of disease against only 3 per cent of health workers (WHO 2006).

As shown earlier, migration from such regions has grown in recent decades and the implications for health care delivery can be very serious. The 'emigration of health professionals affects the capacity of governments to manage health sector human resources efficiently, *that is*, their capacity to predict the number of people that would need to be trained in each specialization, in order for the health system to work properly' (OECD 2003: 136). This has repercussions on (a) the availability of health professionals, and (b) the real cost of training, if people are trained and then do not work in the country. More than this, emigration can affect both the quantity and quality of skilled health workers but as Connell (2010) points out this is notoriously difficult to substantiate empirically.

(1) Lack of Access to Health Practitioners in Poor Sending Countries

The most obvious outcomes of a shortage of health workers are high vacancy rates and the closure of health facilities. Nurse vacancy rates of over 50 per cent in parts of the Caribbean (Caribbean Commission on Health and Development 2006) and Kenya and Ghana (Buchan et al. 2004, Volqvartz 2005) and medical vacancies of 47 per cent in Ghana in 2002 (Buchan and Dovlo 2004) provide some data on shortages. It follows that an absence of health workers will lead to a lack of access to services or longer waiting periods, both of which will be reflected in increased mortality or morbidity rates. For example, in Zambia maternal mortality has increased due to a shortage of doctors and nurses. Garrett (2007: 32) states that 'when doctors and nurses leave a health system the first death marker to skyrocket is the number of women who die in childbirth'. The final outcome of shortages will be the closure of facilities and there is evidence of this having happened in many countries. For example, provincial hospitals and rural clinics have been closing down in the Philippines because of the departure of nurses (Asis 2008).

Workforce planning becomes highly problematic if emigration is ongoing and governments have no way of predicting future movements, either in terms of numbers or regions of origin within a country. Professionals who are considering emigration do not normally flag this with their employers and most are secretive about their plans, as they know the implications for their fellow workers and employers (Iredale et al. forthcoming).

(2) Quality of Health Services Suffers in Poor Sending Countries

The skilled migrants most likely to emigrate from countries are those who are the most highly qualified. Empirical studies generally confirm that the majority of health workers moving from developing into industrialized countries are better educated than the average workforce remaining behind (Connell 2009, Kategekwa 2008, Kaushik et al. 2008, Labonté et al. 2006). The impact on the quality of service provision and training is self-evident. Not only are the less skilled left behind but skilled health workers may be replaced by less skilled workers: for example, nurses replaced by nurse aides and young recruits placed in positions that are beyond their expertise (Awases et al. 2004).

The quality of training can also be impacted. It is alleged that the best nurse trainers have left the Philippines for overseas, leaving less capable professors in institutions. Another possible consequence is that countries in critical shortage (for example, South Africa) have considered the tailoring of health training to meet local needs, as one option for minimizing emigration. This could involve:

> revising curricula and adjusting the length of studies. The aim is both to train providers of basic healthcare more quickly, and to ensure that the training is better matched to the needs of the population and the realities of medical practice in South Africa. Indirectly, some also hope to make the skills acquired by health professionals less easily transferable, and hence more difficult to export (OECD 2003: 133).

Whether this reduces the quality of training is open to debate. It is strongly criticized by some within the medical profession who argue that medicine is a universal science and see this as compromising the quality of training (Cohen 2001). Others see it as a realistic option. For example, (Collyer 2001) put forward a proposal which consists of reorganizing curricula into two blocks: (1) basic training according to international standards, and (2) medical training specific to the typical conditions in each country. This would tailor training to meet specific needs but whether it would lead to less possibility for emigration is not known. In relation to nurses, another option under consideration is to fit nurses' training into three years, rather than four. Such an approach would make them immediately unacceptable in many health systems that now require four years of university training. 'Such measures are likely to preserve the national health system from over-exposure in international demand, without being excessively protectionist, and without undermining the professionalism of health workers' (OECD 2003: 134). The latter point would be contested by some.

One approach that has been effective in some countries is the creation of new positions: non-physician clinicians or nurse practitioners and community health workers. The former have recently become prominent in developing countries, and developed countries, and half of all SSA countries have non-physician clinicians. In Mozambique, Uganda, Kenya and Malawi, they have become the core of the health system (Connell 2010: 180).

(3) Loss of Health Worker Skills to the Global Community as a Whole

The loss of skilled workers from developing countries may be compounded by the fact that skilled migrants who leave are not able to fully utilize their skills in the destination. The absence of fair and equitable mechanisms for assessing and employing overseas-trained health practitioners has often been a feature of the traditional immigrant-receiving countries, such as Australia, New Zealand, Canada and the US. The outcome has sometimes been the unfair treatment of overseas-trained health professionals by countries, in denying them access to the profession, confining their practice to certain disadvantaged areas and/or impeding their progress or career advancement once in the workforce. Those who move independently or as permanent migrants often find themselves under- or unemployed. As Redfoot and Houser (2005: 13) state, nations 'establish education and credentialing requirements to help assure quality of care; these requirements can also be used as a method for limiting the admission of long-term care workers, especially nurses'. In spite of these problems, few countries have adequate initiatives to assist foreign health workers to integrate into their labour markets.

A growing phenomenon is that of temporary migration. Those who are recruited for specific contracts are more likely to be able to fully utilize their skills but, even here, there is 'evidence of downgrading, marginalisation and racism' (Connell 2010: 135–137). This represents an economic and personal loss to the individual as well as a wider societal economic loss.

Policies and Practices for the Socially Acceptable Management of Health Worker Mobility

The issues highlighted in this chapter clearly point in the direction of a coordinated approach now being required to address critical health shortages that have often been exacerbated by a loss of health workers to emigration. The various options available at the national, regional and global level will be examined. Policies refer to both sending and receiving countries, though the discussion will focus mainly on sending countries. Unless receiving countries address the same set of issues, however, there will be no solution.

National Measures

(a) Measures to improve domestic working conditions which will favour retention A survey conducted by The Alliance in 51 out of 57 priority countries found that 32 (63 per cent) reported having undertaken some measures to improve domestic working conditions since 2008, such as an adjustment to the salary scale or an increase in allowances or benefits for health workers in remote or hardship areas. The majority of countries (35 out of 51) reported an improvement in career development for doctors, while 31 reported an improvement for nurses and 27 for midwives.[8] However, only 18 countries (35 per cent) reported improvements in career development for community health workers (The Global Health Workforce Alliance 2011b: 36–37). The report concluded that countries may be focusing

8 Anecdotal comments suggest that the improvements are marginal.

on improving the conditions of categories of staff who are more internationally mobile. However, direct evidence on whether migration flows have increased or reduced is not available.

(b) Other measures for tackling domestic workforce challenges The Alliance pays very careful attention to the fact that domestic shortages and the mobility of health workers are not just a result of poor working conditions and remuneration rates. Many other factors are crucially important in tackling health workforce issues. They include:

- A coherent national and global leadership.
- Capacity for an informed response based on evidence and joint learning.
- Scaled-up health worker education.
- Retention of an effective, responsive and equitably distributed health workforce.
- Securing additional and more productive investment in the health workforce (The Global Health Workforce Alliance 2011a: 16).

Where 'packages' have been implemented that include a range of policies (financial, introducing new categories of workers, improving status, increasing recruitment capacity, providing housing, offering clear career structures and continuing education), such as in Malawi and Swaziland, there is evidence of improved job satisfaction and retention (Connell 2010: 171). The overwhelming factor, however, is the shortage of financial resources in many poor countries to put in place such measures. Most international organizations agree that higher amounts of overseas aid are required to fund such improvements.

In this context, sending countries have tried various measures to stop their losses of resources – including bans, taxes and bonds. In the light of the failure of these policies, some request that they be compensated for the loss of their resources, when their skilled health workers go offshore permanently. To date, calls for compensation from receiving countries have been unsuccessful as they are regarded as too idealistic and impractical. The question of the real cost of training is a much debated issue. Many people maintain that the emigration of professionals can lead to remittances and new technologies and skills being returned to the country of origin. These are all positive outcomes, if and when they occur. The problem is that in many instances they do not eventuate, especially when applied to poorer sending countries. Thus, the flow of skilled health workers from developing to developed countries results in a gift of many millions of dollars. The outcome is that poor countries are required to continue devoting scarce resources to training more health workers.

These same elements are essential in receiving countries so that they stop relying on overseas trained health workers and plan to meet their own needs. At the same time, they have other options of schemes to encourage their own nationals to return on either a temporary or permanent basis. Such schemes are much less viable for poor developing countries where return migration or using the diaspora is often difficult to achieve.

(c) Opening up to trade in services There is significant debate about whether developing countries that are already short of health human resources should be engaging in trade in services, as spelled out by the WTO. Trade in services incorporates four modes, as we saw earlier, and two of them impact particularly on the provision of health services and universal access to health services for all, in developing countries. One is Mode 3, commercial presence, which allows foreign firms to enter a country and set up health services. The terms of foreign business presence and operation are defined in countries' horizontal and vertical schedules of commitments. Kategekwa (2008: 29) argues that the terms/regulations for foreign-established health facilities could include conditions such as: the minimum number of locals to be employed; all health suppliers working at a certain level (for example, doctors) to also serve hours in public facilities; the provision of free treatment to those with communicable diseases; and the provision of training for local health workers. These regulations are possible but they should not be too harsh as to deter foreign investors.

Mode 4, the movement of natural persons (mainly independent professionals and contract service suppliers), poses a greater challenge. In the event that people cannot be discouraged from leaving, the provision of opportunities for short-term contracts overseas may offer an avenue for extra money to be earned and remitted, and foreign experience and skills to be gained and brought back home. This, hopefully, sets up more temporary circulation, something that is often lacking in the permanent migration patterns between developing and more developed economies. The selection of countries for the movement of natural persons could be based on which offer the best conditions and options for benefiting the sending country (Mayer et al. 2009).

(d) Bilateral or regional arrangements Some governments are managing their migration of health care workers through specific bilateral or regional arrangements. Increasingly sending countries see no possibility for stemming the outflows and they see bilateral and multilateral arrangements as one way of at least managing the flows. For example, the Philippines-UK Memorandum of Understanding is an example of a north–south partnership that is intended to ensure protection for both countries.[9]

International Measures

(a) Commonwealth secretariat code of practice for the international recruitment of health workers (2003) The code provides guidelines for the international recruitment of health workers in a manner that takes into account the potential

9 200 nurses were recruited in 2002 through the Philippines Overseas Employment Agency to work in the UK for at least a year.

impact of such recruitment on services in the source country. Its intention was to discourage the targeted recruitment of health workers from countries that were experiencing shortages. It also sought to safeguard the rights of recruits, and the conditions relating to their profession in the recruiting countries. The code had limited effect as it did not cover private recruiters.

(b) Other international initiatives The IOM has identified a range of actions to pursue with the WHO, ILO, World Bank and others to move the agenda forward: provide technical assistance to governments to improve national health information systems, including data collection and analysis and the use of a sound evidence base to develop strategies to manage the migration of health care workers; establish an observatory to track/monitor the global migration of health care workers; establish a global alliance for the management of human resources for health to bring together relevant stakeholders for dialogue, to share experiences and to develop action plans and strategies; create an online platform to facilitate information exchange on best practices, innovative policies and programmes for the management of health care worker migration; establish and maintain a database of current health workforce resources in diasporas; and establish an international public-private financing mechanism for human resource development for health (IOM 2006b).

(c) WHO Global Code of Practice on the International Recruitment of Health Personnel (2010) The worldwide increase in health worker migration in the past two decades led members of the WHO to become particularly concerned about mobility from 'lower income countries with already fragile health systems' (WHO 2010b). The view that national gains would not outweigh losses in poorer sending countries has won precedence over the 'internationalist perspective' that brain drain losses will eventually be compensated by remittances and more highly skilled returnees (Connell 2010: 164–166). Thus, policies and practices to remedy the impact of migration have been urgently and widely sought.

The *WHO Global Code of Practice on the International Recruitment of Health Personnel* was adopted by the 63rd World Health Assembly on 21 May 2010. This groundbreaking instrument marks the first time that WHO Member States have used the constitutional authority of the WHO to develop a code in 30 years. The code aims to establish and promote voluntary principles and practices for the ethical international recruitment of health personnel and to facilitate the strengthening of health systems. The most important component is that Member States should discourage the active recruitment of health personnel from developing countries facing critical shortages of health workers. Other key components of the code include:

- greater commitment to assist countries facing critical health worker shortages in their efforts to improve and support their health workforce;

- joint investment in research and information systems to monitor the international migration of health workers in order to develop evidence-based policies;
- Member States to meet their health personnel needs with their own human resources as far as possible and thus take measures to educate, retain and sustain their health workforce;
- migrant workers' rights enshrined and equal to domestically trained health workers (WHO 2010b).

The WHO Code was designed by Member States to serve as a continuous and dynamic framework for global dialogue and cooperation. In this way it is more inclusive than other international codes and therefore may have a greater chance of implementation. Codes such as these do not have a good record of achievement but the attention that it has brought to the issue will hopefully be beneficial. The single most important factor, however, is encouraging developed countries to adopt a range of initiatives that would enable them to meet their own domestic needs and be self-sufficient in terms of health workers. The OECD is particularly strong on this aspect of the issue but only a few countries are seriously trying to adopt this approach. It continues to be cheaper to import health professionals than to train the requisite number in many countries.

Conclusion

The evidence shows that 57 priority countries are suffering severe health worker shortages and this is often compounded by the out-migration of their precious health workers. There is now widespread agreement that the cooperation of all stakeholders is needed to ensure that migration factors are addressed coherently to have a positive impact on the management of the movement of health care workers.

The discussion of policy implications has canvassed the major options for countries experiencing extreme shortages, such as improving national health sectors with additional (obviously limited) finance, training to meet local needs, creating new types of practitioners to fill specific roles, bans, bonds and taxes and more managed migration schemes. They may have some impact on improving the quantity and quality of health workers. The negotiation of GATS Mode 4 arrangements that are mutually beneficial to both sending and receiving countries also offers some scope.

On the other hand, recipient country policy options include improving workplace conditions, increasing training and reducing attrition, compensating sending countries for the training costs embedded in their health workers, encouraging return migration and making use of their diasporas. Compensation for scarce skills gained from overseas could be addressed by more generous overseas aid to specific countries. These options are the most important as they will ensure that demand is met from within rather than relying on other countries.

International solutions, such as codes of practice, have limited chance of having much effect though the WHO code is unique in its broad focus. Its emphasis on more overseas aid to support struggling health systems and self-sufficiency in developed countries is unique. The focus within regions on data collection will help to monitor future trends.

However, as long as structural inequalities continue to exist, global inequalities and critical shortages of health workers will continue. Ultimately, the solutions lie outside of the health sector and involve global reforms in international trade, more effective development assistance, the extension debt relief and the recognition of health as a human right. In the meantime, Connell (2010) is not optimistic and argues that even though migration may be more managed and structured, it will continue to be as damaging in its outcomes, as it has in the past. What exists now is a surfeit of conflicting policies and limited political will on the part of receiving countries to address their own needs.

References

Adelman, H. and Klass, D. 2006. Governance of physicians in a globalized world: developing a transnational research program for medical regulation. Paper to the International Association of Medical Regulatory Authorities (IAMRA) 7th International Conference on Medical Regulation, Wellington, New Zealand, November 2006.

ASEAN-ANU Research Team 2005. Movement of workers in ASEAN: health care and IT sectors. ASEAN Secretariat, REPSF. Project No. 04/007, June.

Asis, Maruja M.B. 2008. How international migration can support development: a challenge for the Philippines, in S. Castles and R.D. Wise (eds), *Migration and Development: Perspectives from the South*, 175–202.

Awases, M., Gbary, A., Nyoni, J. and Chatora, R. 2004. *Migration of Health Professionals in Six Countries*. Brazzaville: WHO.

Bach, S. 2003. *I*nternational migration of health workers: labour and social issues. Working Paper 209, Sectoral Activities Programme. Geneva: ILO.

Bartsch, W. 1974. *The Skill Drain from Fiji. Situation and Possible Remedies*. Suva: Central Planning Office.

Brush, B.L. 2010. The potent lever of toil: nursing development and exportation in the postcolonial Philippines. *American Journal of Public Health* [Online: 15 July 2010]. Available at: http://ajph.aphapublications.org/cgi/content/short/AJPH.2009.181222v1 [accessed: 20 March 2011].

Buchan, J. and Calman, L. 2004. Skill mix and policy change in the health workforce: nurses in advanced roles. OECD Health Working Paper, No. 17. Paris: OECD.

Buchan, J. and Dovlo, D. 2004. *International Recruitment of Health Workers to the UK: A Report for the Department of International Development*. London: DFID.

Buchan, J., Parkin, T. and Sochalski, J. 2004. *International Nurse Mobility: Trends and Policy Implications*. Geneva: WHO, ICN and RCN.

Caribbean Commission on Health and Development. 2006. *Report of the Caribbean Commission on Health and Development*. Kingston: PAHO and Caribbean Community Secretariat.

Clemens, M. and Pettersson, G. 2008. New data on Africa health professionals abroad. *Human Resources for Health*, 6(1), 1–11.

Cohen, J. 2001. The argument for global standards for medical education. *The Meducator*, 1(3).

Collyer, F. 2001. Corporate control of healthcare in Australia. Discussion Paper Number 42, The Australia Institute, October.

Connell, J. 2009. *The Global Health Care Chain: From the Pacific to the World*. New York: Routledge.

Connell, J. 2010. *Migration and the Globalisation of Health Care*. Cheltenham, UK, and Northampton, MA, USA: Edward Elgar.

Cooper, R. and Aiken, L. 2006. Health services delivery: reframing policies for global migration of nurses and physicians – a U.S. perspective. *Policy, Politics and Nursing Practice*, 7, 66S–70S.

Dodson, B. 2002. Gender and the brain drain from South Africa. Migration Policy Series No. 23, South African Migration Project (SAMP).

Dumont, J.C. and Meyer, J.B. 2004. The international mobility of health professionals: an evaluation and analysis based on the case of South Africa, in *Trends in International Migration*, SOPEMI. 2003 Edition, Annex 1, 115–151.

Garrett, L. 2007. The challenge of global health, in *Foreign Affairs*, 86(1), 14–38.

Gish, O. 1971. *Doctor Migration and World Health*. London: Bell.

Global Health Workforce Alliance. 2011a. Reviewing progress, renewing commitment, progress report on the Kampala declaration and agenda for global action [Online: 2011]. Available at: http://www.who.int/workforcealliance/knowledge/resources/KDAGAprogressreport–2011.pdf [accessed: 15 March 2011].

Global Health Workforce Alliance. 2011b. Outcome statement of the second global forum on human resources for health Bangkok, 27–29 January 2011 [Online: 2011]. Available at: http://www.who.int/workforcealliance/forum/2011/Outcomestatement.pdf [accessed: 15 March 2011].

Hawthorne, L. 2007. Growth in two-step migration to Australia. Paper presented at First Asia-Pacific Skilled Migration to Australia Workshop, Macquarie University, Sydney, 19–20 April.

Horn, J. 1977. The medical brain drain and health priorities in Latin America. *International Journal of Health Sciences*, 7, 425–442.

IOM (International Organization for Migration). 2006a. Managing the migration of health care workers the need for action [Online: 2006]. Available at:

http://publications.iom.int/bookstore/index.php?main-page=product-infoandcPath=35–34andproducts-id=471 [accessed: 14 March 2011].

IOM (International Organization for Migration) 2006b. Migration and human resources for health: from awareness to action [Online: 2006]. Available at: http://publications.iom.int/bookstore/index.php?main-page=product-infoandcPath=35–34andproducts-id=474 [accessed: 14 March 2011].

Iredale, R.R. 2009. Luring overseas trained doctors to Australia: issues of training, regulating and trading. *International Migration*, 47(4), 31–65.

Iredale, R., Voigt-Graf, C. and Khoo, S-E. Trends in international and internal teacher mobility in three Pacific Island countries. *International Migration*, forthcoming.

Kategekwa, J. 2008. Liberalisation of trade in health services: balancing mode 4 interests with obligations to provide universal access to basic services. Research Paper 16, South Centre [Online: January 2008]. Available at: http://www.southcentre.org/publications/researchpapers/ResearchPapers16.pdf [accessed: 20 February 2011].

Kaushik, M., Jaiswal, A., Shah, N. and Mahal, A. 2008. High-end physician migration from India. *Bulletin of the WHO*, 86, 40–45.

Khadria, B. 2004. Migration of highly skilled Indians: case studies of IT and the health professionals, OECD Science, Technology and Industry Working Papers, 2004/6, OECD Publishing. doi:10.1787/381236020703 [Online: 2004]. Available at: http://titania.sourceoecd.org/vl=1423234/cl=13/nw=1/rpsv/cgibin/wppdf?file=5lgsjhvj7kd7.pdf [accessed: 18 September 2008].

Khadria, B. 2006. International recruitment of nurses in India: implications of stakeholder perspectives on overseas labour markets, migration, and return. Asia Research Institute, Working Paper No 68, National University of Singapore.

Klass, D. 2005. Professional competence; current change in its meaning and regulation. *College of Physicians and Surgeons of Ontario*, 9(3), 16 September.

Labonté, R., Packer, C. and Klasse, N. 2006. Managing health professionals' migration from sub-Saharan Africa to Canada: a stakeholder inquiry into migration options. *Human Resources for Health*, 4(22), 1–15.

Martineau, T. and Martinez, J. 1997. Human resources in the health sector: guidelines for appraisal and strategic development, Health and Development Series No. 1. Brussels: European Commission.

Martinez, J. and Martineau, T. 2002. Human resources in the health sector: an international perspective. DFID Issues Paper.

Mattes, R., Crush, J. and Richmond, W. 2000. The brain gain: skilled migrants and immigration in post-apartheid South Africa. OECD Migration Policy Series, No. 20, SAMP.

Mayer, J. 2009. Trade trends and what they mean in terms of income gains for developing countries, in *Debt and Trade: Making Linkages for the Promotion of Development*. Report from a Policy Roundtable (ed.) A. Caliari. Geneva: South Centre and Centre of Concern, 29–36. [Online: October 2010]. Available at: www.southcentre.org/index.php?option=com-docmanandtask=cat-viewandgid=45andlimit=5andlimitstart=20andorder=dateanddir=DESCandItemid=313andlang=en [accessed: 20 March 2011].

McCoy, D., Bennett, S., Witter, S., Pond, B., Baker, B., Gow, J., Chand, S., Ensor, T and McPake, B. 2008. Salaries and incomes of health workers in Sub-Saharan Africa, *The Lancet*, 371, 675–81.

Mejia, A., Pizurski H. and Royston, E. 1979. *Physician and Nurse Migration: Analysis and Policy Implications*. Geneva: WHO.

Nyonatar, F. and Dovlo, D. 2005. The health of the nation and the brain drain in the health sector, in (ed.) T. Manuh *At Home in the World: International Migration and Development in Contemporary Ghana and West Africa*. Accra: Sub-Saharan Publishers.

OECD (Organisation for Economic Cooperation and Development). 2003. The international mobility of health professionals: an evaluation and analysis based on the case of South Africa, in *Trends in International Migration*, SOPEMI, Part III. Paris: OECD, 115–145.

OECD (Organisation for Economic Cooperation and Development). 2007a. Immigrant health workers in OECD countries in the broader context of highly skilled migration, in *International Migration Outlook*, SOPEMI, Part III. Paris: OECD, 161–228.

OECD (Organisation for Economic Cooperation and Development). 2007b. Statlink [Online: 2007]. Available at: http://dx.doi.org/10/1787/022648458554 [accessed: 10 July 2009].

OECD (Organisation for Economic Cooperation and Development). 2008. The looming crisis in the health workforce: how can OECD countries respond?, *OECD Health Policy Studies*. Paris: OECD.

OECD (Organisation for Economic Cooperation and Development). 2010. *International Migration Outlook*, SOPEMI. Paris: OECD.

Osunkoya, B. 1974. Postgraduate medical education in developing countries. *British Journal of Medical Education*, 8, 69–73.

Redfoot, D.L. and Houser, A.N. 2005. 'We shall travel on': quality of care, economic development, and the international migration of long-term care workers, AARP Public Policy Institute [Online: July 2005]. Available at: www.aarp.org/research/longtermcare/quality/inb104–intl-ltc.html [accessed: 12 November 2005].

Simoens, S., Villeneuve, M. and Hurst, J. 2005. Tackling nurse shortages in OECD countries, OECD Health Working Paper No 19 [Online: July 2005]. Available at: www.oecd.org/dataoecd/11/10/34571365.pdf [accessed: 5 October 2006].

Thomas-Hope, E. 2002. Skilled labour migration from developing countries: study on the Caribbean region, *International Migration Papers 50*, International Migration Programme. Geneva: ILO.

Volqvartz, J. 2005. The brain drain. *The Guardian*, 11 March.

WHO (World Health Organization). 2006. *Working Together for Health*. Geneva: WHO.

WHO (World Health Organization) 2010a. Migration of health workers, Fact sheet No. 301. [Online: July 2010]. Available at: www.who.int/mediacentre/factsheets/fs301/en/ [accessed: 14 March 2011].

WHO (World Health Organization) 2010b. WHO global code of practice on the international recruitment of health personnel [Online: July 2010]. Available at: www.who.int/hrh/migration/code/practice/en/index.html [accessed: 11 March 2011].

Chapter 3
Building an Ethical and Sustainable Model for Health Professional Recruitment

William Ransome and Charles Sampford

At a fundamental level, ethics is about how we should live our lives. When applied to the ways we live our collective lives through the institutions we design and run, it is about how we treat our fellow human beings and the world in which we live. A practice is sustainable, very broadly, when it may be pursued indefinitely without either internal failure or significant harm to lasting value – and in a sense, what is commonly called 'sustainability' is that part of applied ethics that links current or proposed practices to their overall long-term consequences. As has been the case for many other skilled professions, the present era of globalization has witnessed a dramatic surge in the international mobility of health professionals, with the direction of movement being largely – but not exclusively – from the developing to the developed world, as is extensively discussed in Chapter 2. Rising concern about the ethical status and sustainability of ad hoc developed world recruitment practices, and especially their perceived and potential effects on developing world health systems, have led to the development of codes of practice intended to crystallize the values inherent in, and define the appropriate ethical boundaries of, international health professional recruitment (see OECD 2010, WHO 2006, Willetts and Martineau 2004). These codes have culminated in the adoption by World Health Organization (WHO) Member States at the 63rd World Health Assembly in May 2010 of a 'WHO Global Code of Practice on the International Recruitment of Health Personnel' (WHO 2010).

In this chapter we introduce and explain the 'integrity systems' approach to ethical and sustainable governance, and outline its application to global health professional recruitment. After briefly summarizing key elements of the new WHO code, we describe the 'integrity systems' approach and illustrate its application in reforms to the Australian state of Queensland governance in the wake of that state's *Fitzgerald Report* (Fitzgerald 1989). We argue that making a public commitment to good ethical practice in health professional recruitment, as WHO Member States have in adopting the code, presents an important challenge to those who make it: to live by, and to be publicly accountable for living by, the defining values to which they have committed. To achieve these aims, we claim, is to possess integrity. We argue that building and strengthening the existing integrity system presents a significant set of challenges, especially for key subnational health sector institutions: the system is complex and multidimensional, encompassing the interests of many stakeholders, and covering a broad range of ethically germane considerations operating on and between global, regional, bilateral, national, subnational, local and individual levels. A first step in embarking on an ethical and sustainable model of health professional recruitment, we conclude, involves detailed 'integrity mapping' of current systems aimed at highlighting areas of prevailing and potential ethical tension and dislocation inherent in existing recruitment regimes.

A Global Code of Practice on the International Recruitment of Health Personnel

The WHO code was drafted in response to emerging and continuing global shortages of health professionals in both developed and developing world health systems, and to the threat this shortage poses for both the provision of health services in general and the ability of developing countries to meet health-related targets of multilateral development agreements, such as the Millennium Development Goals. As such, the code is intended to 'be a core component of bilateral, national, regional and global responses to the challenges of health personnel migration and health systems strengthening', and 'to establish and promote voluntary principles and practices for the ethical international recruitment of health personnel, taking into account the rights, obligations and expectations of source countries, destination countries and migrant health personnel' (WHO 2010: 2, 3).

The second of ten articles in the WHO code outlines its nature and intended scope. Being voluntary and very broad in scope, the code's focus falls overwhelmingly upon the agency of Member States in encouraging stakeholder engagement, and in embedding ethical recruitment practices in institutional settings, multilateral and bilateral agreements and relevant legal instruments:

> 2.2 The code is global in scope and is intended as a guide for Member States, working together with stakeholders such as health personnel, recruiters, employers, health-professional organizations, relevant subregional, regional and global organizations, whether public or private sector, including nongovernmental, and all persons concerned with the international recruitment of health personnel (WHO 2010: 3).

Throughout the code, an especially strong link is drawn between ethical recruitment practices and the effects of international health personnel recruitment upon source countries' health systems:

> 2.3 The code provides ethical principles applicable to the international recruitment of health personnel in a manner that strengthens the health systems of developing countries, countries with economies in transition and small island states (WHO 2010: 3).

Article 3 details the code's 'Guiding principles'. Article 3.1 links good human health to peace and security, establishes that governments are ultimately responsible for the health of their people, 'which can be fulfilled only by the provision of adequate health and social measures', (WHO 2010: 4) and urges Member States to take the code into account in developing national health policies. Article 3.2 seeks to establish an ethical foundation for recruitment on the basis of the need to ameliorate present and expected shortages in the health workforce, and the capability of the international health workforce flow to develop and strengthen participating health systems 'if recruitment is properly managed' (WHO 2010: 4). Article 3.3 emphasizes again that source countries' 'needs and special circumstances' should be considered, and recommends that developed destination countries 'should, to the extent possible, provide technical and financial assistance' to developing source countries 'aimed at strengthening health systems, including health personnel development' (WHO 2010: 4). Article 3.4 outlines two areas in which people's rights must be taken into account in ethical recruitment, including 'the right to the highest attainable standard of health of the populations of source countries', and 'individual rights of health personnel to leave any country', noting that 'nothing in this code should be interpreted as limiting the freedom of health personnel, in accordance with applicable laws, to migrate to countries that wish to admit and employ them' (WHO 2010: 4).

The central statement of the code's guiding ethical principles occurs in article 3.5, which establishes transparency, fairness and sustainability as the defining ethical ideals for international health personnel recruitment.

> 3.5 International recruitment of health personnel should be conducted in accordance with the principles of transparency, fairness and promotion of sustainability of health systems in developing countries. Member states, in conformity with national legislation and applicable international legal instruments to which they are a party, should promote and respect fair labour practices for all health personnel. All aspects of the employment and treatment of migrant health personnel should be without unlawful distinction of any kind (WHO 2010: 5).

These three core principles are left undefined in the code. However, we believe the principle of sustainability in relation to developing world health systems may be defined, in general terms, with reference to their capacity to endure and be maintained in a well-functioning state indefinitely into the future. The principle of transparency in this context involves institutions publicly stating the values they claim to further in both general and specific terms, the means by which they intend to achieve them, and the extent to which they have been achieved (see Head et al. 2008, Pope 2000, Sampford et al. 2005). The principle of fairness – a derivative of justice more generally understood as giving each person their due – is definable in terms of equitable recruitment practices. An equity-based definition of fairness is closely related to justice understood as a virtue: according to John Rawls, the 'first virtue of social institutions' (Rawls 1971: 3). Being fair – equitable – in the relevant sense, requires sensitive and fine-grained deliberation that is capable of reaching beyond the strictures of formal justice, seeking to understand and balance all relevant considerations in a particular case before a course of action is undertaken or recruitment practice instituted (see Nussbaum 1993).

The principle of mutual benefit is introduced later, in article 5.1, and applies to source and destination health systems rather than individuals – although article 4 ('Responsibilities, rights and recruitment practices') sets out rights and responsibilities of stakeholders in relation to migrant health personnel, emphasizing their right to just and equal treatment in recruitment and terms of employment (WHO 2010: 5–6). Articles 4 to 10 concern the application of the code, prescribing ethical norms for health personnel in general terms and for all stakeholders, although focusing on Member States – and especially on the responsibilities and obligations of recruiting countries, and the rights and needs of source countries' health systems. These prescriptions cover 'responsibilities, rights and recruitment practices' (Article 4); 'health workforce development and health system sustainability' (Article 5); 'data gathering and research' (Article 6); 'information exchange' (Article 7); 'implementation of the code' (Article 8); monitoring and institutional arrangements (Article 9); and 'partnerships, technical collaboration and financial support' (Article 10).

A Global Approach for Assessing Ethics and Sustainability: 'Integrity Systems'

The WHO code is global in scope and has been adopted at national government level by Member States. Yet the formulation and adoption of legal rules, bilateral and multilateral agreements and formal ethical norms is unlikely to be sufficient for building an ethical and sustainable recruitment regime in any of these countries per se. While the code is global in scope, responsibility for planning, implementation, execution and day-to-day administration and oversight of international health professional recruitment regimes in the developed world is likely to continue to be subnational (that is, falling on institutions such as state, provincial and local health agencies, regulators, professional organizations and health sector employers). Unfortunately, ethical guidelines such as those represented in the WHO code have in the past been seen by reviewers to be abstract, rigid, and ineffective (Buchan and McPake 2007, Willetts and Martineau 2004), and to lack grounding and support within a sustainable governance regime (Buchan 2010, Willetts and Martineau 2004).

Some key elements are needed to ensure national and sub-national implementation builds ethical and sustainable recruitment regimes. The formal elements of a well-functioning governance system, firstly, need to be consistent. Ethical norms without the mutual support of legal rules to impose appropriate sanctions on those who do not respect their own publicly stated values are impotent;

but legal rules, too, are ineffective unless they are informed by ethical standards which give them meaning and guide their interpretation. Accordingly, ethical standards and legal rules need to be mutually supportive, and must especially seek to avoid giving contrary guidance in their practical application. Furthermore, legal and ethical norms require supportive institutional arrangements. Such arrangements seek to keep ethical and legal norms consistent, guide agencies and officials in the execution of their duties, ensure that relevant rules are observed, and confirm whether or not reputed outcomes and benefits are in fact forthcoming.

Ethical and sustainable governance on a global scale requires a robust and reliable combination of ethical standard setting, legal regulation and institutional design. 'Institutional ethics' offers a way of integrating these elements (see Sampford 1990). From the point of view of institutional ethics, institutions, including government agencies, corporations and professions, need to justify themselves to the communities in which they operate for a number of reasons, including the privileges, benefits and rights accorded them by, and legally protected within, those communities (Preston et al. 2002, Sampford 1990).

From an ethical point of view, making a public commitment to good ethical practice – as WHO Member States have in adopting the code – presents an important challenge to those who make it: to live by, and to be publicly accountable for living by, the defining values to which they have committed. To do so, on a common interpretation, is to possess integrity. When applied to institutional organizations and others who wield public power, integrity may be defined as the use of entrusted power for publicly justified ends (Dobel 1999, Sampford et al. 2005). The 'integrity systems' approach to ethical governance originally arose out of a recognition that the best way of tackling institutionalized corruption and embedding integrity in governance systems is not through any single legal instrument or purpose-built anti-corruption ethics agency (see Meagher 2005). Rather, what is needed is a combination of state institutions and agencies (in the case of government corruption, for example, parliament, courts, police, prosecutors' offices), official watchdog agencies (ombudsmen, auditors general, parliamentary committees), non-government organizations (NGOs), and the norms and mechanisms by and through which individuals across key institutions operate.

An early example of ethics-based reform under the integrity systems model is furnished by Queensland's *Fitzgerald Report* (or as it is less well-known, *Report of a Commission of Inquiry Pursuant to Orders in Council*) (Fitzgerald 1989). The Report's 121 recommendations contained Fitzgerald's vision for reform of some of Queensland's key public institutions in the areas of: electoral and administrative processes, criminal justice, and policing. The major recommendations of the Report were the establishment of the Electoral and Administrative Review Commission (EARC) and the Criminal Justice Commission (CJC), restructuring of the Police Department along regional lines, 'scrapping' of the Police Department's Internal Investigation Unit, abolishing the police Complaints Tribunal, and revising police rules compelling police to report misconduct to the CJC on a confidential basis

(Fitzgerald 1989). Fitzgerald recommended that the EARC and the CJC report to Parliamentary Select Committees.

What was most striking in the Queensland reform process, however, was that a new model for combating corruption had been developed. Rather than rely upon a single law and a single institution, existing institutions were strengthened and new institutions were created to build a set of mutually supporting and mutually checking institutions, agencies and laws that jointly sought to improve governmental standards and combat corruption. Some of the reforms were versions of those tried elsewhere – involving the creation or strengthening of institutions or the passage of a package of administrative laws following the Commonwealth model. Other reforms were either unique to Queensland or very rare – the Queensland *Public Sector Ethics Act* 1994 and associated regime of ethical standard setting; the Queensland *Legislative Standards Act* 1992 which provided a means for the protection of human rights in the legislative process rather than just a judicial backstop; a powerful Scrutiny of Legislation Committee; an Integrity Commissioner to provide advice on conflict of interest and potentially other ethical issues affecting ministers and their advisors.

When functioning effectively and as intended, this set of interconnecting norms, institutions and mechanisms embeds and promotes integrity in public institutions and reduces the likelihood of systemic ethical failure. This was originally termed an 'ethics regime' (Sampford 1990, Sampford and Wood 1993), and later, when adopted by the Organisation for Economic Cooperation and Development (OECD), an 'ethics infrastructure' (OECD 1996, 1997a, 1997b, 1998) – but in its widest current use (for example, by Transparency International (TI)) it is now known as a 'national integrity system' (Langseth et al. 1997, Pope 2000). Sampford and others have developed a conceptual framework and sophisticated mapping and assessment tools (see for example Head et al. 2008, Preston et al. 2002, Sampford et al. 2005), which have helped shape the preferred models for governance reform within many national and subnational jurisdictions (see for example Acar and Emek 2008, Anechiarico 2010, Behnke and Maesschalck 2006, Huberts et al. 2008). An integrity systems assessment seeks to understand the actual dynamics of an integrity system (Sampford et al. 2005). Ideally, it maps, describes and assesses the effectiveness of the entire set of norms, institutions and mechanisms designed to reduce ethical failure and ensure integrity, examining the extent and strength of interconnectedness, overlaps, conflicts and mutual supports.

As such, an integrity systems assessment aims at providing a granular evaluation of how an integrity system actually works. An assessment of integrity systems modified to apply on a global scale in a specific area, such as to international health personnel recruitment, requires identifying the powers of institutions and individuals to be regulated, the ends to which they are supposed to be devoted, and the potential for ethical failure; identifying the range of norms, institutions and mechanisms that may enhance accountability, raise ethical standards and performance, ensure powers are used for the purposes for which they are intended, and make unethical conduct more difficult; describing each of those norms, institutions and mechanisms in its operational context; and documenting the legal instruments that govern them and the communal values that support them. Such an assessment would also aim at describing the ways in which these elements interrelate and the various kinds of relationships between them that make a set of integrity institutions a 'system', assess the strengths and weaknesses of the current system – focusing on areas of potential risk in which undesirable practices might develop or may already have developed – and make proposals for further improvements and reform, concentrating on ways to make existing integrity institutions more effective.

Integrity in International Health Personnel Recruitment: Stakeholder Interests

Making a commitment to respecting and promoting appropriate guiding ethical principles through an integrity systems framework constitutes a form of 'ethical risk management' (see Sampford and Lui 2004) for stakeholders involved in and affected by international health personnel recruitment. The ethics of developed world recruitment regimes has to date been uncoordinated, piecemeal, ad hoc, and conducive to the 'external shocks' of sporadic and sudden changes in political, social and economic conditions (Buchan and McPake 2007). Recruitment regimes in developed countries have also been viewed as ethical failures – unfair, opaque, lacking in tangible mutual benefits, exploitative, damaging to source countries, and unsustainable – driving the need for a Global Code of Practice on the International Recruitment of Health Personnel (WHO 2006, 2010, Willetts and Martineau 2004). Yet the presumed ethical failings of existing international recruitment regimes in the developed world are understandable: the global integrity system that is gradually emerging in international health personnel recruitment – of which the WHO code now becomes a central element – is irreducibly complex and multidimensional. International recruitment of health personnel covers a very broad range of ethical, political, legal, economic, social, cultural and psychological considerations operating on and between global, regional, bilateral, national, subnational, local and individual levels. And the ethics and sustainability of recruitment practices unifies, interpenetrates, and is expressed through each of its other dimensions: the political, the legal, the economic, social and cultural dimensions, too, are all also ethical dimensions.

A hierarchy of influence operates throughout a heavily layered global health personnel recruitment system. Core integrity system 'macro' elements for international health personnel recruitment, including ethical codes, multilateral and bilateral legal instruments and institutional settings, are determined at a macro-political level, but these global 'top-down' elements are ultimately aimed at influencing a great number of individual subnational and local ethical decisions across a vast and complex global-scale multi-institutional landscape, much of which occurs at and between stakeholders from the 'bottom-up' both inside and between countries. Yet governments, their agencies, other institutional stakeholders and individuals at these levels, who are putatively responsible for implementing principles such as those represented in the WHO code, represent a broad range of different interests themselves, and often operate primarily in the light of their own already well-established norms, legal rules and institutional settings aimed at securing a variety of different (and in practice sometimes conflicting) ends. Within the international health personnel recruitment integrity system, top-down prescriptions derived from global principles meet the bottom-up functions, responsibilities, interests and loyalties of many stakeholders. This layered meeting of different interests represents the multifaceted cutting edge of 'ethical risk management' within the international health recruitment integrity system.

Key stakeholders in international health personnel recruitment regimes – including those directly involved and those indirectly concerned with the recruitment process, and those who have power to act and those whose interests are affected – represent a very broad range of overlapping and often conflicting interests (Xu and Zhang 2005) operating across global, regional, multilateral, bilateral, national, subnational and individual levels. At a direct individual level, key stakeholder interests are represented by internationally recruited health professionals, the domestic health workforce in destination countries' health systems, and patients. Migrant health professionals represent a uniquely central ethical stakeholder group – their personal circumstances and prospects are directly affected by the consequences of ethical actions taken by others at every level of international health professional recruitment. As Xu and Zhang observe in the case of migrating nurses:

> From the perspective of nurses from source countries, international nurse recruitment is viewed as beneficial and positive since it not only promotes nurses' mobility but also enhances their career opportunities, educational possibilities and quality of life. Moreover, such an opportunity provides a means to improve their financial status, earn money for their families back home or accumulate savings for a more secure retirement, and offers an avenue for immigration. For many nurses from the developing countries, work in a developed country may be the ultimate opportunity to change their lives and enjoy a quality of life of which they could only dream (Xu and Zhang 2005: 573).

On the other hand, colleague health workers in destination countries may have a less positive view of the effects of international recruitment, including 'perceived threat to job security; competition in the workplace; conflict arising from different cultural and educational backgrounds and a different professional scope of practice; clinical protocols, and standards; and barriers to communication' (Xu and Zhang 2005: 573). Patients in destination countries, too, may have concerns – whether soundly based or not – over professional standards, barriers to communication, and cultural and social misunderstandings which might affect patient care. Given the different and potentially conflicting interests – and also given the particular

Table 3.1 Stakeholders involved in and affected by international health personnel recruitment

International	Global and International Intergovernmental Organizations and NGOs, for example UN, WHO, OECD International Health Professional Organizations International Agreements, for example international declarations, codes of practice, bilateral and multilateral treaties and other legal instruments
National	National Government, Departments and Agencies National Health Professional Regulators National Health Professional Groups Migration Agents National Health Professional Standards, Regulations & Codes National Laws, for example Immigration, Employment, Health
Sub national	State/Provincial Governments, Departments and Agencies State/Provincial Health Professional Regulators State/Provincial Health Professional Organizations Health Professional Education and Training Institutions, for example Universities Recruitment Agencies State/Provincial Health Laws, Standards and Regulations State/Provincial Employment Laws, Regulations and Policies
Local	Local Governments Local Health District and Facility Boards, other local health authorities District, facility, floor, ward Managers Health Professionals Local Health Professional Organization representatives Patients and local communities Employment conditions, support services, workplace policies and procedures, culture, professional development, et cetera.

legal, regulatory and institutional environments that may be encountered by internationally recruited health personnel – significant ethical issues regarding the WHO code's principles of fairness, sustainability and mutual benefit are thus likely to arise directly 'at the coal face' in migrant health professionals' places of employment.

At subnational institutional levels in both source and destination countries there are many interests represented, both directly and indirectly, in recruitment regimes. Health agencies and their health facilities in destination countries are directly responsible for the planning and execution of international health personnel recruitment practices in an institutional environment in which many different, competing, and often conflicting official and unofficial, formal and informal obligations, commitments and loyalties operate within and between institutions. Health agencies and facilities operate under legislative and professional regulatory rules and procedures set by national and state governments and regulatory bodies, and within established public and private sector managerial and operational cultures, where health personnel interests are collectively represented by professional associations and workers' unions at local health facility, agency, state and national levels. These institutions seek to influence the governance of international health recruitment regimes in their members' interests and also, in the case of government health agencies, healthcare professions and regulators, in the interests of the overall well-functioning of health systems and, ultimately, their patients. Recruiters, migration agents, educational institutions in destination and source countries, source country health systems, and other government agencies and NGOs also represent various differently motivated interests affected by recruitment regimes at the subnational institutional level, and bring their influence to bear on recruitment policy formulation and practice through negotiation and lobbying efforts. At times there may be significant domestic pressure on publicly accountable subnational government institutions, and especially on responsible destination country health agencies, to produce desired health workforce outcomes in circumstances of urgent need and significant political pressure and public expectation. This pressure may put strain on commitments to broad global principles of ethical and sustainable recruitment such as those embodied in the WHO code.

Internationally, national governments and their agencies, global intergovernmental organizations, such as the United Nations (UN), OECD, WHO and their sub-agencies, and international health regulatory and professional organizations negotiate on their members' behalf, designing, implementing and enforcing the global, multilateral and bilateral agreements, legal instruments and governance frameworks in which ethical and sustainable international health personnel recruitment is intended to take place. Each of these internationally focused institutions represents a distinct set of interests and operates within an established set of legislative and other governance arrangements that sets out the scope and limit of its legitimate exercise of power. National governments, obviously, are expected to act in their own national interest, whereas global institutions such as the UN, WHO and OECD operate with a broader set of global ethical and other relevant principles, yet with limited power and resources to directly represent their interests in member countries. Other international professional organizations and regulators represent their professions' and members' interests, as well as universal principles of health care. Beneath this level, but still internationally operative and of international-level importance, are the subnational institutions – such as state and provincial governments, their health agencies, recruiters, employer health facilities, domestic regulators and professional associations, educational institutions and migration agents – which are directly involved in international recruitment regimes. In fact, as has already been mentioned, responsibility and accountability for the implementation of ethical and sustainable recruitment practices is largely being placed with these intermediating subnational – but also internationally operative – institutions.

Integrity System Vulnerabilities: Areas of Ethical Tension and Dislocation

In an era of global skilled labour movements across a range of professions, building an ethical and sustainable model of international health personnel recruitment becomes a matter of improving and strengthening its integrity system – a system which has emerged organically out of existing international, national and subnational institutional settings in response to global shortages and misdistributions of health personnel – in a number of crucial areas of actual and potential ethical failure. With global institutional commitment to principles of fairness, transparency, mutual benefit and sustainability now in effect via the WHO Global Code of Practice on the International Recruitment of Health Personnel, building, strengthening, and maintaining the integrity system is also a matter of detailing what a public commitment to those values means in practice at each level in each institutional environment – mapping the integrity landscape – and of crafting and instituting, where necessary, recruitment regime reforms which aim at publicly living up to that commitment and those values.

Ethical failure and consequent integrity system weakness may occur on systemic, institutional and individual levels, and between and within source and destination countries throughout international health personnel recruitment regimes. It is crucial in combatting ethical failure and promoting integrity that ethically committed stakeholders and individuals are capable of identifying areas of both actual and potential ethical failure – points of tension and dislocation between practice and principle – throughout recruitment systems and processes. These multiple points of ethical tension and disconnection may be distinguished in a number of ways. A useful distinction can be made between established systemic design features which may cause, enable, or be conducive to unfairness, opacity, failure to secure expected benefits or unsustainable practices, and particular points of ethical tension and disconnection facing institutions and individuals wielding power or influence over various systemic elements, processes and outcomes, and those affected by them. Recruitment regimes may, for various inadvertent reasons, have been effectively 'designed to fail' from an ethical point of view in the past, especially when integrity considerations have not been included from the beginning, as is the case with the escalation of developed world international health personnel recruitment regimes in the current era. This is understandable in a certain sense, since developed world recruitment regimes tend to have been designed and instituted with the instrumental focus of recruiting needed health professionals, with little or no thought to wider issues.

Points of ethical tension faced by stakeholders who act and are acted upon across all levels in existing international recruitment regimes are likely to include both temptations to engage in unethical or ethically dubious practices, and real or apparent ethical dilemmas – circumstances in which it appears that equally valid and compelling ethical principles give conflicting practical guidance. Often, less influential stakeholders will have limited power to change or overcome decisions and systemic design elements instituted at higher levels that cause or exacerbate ethical tensions and dislocations for them and those affected by their decisions. Institutions and individuals may be tempted to cut ethical corners where the integrity system lacks effect and where pressure from other sources of motivation is great, or not to inquire into issues of ethics and sustainability of current settings and practices where the public and honest answers may be disappointing, embarrassing or awkward. Alternatively, they may simply not recognize that recruitment processes have ethical dimensions. Dilemmas may appear to arise at various levels, especially where defining principles of care, legal and contractual rules and competing loyalties entrenched in institutional frameworks appear to weigh against what codified ethical principles would recommend. In these circumstances, special care must always be taken to distinguish genuinely conflicting basic ethical principles from a clash of ethical principles with very strong temptation, for example the need to 'get results'. There may arise, for example, a strong temptation to misrepresent clashes of instrumentally urgent but ethically weak reasons with sound ethical principles as 'ethical dilemmas' when, from an ethical point of view, no dilemma obtains and the ethical principle clearly applies.

Ethical dislocations may occur where publicly entrusted power and accountability have become separated, or where there are ethical blind spots, oversights and broken or absent links in integrity systems which allow ethical failure – opacity, unfairness, lack of mutual benefit, unsustainable practices – to flourish. An area of dislocation, for example, may open up when changes in national immigration policy, aimed at broader economic and social goals, close off previously established recruitment pathways for international health personnel, force policy changes at subnational levels, and affect health systems, employers, recruiters, migration agents, educational institutions in both source and destination countries, and migrating health personnel. Another ethical dislocation may open up between employers and recruiters, where recruitment is contracted out by the health facilities or agencies with whom ethical accountability traditionally rests. Unfairness, lack of mutual benefit and unsustainable practices may emerge and become entrenched without effective oversight in a recruitment regime that, thanks to structural dislocation, lacks full transparency and accountability. Once again, there may also be many potential dislocations between the national governments of member states who sign international ethical agreements and set legislative agendas, the subnational agencies expected to implement them, and stakeholders across the integrity system. This is especially the case where institutional ethics have not been explicitly considered or embedded previously, and where integrity systems are consequently underdeveloped.

Conclusion: Pathways and Models for Integrity System Mapping

The weight of responsibility for oversight of the ethics and sustainability of international health personnel recruitment falls overwhelmingly on subnational health agencies in destination countries. From the point of view of integrity system reform, it is therefore important for those stakeholders most directly responsible for international health personnel recruitment regimes – these same subnational health agencies in destination countries – to have available for reference what might be called an 'integrity map' describing in detail the relevant integrity landscape: the legal rules, institutional settings, powers, roles, responsibilities, policies, practices, stakeholder interests and influence, structural policy changes and their effects; and an ethical 'key': a practical grasp of how each of these elements and the system overall relate to the defining principles of ethical recruitment. One central region of the integrity map which may need to be traced in greater detail from an ethical point of view includes the range of pathways migrant health personnel follow throughout the recruitment process from source country into destination country employment, the challenges and obstacles they may face, and the relationship of these experiences with the principles that guide their fair treatment, as is emphasized in the WHO code. Another region, which the WHO code also emphasizes in terms of developing world health system benefits and recruitment practice sustainability, is the often uncharted (by destination agencies and employers) ethical landscape of source countries' stakeholder experiences and institutional conditions.

A simple determination concerning at what level – and with which institutions and individuals – responsibility rests for maintenance and reform of the international health professional recruitment integrity system cannot be made, we believe, in advance of a detailed case-by-case understanding of both broader institutional landscapes and the specific ethical, legal and institutional dynamics of existing regimes. The areas in which ethical tensions and dislocations exist or are likely to arise will be different in different integrity systems, and reforms, to have a realistic chance of being effective, must be tailored to suit the particular circumstances. However, in the light of our argument in this chapter, two general observations can be made. The first is that when an international health professional recruitment regime is in need of rebuilding, repair or strengthening, those subnational institutions most closely involved in recruitment will shoulder much of the responsibility. Second, without the good will and appropriate support of other stakeholders across the integrity landscape – especially those with significant influence over the success or failure of international health professional recruitment models designed in favour of ethics and sustainability – lasting changes for the better are less likely to be achieved.

Acknowledgements

This research was supported by an Australian Research Council Linkage Grant: Building an Ethical and Sustainable Model for Health Professional recruitment to Australia: Case study of the Philippines (2010–2012).

References

Acar, M. and Emek, U. 2008. Building a clean government in Turkey. *Crime, Law and Social Change*, 49(3), 185.

Anechiarico, F. 2010. Protecting integrity at the local level. *Crime, Law and Social Change,* 53(1), 79.

Behnke, N. and Maesschalck, J. 2006. Integrity systems at work: theoretical and empirical foundations. *Public Admininstration Queensland*, 30(3), 263.

Buchan, J. 2010. Can the WHO code on international recruitment succeed? *British Medical Journal*, 340(7750), 791.

Buchan, J. and McPake, B. 2007. *The Impact of the Department of Health, England, Code of Practice on International Recruitment: Report to Department for International Development, and Department of Health.* United Kingdom: Government of the United Kingdom.

Dobel, J.P. 1999. *Public Integrity*. Baltimore: Johns Hopkins University Press.

Fitzgerald, G.E. 1989. *Report of a Commission of Inquiry Pursuant to Orders in Council*. Brisbane: Queensland Government.

Head, B., Brown, A. and Connors, C. 2008. *Promoting Integrity: Evaluating and Improving Public Institutions*. Farnham: Ashgate.

Huberts, L.W., Maesschalck, J. and Jurkiewicz, C. 2008. *Ethics and Integrity of Governance*. Cheltenham: Edward Elgar Publishing.

Langseth, P., Stapenhurst, R. and Pope, J. 1997. Role of national integrity systems in fighting corruption. *Commonwealth Law Bulletin*, 23, 499.

Meagher, P. 2005. Anti-corruption agencies: rhetoric versus reality. *The Journal of Policy Reform*, 8(1), 69.

Nussbaum, M. 1993. Equity and mercy. *Philosophy and Public Affairs*, 22(2), 83.

OECD. 1996. *Ethics in the Public Sector: Current Issues and Practices*. Paris: OECD.

OECD. 1997a. PUMA draft checklist. *Symposium on Ethics in the Public Sector: Challenges and Opportunities for OECD Countries*. Paris: OECD.

OECD. 1997b. Survey of anti-corruption mechanisms in OECD countries. *Symposium on Ethics in the Public Sector: Challenges and Opportunities for OECD Countries*. Paris: OECD.

OECD. 1998. *Council Recommendations on Improving Ethical Conduct in the Public Service – Background Note.* Paris: OECD.

OECD. 2010. *Policy Brief – International Migration of Health Workers: Improving International Co-operation to Address the Global Health Workforce Crisis.* Paris: OECD.

Pope, J. 2000. *Confronting Corruption: The Elements of a National Integrity System (TI Source Book).* Berlin: TI.

Preston, N., Sampford, C. and Connors, C. 2002. *Encouraging Ethics and Challenging Corruption.* Sydney: Federation Press.

Rawls, J. 1971. *A Theory of Justice.* Cambridge: Harvard University Press.

Sampford, C. 1990. Law, institutions and the public private divide. *Federal Law Review,* 20(2), 185–222.

Sampford, C. and Lui, R. 2004. Australian media ethics regime and ethical risk management. *The Journal of Mass Media Ethics*, 19(2), 86.

Sampford, C., Smith, R. and Brown, A. 2005. From Greek temple to bird's nest: towards a theory of coherence and mutual accountability for national integrity systems. *Australian Journal of Public Administration,* 64(2), 96.

Sampford, C. and Wood, D. 1993. The future of business ethics: legal regulation, ethical standards setting and institutional design, in *Business Ethics and the Law*, edited by C. Sampford and C. Coady. Sydney: Federation Press.

WHO. 2006. International migration of health personnel: a challenge for health systems in developing countries, provisional agenda item 11.12, Fifty-Ninth World Health Assembly. Geneva: WHO.

WHO. 2010. *The WHO Global Code of Practice on the International Recruitment of Health Personnel.* Geneva: WHO.

Willetts, A. and Martineau, T. 2004. *Ethical International Recruitment of Health Professionals: Will Codes of Practice Protect Developing Country Health Systems?* Liverpool: Liverpool School of Tropical Medicine.

Xu, Y. and Zhang, J. 2005. One size doesn't fit all: ethics of international nurse recruitment from the conceptual framework of stakeholder interests. *Nursing Ethics*, 12(6), 571.

Chapter 4

The Global Health Workforce 'Crisis' and Inequities in Health Care Access: Advancing a Gender and Organisations Approach to Policy, Research and Practice

Toni Schofield

The Global Health Workforce 'Crisis' and Health Care Access

Governments in high-income countries, such as members of the Organisation for Economic Cooperation and Development (OECD), have been reporting an impending 'crisis' with health workforce shortages expected to intensify over the next decade (AHMC 2004: 5, Derksen and Whelan 2009, O'Brien and Gostin 2008/09, WHO 2006). With them will come unwanted public health consequences, primarily contraction and even disappearance of health services. In OECD countries, such as Australia, for example, these contractions and disappearances will mainly occur in remote and rural regions, and the more socially and economically marginalised areas in urban centres (Duckett 2007, Palmer and Short 2010. Those most adversely affected will be Indigenous, low-income and older Australians who already have the worst health (AIHW 2010, Baum 2008). The predicted health workforce shrinkage in high-income countries, then, will pose formidable challenges to policy aspirations to 'close the gap' in *access to health and for advancing health equity*.

As the World Health Organization (WHO) (2006) has reported, however, the problem is not confined to privileged nations. Indeed, health workforce shortages pose a markedly graver challenge outside the 'global north' and are predicted to deepen significantly. According to the WHO (2006), the most severe impacts will be felt in those countries with greatest relative need, or where shortages of health service providers (doctors, nurse and midwives) are already defined as 'critical' (WHO 2006: 11–13). These countries are mainly in South-East Asia, especially Bangladesh, India and Indonesia, and sub-Saharan Africa. In sub-Saharan Africa, for example, with only 3 per cent of the world's health workers but 24 per cent of the world's burden of disease, the more than 50 countries that comprise the region are expected to suffer a catastrophic decline in the survival rates of women in childbirth and children in early infancy (WHO 2006). OECD countries, by contrast, are not facing critical shortages. So while health workforce shortfalls will be accompanied by significant barriers to achieving national health goals across the world, they will impact even more heavily on *global* health goals. The forthcoming health workforce 'crisis', then, is expected to widen rather than narrow the already entrenched health inequities between the 'global north' and 'global south'.

So what do health workforce policy makers 'make' of the problem? How do they understand or make sense of it? As significantly, how do they intend to address and redress it? This chapter critically examines prevailing international approaches to the impending 'crisis' and argues that one of the major obstacles to an effective solution lies with the failure of wealthy nations, such as members of the OECD, to develop a better, research-based understanding of, and interventions to address, the exodus of workers from their own health workforces. This problem, the chapter proposes, is directly related to how health workforce shortages are represented and understood by policy makers in high-income countries. In the face of such limitations, the chapter calls for a new approach: one that focuses on the complex social dynamics involved in generating the problem, in particular, those associated with the institutional organisation of the health workforce in high-income countries. In illustrating and discussing the problem, the chapter draws on the Australian context.

Representing the Problem of Global Health Workforce Shortages: the WHO and Health Workforce Policy

It is important to note, as many policy researchers have observed (see, for example, Barraclough and Gardner 2008: 4, Hill 2005, Parsons 1995), that recognising and identifying a policy problem is fundamental to policy formation or formulation. It establishes the parameters or boundaries for possible solutions (Dery 1984, Parsons 1995). As significantly, as Carol Bacchi (1999: 1–2) explained to us a decade ago, 'what the policy problem is represented to be' is an interpretation that 'involves judgement and choices' and that has 'programmatic outcomes; that is, the interpretation offered will line up with particular policy recommendations'. This means that policy 'problems' are not simply apprehended as pre-existing 'objects' but are actually brought into being as 'problematisations'. The ways in which issues are problematised or represented 'limits what is talked about as possible or desirable, or as impossible or undesirable' (Bacchi 1999: 3). Policy representations or constructions are thus crucial in determining the nature of public interventions and their consequences. From this perspective, policy may be understood as a discourse in which both problems and solutions are created. This is not to say that policy is *only* discourse or 'ideation' – 'the name given to the imagining or conceiving of something' (Lewis 2005: 13). As numerous public policy scholars have demonstrated, policy is a process that involves complex human action, but ideas and meaning are foundational. The power of the policy story line, or the way in which the problem is represented in policy discourse, is not only influential but *constitutive* of policy actions or interventions (Fairclough 1995, Fraser 1989, Wodak 2008).

The following turns to a discussion of how *The Working Together for Health* report, produced by the WHO in 2006, *represents the problem* of health workforce shortages and the strategies for addressing it. The report outlines the main international public policy and planning approach to the expected shortfall in the global health workforce. According to the report the health workforce is comprised of two main groups: 'health service providers' (doctors, nurse and midwives) and 'health management and support workers' (WHO 2006: xvi). The former constitute about two thirds of the global health workforce while the latter account for one third. The WHO estimates that there are 59.2 million full-time paid health workers in total (WHO 2006: xvi).

From the outset, the report is emphatic: the global health picture is one of polarised extremes with growing fears of grave new health threats 'in rich and poor countries alike'. Though it stops short of a global health armageddon, the WHO's report leaves no doubt that the world's health fortunes are imperilled and that access to 'capable, motivated and supported health workers is essential for overcoming bottlenecks to achieve national and global health goals' (WHO 2006: xv). The main problem is that the biggest 'bottlenecks' are in regions with the most critical shortages of health service providers and health systems that are the most poorly resourced and managed (WHO 2006: 1–39). What is to be done? Basically, 'national leadership must … be complemented by global solidarity on … three (main) fronts: knowledge and learning; cooperative arrangements; and responsiveness to workforce crises' (WHO 2006: xxiv). According to the WHO, in practical terms this strategy amounts to: more and better global 'pooling' of 'diverse technical expertise and breadth of experiences' related to mapping and planning the nature and distribution of international health resources so that there is a shift from 'assistance and gap-filling to exchange and joint learning' (WHO 2006: 142); adoption of 'ethical workforce recruitment practices' so that those with the least shortages do not 'poach' (through migration programmes) health service providers from countries with the most pressing shortages such as those in sub-Saharan Africa and South-East Asia (principally Bangladesh, India and Indonesia); and the allocation of 50 per cent of all international assistance by high-income countries to the world's poorest countries as funding specifically for health systems, 'with half of this devoted to national health workforce strengthening strategies' (WHO 2006: xxiv).

In telling this story the WHO's global health workforce report identifies key health system challenges that need to be addressed in advancing its strategic approach. *First is the training and recruitment of the health workforce*, and how the institutional landscape in which this occurs has a major impact on the number, diversity and competencies of its graduates. As the report comments, the prevailing institutional organisation takes the shape of a 'pipeline to generate and recruit the health workforce' (WHO 2006: 42), and determines how many and who get to join. According to the report, there is a severe mismatch between those who get to enter training institutions and are subsequently recruited to the health workforce, and the populations and 'clientele' with the most pressing health needs. At present, 'entrance to most training programmes for health professions requires a secondary education … (so) students are disproportionately admitted from the higher social classes and dominant ethnic groups' (WHO 2006: 46). As a result 'students entering health professions rarely reflect national profiles of social, linguistic and ethnic diversity' (WHO 2006: 46). A new approach is suggested – one that is more closely attuned to 'giving the right training to the right people to create an effective workforce' (WHO 2006: 41). This not only involves more relevant curricula that are aligned with the health needs of local populations, and that are taught to a variety of students representative of these populations. It also requires the establishment of more public health-focused education and training in those regions suffering the greatest health workforce shortages – primarily sub-Saharan Africa and South-East Asia. Such training should produce workers who are better able to apprehend and understand specific and local health problems, and to act more effectively in planning and managing responses and interventions.

As significant as training and recruitment of future health workers in obstructing the advancement of its global health workforce strategy, according to the WHO, is *institutional organisation and management of the current health workforce*. An effective health workforce strategy, the report states, 'has to focus on three core challenges: improving recruitment, helping the existing workforce to perform better, and slowing the rate at which workers leave the health workforce' (WHO 2006: 67). These imperatives arise from significant limitations in prevailing approaches to organising and managing health workers throughout the world. In short, as the WHO report proposes, these approaches do not focus on employing and training enough people with the right skills to work in areas with the greatest need; nor do they support health workers sufficiently to optimise their output and effectiveness; and nor are they doing enough to encourage them to remain in the health workforce.

As the WHO (2006: 144) concludes its magisterial review of global health workforce challenges, 'an extraordinary global response is needed'. Central to the response is 'global solidarity' (WHO 2006: 149) enacted through a massive redistribution of financial and human resources from the wealthy to what the WHO report describes as the 'crisis countries'. This is not to say that the WHO's report ignores the role of *national* health workforce policy in addressing the crisis. Indeed, according to the WHO (2006: 148), 'strong country strategies' are vital in building and strengthening national 'institutional capacities to deal with their own predicaments and problems of human resources for health'. The absence of 'national leadership' in health workforce policy and planning, according to the WHO, seriously jeopardises the chances of global efforts to manage and reduce critical shortages. It is evident from the WHO's perspective that effective national leadership in health workforce policy and planning in wealthy countries can no longer rely on the importation, through migration, of health workforce personnel from the 'crisis countries' of South-East Asia and sub-Saharan Africa. As mentioned above, 'ethical recruitment practices' that eschew negotiation related to the migration of health workers from the poor to the rich countries of the world are fundamental to the WHO's proposed global strategy to intervene effectively in the health workforce crisis. Yet, as the WHO's report makes clear, effective national health workforce strategies involve more than this.

Although it rejects the idea of a 'global blueprint', the WHO advances specific goals and a set of principles to guide national health workforce strategies. 'Guarantee(d) universal access to health care and social protection to all citizens in every country', according to the WHO (2006: 119), is the 'ultimate goal' of such strategies; and 'mobilising political commitment to tackle workforce challenges' is the 'key' to achieving it. As the WHO's report (2006: 119) comments, this is no easy task because health workforce problems inevitably extend beyond election cycles; they are emotionally charged because of professional status issues; and they involve divergent and often conflicting interests such as those within and between professional organisations, state regulatory and insurance agencies, and citizens' groups such as health consumer/user organisations. Political inaction, however, is not really an option given the severity of health workforce challenges, and policy makers, according to the WHO (2006: 129), must be inclusive of all 'key stakeholders' in order to establish trust in health systems and the development of cooperative governance. As significantly, to carry out policy formulation related to health workforce reform, policy makers must have the 'capacity to base policy on a proper understanding of the nature of the problems' (WHO 2006: 129).

National Policy and Planning Approaches to Understanding and Acting on Health Workforce Shortages in High-income Countries: Australia as a Case Study

It is evident that high-income countries such as Australia, Canada, New Zealand, the United Kingdom and the United States are not self-sufficient in terms of securing enough health workers to ensure universal healthcare access (AHMC 2004, ANHWT 2009, O'Brien and Gostin 2009). According to the OECD (2002 cited in Liese and Dussault 2004: 12), 'foreign-trained health professionals are estimated to represent more than a quarter of the medical and nursing workforces of Australia, Canada, the UK, and the US'. At the same time, the health systems of these countries are experiencing major difficulties in *retaining* the health workers they educate and train for their respective health workforces (see, for example, ANHWT 2009). But how is the problem of workforce shortages conceptualised or understood in high-income countries? Further, do such representations reflect what the WHO (2006:129) describes as a 'proper understanding of the nature of the problem?' Drawing on the Australian context as a case study, the following suggests that prevailing policy understandings of the nature of health workforce shortages in high-income countries are beset by significant limitations associated with narrow, technocratic approaches to the problem. In the face of such limitations, a new approach that focuses on the complex *social dynamics* of healthcare institutions in organising and managing their workforces is proposed.

In addressing the problem of health workforce shortages, Australian health policy makers and planners have focused their efforts on doctors and nurses – the members of the workforce who deliver most of the services within the 'formal health care system' (Duckett 2007). However, increasing policy attention has been paid to the allied health workforce because of the contribution its members could make in addressing the anticipated shortfall in medical and nursing personnel (AHWAC 2006). At present, according to the Australian Institute of Health and Welfare (AIHW 2009: 4–5), doctors comprise around 10 per cent of the health workforce, nurses 41 per cent and allied health workers approximately 10 per cent. While all three sectors have sustained growth rates over the last decade that have exceeded population growth (AIHW 2009: 4–5), there are various trends in the participation of the health workforce that signal impending and significant shortages. In conventional workforce policy and planning terms, such trends are associated with *supply* and *demand* factors. An unprecedented rise in population ageing over the next 20 years (Access Economics 2001) that will be accompanied by increased rates of chronic illness (Leeder 2004) are understood to be the main demand factors. The supply factors involve expected rates of participation by the health workforce that will see its members increasingly: (i) relinquishing health professional employment and moving to other occupations; (ii) moving from full-time to part-time or casual employment as a health professional; (iii) retiring from paid work in the health sector completely; and (iv) choosing to work in large urban or regional centres that offer diverse social amenity (Boyce 2008:108). These trends are expected to exacerbate already pressing shortages across a wide range of health occupations.

One of the outstanding characteristics of the Australian health workforce, like its counterparts in other comparable high-income countries, is that it is highly feminised. Women account for 76 per cent of all employed allied health workers (excluding radiographers) (AIHW 2009: 33) and 91 per cent of employed nurses (AIHW 2009: 31). Though they are a minority in medicine – 39 per cent of general medical practitioners and 29 per cent of specialist medical practitioners (AIHW 2009: 29) – women constitute around a third of the medical workforce. The gendered nature of the health workforce is acknowledged by a range of Australian health workforce reports investigating anticipated shortages in the medical, nursing and allied health workforces (see, for example, Productivity Commission 2005, AHWAC 2006, ANHWT 2009) but none of them provides any critical analysis and discussion of the role it might play in the anticipated shortage of health workers, as the following section discusses in more detail. How, then, does mainstream health workforce policy and planning understand the problem of anticipated shortages of health workers?

Technocratic Dominance

Most Australian health workforce policy reports focus on workforce planning and are designed to inform and advise the Australian Health Ministers Advisory Council (AHMAC) about the 'required supply of health care practitioners to meet an expected future level of service requirement as defined by population need and/or demand and the development of strategies to meet that requirement' (AHWAC 2006: 34). Most of the current data on which Australian health workforce planning depends focuses on 'supply-side' factors (AHWAC 2006: 36, ANHWT 2009: 40–41). What is known about the health workforce is largely informed by descriptive statistical data that permit policy makers and planners only to identify: (i) workforce numbers, characteristics, participation, distribution, productivity, types and quantity of service provision, and skills and tasks; (ii) trends in the recruitment process, such as the number and characteristics of those undertaking training in Australia; and (iii) the extent of 'wastage' arising from workforce exits, such as those arising from adoption of other careers and migration.

The dominant approach in health workforce planning is 'profession-centred' or profession-specific and focuses on 'front end', supply-focused, policy instruments such as creating more student places (Boyce 2008: 109). From this perspective, workforce shortages are like droughts, and the major policy and planning response is to turn on the taps to increase the volume of workers through the education and training pipeline. The underlying assumption is that the dams are full – lots of potential students – and that better provision of pipeline and associated infrastructure – education and training – will significantly relieve or end the drought. Such an approach discloses the operation of a kind of engineering mentality that has dominated the development of public policy on water, roads, transport, housing and so on in Australia at least since the late nineteenth century. It is fundamentally *technocratic* in character insofar as the organisation, management and distribution of the resources involved in public governance are heavily influenced by the knowledge and understanding of technical experts. Problems and solutions that arise in the course of public governance and policy making derive from the ways in which technical specialists and technocratic discourse frame and understand them (see, for example, O'Donnell, Allan and Peetz 1999, Power 1997: 78–82). Tom Christensen and Per Laegreid (2007) suggest that this technocratic approach to public governance developed as part of the tide of rationalisation that shaped public sector management in the twentieth century, particularly after WWII (Christensen and Laegreid 2007: 223). Indeed, according to them, technocracy is the 'quintessential rationalization of government itself' (2007: 223) and the New Public Management its latest and most robust incarnation. Technocratic governance is an approach to organising, managing and distributing resources that frames problems and solutions in terms of conceptual tools and frameworks informed by positivist science. As a consequence, problem identification and analysis typically focus on linear cause-and-effect relationships and measurable patterns and outcomes. The adoption of such an approach is understood not only to enhance the calculability of results but also to ensure objectivity and neutrality since interpretive, and therefore partisan, judgements are presumed to be excluded (Christensen and Laegreid 2007). Recent Australian policy analysis has identified its dominance across a wide range of major policy and planning arenas in Australia such as health services (Schofield 2008), occupational health regulation (Schofield 2007) and other human services (Schofield and Goodwin 2005). It also predominates in health workforce policy and planning through the identification of demand and supply factors that are based mainly on population and workforce characteristics that can be measured, as outlined above.

So why is technocratic governance a problem? In relation to health workforce shortages, the application of such an approach does not permit policy makers and planners to identify and understand the *social dynamics* responsible for producing the problem. For example, responding to measurable decreases in workforce participation by health professional groups by creating and funding increased health student places leaves unaddressed why graduates of health education and training programmes do not stay in the health workforce and are reluctant to work outside urban and regional centres. It is an approach that relies on assumptions about workforce motivations rather than empirical evidence on precisely who its members are, what they do, the relations and conditions under which they are employed, and their occupational and professional inter-relationships. This is particularly apparent in relation to the 'leakage', or problem of retention, of the health workforce as several health workforce reports show. The Australian National Health Workforce Taskforce (ANHWT) (2009:30) report on 'factors for current shortages', for example, cites the increasingly female character of general practitioners as significant, stating that 'women tend to work fewer hours … especially during their child-rearing years and are more likely to retire early'. The Australian Allied Health Workforce report (AHWAC 2006: 72) also draws on the female-dominated character of the allied health workforce as central to problems of workforce retention. The report comments allied health workers are 'relatively young and predominantly female'. The implication here is that such a workforce poses retention problems because being 'relatively young and predominantly female' means leaving full-time, paid employment to establish and prioritise family life. Such an approach to health workforce planning operates on the basis of assumptions about workforce participation rather than on critical analysis of the evidence of what is happening in the workplace and why.

Yet, as mentioned previously, the evidence currently used in health workforce policy and planning mainly lends itself to descriptive, not explanatory purposes. In fact, as the ANHWT (2009) and Australian Health Workforce Advisory Council (AHWAC) (2006) reports suggest, there is virtually no other kind of data. So it is not known what the diverse segments of the health workforce are actually doing in their workplaces, at what stages of their lives, under what circumstances, in what kinds of inter-professional relationships and organisational contexts, and with what consequences at personal, professional and organisational levels. In other words, there is basically no large-scale, systematic social scientific research that provides policy makers and planners with a basis for understanding how and why health workforce participation assumes the patterns that it does. This is not to say that health workforce policy and planners are the only actors involved in framing the policy problem of health workforce shortages and in posing solutions to it. There is now a substantial body of recent Australian research, both quantitative and qualitative, that has addressed the nursing shortage, for example, by examining why fewer people are choosing nursing as a career (Dockery and Barnes 2005, McCabe, Nowak and Mullen 2005, Preston 2005), why nurses have left the occupation and what might encourage them to return (Buchanan and Considine 2002, Buchanan et al. 2004, Dockery 2004, Flavel 2007, Horner 2002, Naude and McCabe 2005, Nowak 2005). In contrast to the technocratic approach adopted by workforce policy and planners, this research investigates what nurses do in the workplace, the conditions under which they do it, and how their work is managed. It offers an alternative framing of workforce shortages. Among the reasons it identifies for nurses leaving the system are work intensification, lack of recognition and autonomy, lack of professional development as well as unsocial hours and lack of childcare. The findings yielded by such an approach point to the centrality of specific workplace factors involved in producing the problem of health workforce shortages and, in turn, their significance for strategies to address it.

Gendered Organisational Dynamics

A further relevant body of research that transcends the merely descriptive approach evident in technocratic representations of the problem of health workforce shortages and that provides an alternative explanatory framework is that which has emerged from the field of organisational studies. A major development in the field has been the scholarly work on gender as an in-built feature of organisations both in Australia and internationally. Much of this research has focused on how gender operates within organisations, including large public institutions where gendered hierarchies have persisted despite determined policy interventions to redress the problem. Clearly, gender is a significant force in the pattern of health workforce participation in Australia as indicated by the high numbers of women who work in it. Yet technocratic understandings of gender, of the kind evident in health workforce policy and planning approaches, tend to be categoricalist in character (Connell 2009). In other words, gender is understood as a reproductive sexual characteristic – male or female – and applied as a static descriptor of biological difference. Contributors to gender and organisational studies, on the other hand, take a more dynamic approach that provides a framework for developing explanations of how gender operates in relation to health workforce participation patterns, including shortfalls in 'supply'.

Within 'mainstream organisational studies', as Colleen Chesterman and her colleagues have written (2005: 73), gender has been recognised as a problem but largely in terms of women and their femininity, and how they impact on organisations. The focus of the approach is on gender as 'a property of the individuals who appear in the organisational slots' (Connell 2005: 5). So organisational problems in which there are disproportionate numbers of women involved, such as workforce shortages in the health sector, will tend to be viewed in terms of alleged deficits associated with being a woman – fewer and less valued qualifications, inadequate training, having children or thinking about doing so, being more committed to family than career, not being tough and competitive, and so on. Since the 1990s, this approach has been challenged both in organisation studies and gender studies. As a result, the problem of gender in organisations is now seen as a problem of 'gendered organisation' as the US sociologist, Joan Acker (1990: 146), famously described it, meaning that organisations operate on the basis that: 'advantages and disadvantages, exploitation and control, action and emotion, meaning and identities are patterned through, and in terms of, distinctions between what is constructed as male and female, masculine and feminine'. How this happens has been the subject of numerous studies since – more so in the corporate world than in the public sector (Connell 2006: 838). Nevertheless, there are sufficient examples in a growing international literature to show that gendered organisational dynamics in public sector workplaces are not all of a piece. They are diverse, uneven and sometimes internally contradictory (Connell 2006: 838). This means that, as a recent Australian collection of research on gender and public sector organisations found, while there are formidable barriers to developing strategic interventions to address and resolve problems of gendered organisation in public sector contexts, there are also significant opportunities (Bacchi and Schofield 2005: 1–4).

What might this mean in relation to understanding the organisational dynamics of public sector workplaces in which health workers are employed and how might it help in addressing the problem of predicted shortages among them? Basically, the study of gender and public sector organisation has generated significant and innovative theoretical and methodological tools for identifying how organisational processes create barriers and opportunities for women's participation in public sector employment and workplaces. Since women comprise the overwhelming majority of health workers in the public sector and are demonstrating an increasingly precarious relationship to participation in the health workforce throughout Australia, the application of recent theoretical and methodological advances in gender and organisation studies may prove useful in understanding and responding to the problem more effectively. This may be illustrated with reference to a recent Australian ethnographic study that explored the barriers to democratic participation in clinical decision-making and practice within a public hospital setting (Long et al. 2006). It found that although all members of the health services team were committed to democratised clinical practice, 'the medical voice was often dominant, and non-medical voices were often muted. Medical time was valued over non-medical time, both within the team and the broader hospital environment. The medical voice had more authority and autonomy than the non-medical voice' (Long et al. 2006: 516). These findings suggest that in spite of team members' intentions, there was an organisational dynamic that produced hierarchical differentials between medicine and other health professionals in the exercise of clinical skills, knowledge, experience, authority and autonomy. These differentials, according to the researchers, appeared to be closely associated with organisationally based practices of esteem and recognition, particularly in relation to the time and specific clinical contribution of team members. As the researchers commented, this was evident in what they called 'waiting hierarchies':

> In clinic … surgical waits for no one, medical waits for surgical, but not for allied health or nursing; physiotherapist and occupational therapist wait for medical and surgical, but not for nursing, social work, peer support or dietician. Nursing waits for surgical, medical, physiotherapist and occupational therapist and occasionally for social work and dietician, but not for peer support. Social work, dietician and peer support most frequently do their work when everybody else is finished, or when the team are waiting for people further up the hierarchy to arrive (Long et al. 2006: 513).

Yet closer examination of the hierarchical differentials between medicine and other health professionals suggests they were simultaneously gendered. For example, two key structures of work organisation that prevailed – the division of labour (between medical specialist and other health professionals) and relations of power and authority (between team leader and team members) – were distinctly gendered. The medical specialist/team leader was a man while all the other health professionals, except the social worker, were women. (This was evident in the data presented in the published paper of the study's findings.) As significantly, the embodied dimensions of the interactions between them, such as the exercise of voice, were also gendered. Further, though the authors did not recognise it, they inferred that the work of the allied health and nursing staff was symbolically equivalent in gendered terms to the unpaid work that women typically perform outside the labour market and that, as Marilyn Waring (1988) calculated more than two decades ago, usually 'counts for nothing' in terms of economic production and productivity. The authors commented:

> in terms of hospital accounting practices, many of the tasks which allied health and nursing staff undertake are valued differently, or are not provided with a descriptive vocabulary so that they can be measured, counted and accounted for in hospital budgets (Long et al. 2006: 514).

The hierarchical relations that the study identified as prevailing in the team's work and organisation, then, were not simply associated with differentiations in esteem and recognition related to occupation and authority, but also to gender. How might such an approach contribute to explaining health workers' participation patterns and their exodus from the workforce?

An Alternative Framing of Health Workforce Shortages

At present, there is no published research specifically investigating institutionalised gender dynamics related to health workforce participation and the problem of retention in Australia. There is, however, a small but cogent sociological examination and analysis of health workers in Australian healthcare institutions that has explored the social dynamics involved in the development, organisation and operation of the health professions, and of the relations between them. The findings of this work are very useful in building a framework and method for developing 'a proper understanding of the nature of the problem of health workforce shortages' as the WHO proposes.

Informed by the approach of the US sociologist, Eliot Freidson (2001), Australian sociologist, Evan Willis (1989), has identified the dominance of the medical profession in the division of labour in health care as foundational to the organisation and management of healthcare institutions. According to Willis, the assertion of occupational interest and professional boundaries by medicine has been the central dynamic in rendering other health workers subordinate and their contribution to patient care as subsidiary. Though Willis is recently more equivocal about medical dominance, acknowledging persuasive evidence of its decline, he nevertheless argues that 'the medical profession retains very significant power and authority. Boundaries between health occupations have become more fluid and less entrenched but that does not mean they do not exist' (Willis 2006: 427). One of the principal outcomes of this process, according to Willis, is that the non-medical sectors of the health workforce continue to enjoy far less institutional autonomy and control over their work, more limited financial rewards, and significantly more constrained opportunities for career advancement and recognition of their contribution to patient care and health.

Based on sustained sociological research of the allied health workforce in Australia, Rosalie Boyce (1996, 1997, 2001, 2006) concurs with Willis's approach and conclusions regarding medical dominance in the organisational dynamics of professional boundary maintenance within healthcare institutions. According to Boyce these dynamics establish structural impediments to the development of allied health workforce capacity (Boyce 2008: 114). She argues that medical dominance still exerts significant influence in the current organisation of the health workforce and its expected shortages by imposing barriers to the full and effective utilisation of the skills of health workers. This dominance, as Boyce points out, was evident in a submission by the Australian Medical Association (AMA) to an investigation by the Productivity Commission of the health workforce in 2005–2006. The AMA's submission openly opposed 'professional substitution' – whereby a range of health professionals other than doctors receive public funding to provide bulk-billed health services and prescribe medications – as recommended by the Productivity Commission. Professional substitution was seen as an intervention that might address shortages in the medical workforce, particularly in regional, rural and remote areas. The AMA (2005: 5) favoured 'delegation (by doctors) to appropriately trained nursing and allied health colleagues'– a recommendation that the Council of Australian Governments (COAG) subsequently adopted and implemented, despite the Productivity Commission's support for professional substitution.

So while medical dominance plays a major role in allied health workforce shortages by constraining the release of workforce capacity, Boyce (2008: 114) speculates that it also contributes significantly to the low retention rates of allied health professionals because they leave their jobs in frustration at being prevented from using the full range of skills they have acquired in their education and training. Australian nursing workforce research (cited above) certainly provides ample evidence for the role that skills under-utilisation plays in nurses' departure from the workforce. So, too, does a comprehensive review of 'factors influencing turnover and retention of midwives and consultants' in the UK. According to the review, midwives, for example, will only stay in, or return to, the profession 'if their skills and experience are valued and their promotion prospects and career paths are improved' (Shen, Cox and McBride 2004: 255). On the other hand, they leave in droves if they experience job dissatisfaction arising primarily from a lack of recognition of their contribution, a stressful working environment, a heavy workload, unsocial hours and a lack of child care (Shen, Cox and McBride 2004: 254–256). As the authors of the review concluded, its implications 'mainly lie in how to deal with job dissatisfaction caused by workload/working pattern and lack of perceived recognition' (Shen, Cox and McBride 2004: 257). Recognising and valuing staff contribution, they added, is basically an issue of 'organisational culture', and the problem of retention, one requiring organisational solutions.

While Boyce (2006) proposes that medical dominance is a major organisational barrier, she suggests that the restructuring of public hospitals in the 1990s (Harris 1999) have provided organisational opportunities for allied health workers to increase their institutional authority in relation to medicine. This has not meant a 'substantive change to the overall dominance of medicine' (Boyce 2006: 532) but it operates differently to the way it did prior to the organisational 'reforms' of the 1990s. According to Boyce, medicine used to subordinate the allied health professions. Now it only 'marginalises' them. This putative improvement basically stems from a new kind of management structure in which allied health managers report only to the allied health director. As a result, medical directors no longer directly supervise the allied health professions at a managerial level. The allied health professions are no longer directly answerable to medicine in a hospital-based hierarchy. There is, as a consequence, an aggregate impact on the allied health professions towards the establishment of their own independent, institutional coalescence, 'grounded within a shared meaning of (being) allied to each other …' (Boyce 2006: 531). Yet as Boyce herself acknowledges, at the level of day-to-day *clinical* work and interactions in public hospitals, most allied health workers continue to be subordinate to medicine, and their time and contribution valued significantly less than their medical counterparts. Medicine still dominates in terms of clinical decision-making and the kinds of skills and experience that are used in managing and treating patients. Indeed, recent evidence on the dynamics associated with the professional boundaries between doctors and other health professions in clinical work does not provide much ground for optimism about transforming prevailing hierarchical clinical relations simply through introducing an independent management structure for non-medical health workers such as those in allied health and nursing professions. The establishment of clinical team-based care and collaboration among doctors, nurses and the allied health professions in Australia and comparable countries has typically been accompanied by the appointment of the team's medical practitioner, usually with specialist credentials, as coordinator or director (Bourgeault and Mulvale 2006, Reiger and Lane 2009). Moreover, as recent Australian ethnographic research (cited above) shows, even in situations where the medical team leader is explicitly committed to a 'flat management' structure and democratic decision-making in the interests of better health outcomes, medicine still dominates (Long et al. 2006).

Yet detailed sociological research drawing on historical and ethnographic case studies of the development of nursing in Australia suggests that medical dominance is far from hegemonic, and that the organisational dynamics associated with the professional relationship between medicine and nursing is more complex and nuanced than the medical dominance thesis would suggest. Deidre Wicks' (1999) study of the sexual division of labour between medicine and nursing, for example, provides a rich empirical account of the diversity of power relations that prevail in Australian healthcare institutions between the two professions. Her work demonstrates that in many clinical settings in public hospitals, it is not uncommon for senior nurses to prevail over hospital-based medical staff in decision-making regarding patient care. While such a situation is not usual in relations between senior medical specialists and nurses, it is far from infrequent in relations between junior medical and experienced nursing personnel. Professional boundary maintenance between doctors and nurses, then, is more porous than the medical dominance thesis suggests. Despite this diversity and contestation by nurses of medical power in the everyday life of healthcare institutions, Wicks' research concedes that medicine maintains legitimacy in struggles for organisational authority. While the social dynamics of the professional relations between medicine and nursing are complex and gender differentiated, precisely how these dynamics are gendered remains unclear.

If it is the organisational subordination of nursing and allied health workers in public hospitals and other major public health service settings that is primarily accountable for creating the barriers to retaining them, and clinical work is a key site of the dynamics that produce them, then what precisely is the nature of these dynamics and how do they work? While there are increasing numbers of women entering the medical profession, their workforce participation is still concentrated in community-based, fee-for-service, general practice – not hospital-based specialist practice. Men still dominate this field. The hospital-based division of labour between medicine and other health workers remains highly gendered. It is evident then that if it is the organisational dynamics involved in Australian public hospitals that are generating professional hierarchies, then they are simultaneously ensuring that these hierarchies are gendered. Yet the recent Australian sociological research into the organisational dynamics associated with the work of non-medical health workers leaves largely unaddressed and unexamined the *gendered* character of these dynamics. It does not ask how they render professional divisions in health services gendered or how gender operates in health service organisations within the public sector.

This is an important omission if sociological investigation is to challenge technocratic dominance of health workforce policy and planning, particularly in relation to the problem of workforce shortages. One of the hallmarks of technocracy is the effacement of gender and the neutralisation of gender inequality as a workplace and policy problem as recent gendered organisational studies have shown (Connell 2007, Schofield and Goodwin 2005). While the AHWAC (2006) report, for instance, comments on the feminisation of the allied health workforce and infers that this is a factor in allied health workforce shortages, it eschews any mention of its relationship to gendered dynamics in the health services industry and the gendered inequalities associated with them. Similarly, sociological approaches that do not include gender in their analysis of the organisational dynamics associated with professional boundary maintenance and contestation in health service settings imply that it doesn't matter whether the participants involved in the process are men or women. Yet the evidence clearly shows that the hierarchies generated by the dynamics are gendered, and that *being a man or a woman does matter – not only in terms of who does what work but also in relation to who is likely to **stay** doing it.* Gendered dynamics involved in the organisation and practice of health service work may be central in causing health workforce problems such as shortages and low retention rates. Whether this speculative explanation is correct, however, requires systematic social scientific investigation of institutional health service arrangements and dynamics that is informed by recent theoretical and methodological advances in gendered organisational studies.

Conclusions

In the face of an imminent global health workforce 'crisis' as documented by the WHO (2006), workforce policy and planning approaches in high-income countries offer limited solutions. Informed by narrow technocratic understandings of the problem, as illustrated by the Australian context, they have shown little or no interest in examining the social dynamics involved in its making. Recent sociological investigation of the health workforce suggests that organisational dynamics associated with health service provision are fundamental in understanding health workforce participation, including staff shortages, turnover and retention rates. Yet this sociological intervention could arguably make a more critical and effective contribution to redressing the problem if it drew on recent approaches in gender and organisations studies, especially in relation to the Australian public sector. At the heart of these developments are new theoretical and methodological tools for identifying barriers to and opportunities for women's participation in public sector employment. Given the numerical dominance of women in the health workforce, particularly in the public sector, such advances are timely and apt for conducting research to inform policy and planning approaches to anticipated health workforce shortages.

References

Access Economics. 2001. Population ageing and the economy. Canberra: Commonwealth Department of Health and Aged Care [Online]. Available at: http://www.health.gov.au/Internet/wcms/publishing.nsf./Content/ageing-ofoa-research-accessecon.htm [Accessed: 31 August 2011].

Acker, J. 1990. Hierarchies, jobs, bodies: a theory of gendered organizations. *Gender and Society* 4, 2, 139–158.

AIHW (Australian Institute of Health and Welfare) 2010. Australia's Health 2010. Australia's health no. 12. Cat. no. AUS 122. Canberra: AIHW.

AHMC (Australian Health Ministers' Conference). 2004. *National Health Workforce Strategic Framework*. Sydney.

ANHWT (Australian National Health Workforce Taskforce). 2009. *Health Workforce in Australia and Factors for Current Shortages*. KPMG.

AHWAC (Australian Health Workforce Advisory Committee). 2006. *The Australian Allied Health Workforce: An Overview of Workforce Planning Issues*. AHWAC Report 2006.1. Sydney.

AIHW (Australian Institute of Health and Welfare). 2008. *Australia's Health.*

AIHW (Australian Institute of Health and Welfare). 2009. *Health and Community Services Labour Force, 2006.*

AMA (Australian Medical Association). 2005. AMA Submission to the Productivity Commission Review of Health Workforce. Canberra [Online]. Available at: http://www.ama.com.au/web.nsf/doc/WEEN-6EW44C [Accessed: 31 August 2011].

Bacchi, C. 1999. *Women, Policy and Politics: the Construction of Policy Problems*. London: Sage.

Bacchi, C. and Schofield, T. 2005. Introduction. *Policy and Society*, 24(4), 1–4.

Barraclough, S. and Gardner, H. 2008. A problem-oriented approach to health policy analysis, in *Analysing Health Policy*, edited by S. Barraclough and H. Gardner. Melbourne: Oxford University Press, 3–14.

Bourgeault, I.L. and Mulvale, G. 2006. Collaborative health care teams in Canada and the USA: confronting the structural embeddedness of medical dominance. *Health Sociology Review*, 15(5), 481–495.

Boyce, R. 1996. The oganisation of allied health professions in Australian general hospitals, unpublished PhD thesis. Brisbane: Queensland University of Technology.

Boyce, R. 1997. Health sector reform and professional power, autonomy and culture: the case of the Australian allied health professions, in *Concepts of Care: Developments in Health and Social Welfare*, edited by R. Hugman, M. Peelo and K. Soothill. London: Arnold.

Boyce, R. 2001. Organisational governance structures in allied health services: a decade of change. *Australian Health Review*, 24(1), 22–36.

Boyce, R. 2006. Emerging from the shadow of medicine: allied health as a 'profession community' subculture. *Health Sociology Review*, 15(5), 520–534.

Boyce, R. 2008. The health workforce: innovation, substitution and reform, in *Analysing Health Policy*, edited by S. Barraclough and H. Gardner. Melbourne: Oxford University Press, 105–118.

Buchanan, J. and Considine, G. 2002. *Stop Telling Us to Cope! NSW Nurses Explain Why They are Leaving the Profession*. Sydney: NSW Nurses Association.

Buchanan, J., Bretherton, T., Bearfield, S. and Jackson, S. 2004. *Stable, but Critical: The Working Conditions of Victorian Public Sector Nurses*. Sydney: ACIRRT.

Chesterman, C., Ross-Smith, A. and Peters, M. 2005. The gendered impact on organisations of a critical mass of women in senior management. *Policy and Society*, 24(4), 69–91.

Christensen, T. and Laegreid, P. 2007. *Transcending New Public Management: The Transformation of Public Sector Reforms*. Aldershot: Ashgate Press.

Commonwealth Department of Employment and Workplace Relations (DEWR). 2008. Is your occupation in demand? – workers – visas & immigration [Online]. Available at: http://www.immi.gov.au/skilled/general-skilled-migration/skilled-occupations/occupations-in-demand.htm [Accessed: 31 August 2011].

Connell, R. 2005. Advancing gender reform in large-scale organisations: a new approach for practitioners and researchers. *Policy and Society*, 24(4), 5–24.

Connell, R. 2006. Glass ceilings or gendered institutions? Mapping the gender regimes of public sector worksites. *Public Administration Review*, 66(6), 837–849.

Connell, R. 2007. News from the coalface: experiences of gender reform by the staff of public sector agencies. *International Feminist Journal of Politics*, 9(2), 137–153.

Connell, R. 2009. *Gender in World Perspective* 2nd edn. Cambridge: Polity Press.

Derksen, D.J. and Whelan, E.M. 2009. Closing the health care workforce gap: reforming federal health care workforce policies to meet the needs of the 21st century, Center for American Progress [Online]. Available at: http:www.americanprogress.org/issues/2010/01/pdf/health-careworkforce.pdf [Accessed: 31 August 2011].

Dery, D. 1984. *Problem Definition in Policy Analysis*. Kansas: University Press of Kansas.

Dockery, A.M. 2004. Workforce experience and retention in nursing in Australia. *Australian Bulletin of Labour*, 30(2), 74.

Dockery, A.M. and Barnes, A. 2005. 'Who'd be a nurse? Some evidence on career choice in Australia, *Australian Bulletin of Labour*, 31(4), 350.

Duckett, S. 2007. *The Australian Health Care System*, 3rd edition. Melbourne: Oxford University Press.

Fairclough, N. 1995. *Critical Discourse Analysis: The Critical Study of Language*. London: Longman.

Flavel, J. 2007. The aged care workforce: methods to increase supply to remedy possible shortages. *Australian Bulletin of Labour*, 33(1), 106.

Fraser, N. 1989. *Unruly Practices: Power, Discourse, and Gender in Contemporary Social Theory*. Cambridge: Polity Press.

Freidson, E. 2001. *Professionalism: The Third Logic*. Cambridge: Polity Press.

Harris, P. 1999. Changing patterns of governance: developments in Australian public hospitals and universities. *Policy Studies*, 20(4), 255–272.

Hill, M. 2005. *The Public Policy Process*. Harlow: Pearson Education.

Horner, B. 2002. Where have all the aged care nurses gone? *Geriaction*, 20(3), 9–13.

Leeder, S. 2004. *Race Against Time*. New York: Columbia University.

Liese, B. and Dussault, G. 2004. The state of the health workforce in sub-Saharan Africa: evidence of crisis and analysis of contributing factors [Online]. Africa Region Human Development Working Paper Series, The World Bank. Available at: http://info.worldbank.org/etools/docs/library/206769/The%20 State %20of %20Health %20Workforce %20in %20SubSaharan %20Africa. pdf [Accessed: 29 September 2011].

Long, D., Forsyth, R., Iedema, R. and Carroll, K. 2006. The (im)possibilities of clinical democracy. *Health Sociology Review*, 15(5), 506–519.

McCabe, R., Nowak, M. and Mullen, S. 2005. Nursing careers: what motivated nurses to choose their profession? *Australian Bulletin of Labour*, 31(4), 384.

Naude, M. and McCabe, R. 2005. Increasing retention of staff at hospitals: aspects of management and leadership. *Australian Bulletin of Labour*, 31(4), 426.

Nowak, M. 2005. Choosing to be a nurse, remaining a nurse and leaving nursing in Western Australia: nursing workforce issues in the twenty-first century. *Australian Bulletin of Labour*, 31(4), 304.

O'Brien, P. and Costin, L.O. 2008/09. Health worker shortages and inequalities: the reform of United States policy. *Global Health Governance*, II, 2 [Online]. Available at: http://www.ghgj.org [Accessed: 31 August 2011].

O'Donnell, M., Allan, C. and Peetz, D. 1999. *The New Public Management and Workplace Change in Australia*. Sydney: School of Industrial Relations and Organisational Behaviours, UNSW.

Palmer, G. and Short, S. 2010 *Health Care and Public Policy: An Australian Analysis*, 4th edition. Melbourne: Palgrave Macmillan.

Parsons, W. 1995. *Public Policy: An Introduction to the Theory and Practice of Policy* Analysis. Aldershot: Edward Elgar.

Power, M. 1997. *The Audit Society*. Oxford: Oxford University Press.

Preston, A. 2005. Registered nurses: who are they and what do they want? *Australian Bulletin of Labour*, 31(4), 321.

Reiger, K. and Lane, K. 2009. Working together: collaboration between midwives and doctors in public hospital settings. *Australian Health Review*, 33(2), 315–324.

Schofield, T. and Goodwin, S. 2005. Gender politics and public policy making: prospects for advancing gender equality. *Policy and Society*, 24(4), 25–47.

Schofield, T. 2007. Deterring workplace deaths and injuries: legal sanctions and outcomes or institutional process? in *Public Sociologies: Lessons and Trans-Tasman Comparisons: TASA/SAANZ 2007 Joint Conference Proceedings*, edited by B. Curtis, S. Matthewman and T. McIntosh. The University of Auckland: Department of Sociology.

Schofield, T. 2008. Gender and health inequalities: what are they and what can we do about them? *Australian Journal of Social Issues*, 43(1), 139–157.

Shen, J., Cox, A. and McBride, A. 2004. Factors influencing turnover and retention of midwives and consultants: a literature review. *Health Services Management Research*, 17, 249–262.

Sydney, W. 1999. *Demand Management Strategy*. Sydney.

Waring, M. 1988. *Counting for Nothing: What Men Value and What Women Are Worth*. Sydney: Allen &Unwin.

WHO. 2006. *The World Health Report: Working Together for Health*. Geneva.

Wicks, D. 1999. *Nurses and Doctors at Work: Rethinking Professional Boundaries*. Sydney: Allen & Unwin.

Willis, E. 1989. *Medical Dominance: The Division of Labour in Australian Health Care*, 2nd Edition. Sydney: Allen & Unwin.

Willis, E. 2006. Introduction: taking stock of medical dominance. *Health Sociology Review*, 15(5), 421–431.

Wodak, R. 2008. Introduction: discourse studies – important concepts and terms, in *Qualitative Discourse Analysis in the Social Sciences*, edited by R. Wodak and M. Krzyzanowski. Basingstoke: Palgrave Macmillan, 1–29.

Chapter 5
Good Doctors, Safer Patients, Improved Access: the Case of Indonesia

Stephanie D. Short, Hasbullah Thabrany, Valentin D. Hadjiev, Yaslis Ilyas, Robyn R. Iredale, Firman Lubis, Suchaya Thongyoo and Kirsten Harley

Introduction

Governance of the health workforce is an important and pressing issue internationally as demonstrated by major reports published by the World Health Organization (WHO) (2006), World Bank (2008) and in the United Kingdom (UK) (Department of Health 2006, Esmail 2005). We share the view of leading scholars in the field that the 'objective of good global health governance is to strengthen healthcare delivery systems in the developing world with an emphasis on the importance of primary health care' (Sridhar, Khagram and Pang 2008/2009). Thus this chapter focuses on the key medical workforce governance challenges faced by Indonesia, one of the largest and most populous developing countries in the world.

This chapter reports on a collaborative multidisciplinary study of medical workforce governance in Indonesia (Short, Thabrany, Ilyas et al. 2008). Drawing on the expertise of key stakeholders, the study identified key challenges and opportunities for medical workforce governance in Indonesia and collaboratively developed a policy mechanism for establishing and promoting good governance to address these challenges.

Strengthening the Indonesian health sector requires that we address major challenges related to medical personnel in two areas: distribution and quality (Lieberman and Marzoeki 2002, Ministry of Health 1999). The problem of distribution is one of matching supply (medical practitioners) and demand (people's needs and expectations), to remedy the unevenness that presently disadvantages rural and remote regions in particular (Joint Learning Initiative 2004). The quality of the service provided by healthcare professionals depends greatly on the quality of the institutions that train and certify them. Adequate financing and clear governance processes are also important elements in addressing these challenges. Thus the study aimed to improve the capacity of policy makers and regulators to create an integrated governance continuum that addresses the three interlinked aims of health governance referred to in the title of this book (and chapter): accreditation and quality of education programmes to ensure well qualified (*good*) *doctors*; professional standards, *good regulatory practices* and continuing medical education to protect the public (*safer patients*); and reformed governance structures and workforce distribution for *improved access* to high quality health services.

This study was undertaken as an international collaboration between researchers, regulators and health professionals in Australia and Indonesia in a manner consistent with the strategy proposed by O'Brien and Gostin (2008/2009) to assist partner countries to build their health systems. Indonesia, the most populous Moslem country in the world, is Australia's nearest neighbour and the focus for attention in Australia's foreign aid policy. A key priority of the Australian Aid programme, administered by the Australian Agency for International Development (AusAID), is ensuring that the fundamentals of the health system, including human resource issues, are right so that the system can function more effectively (AusAID 2006). The project was undertaken as part of the work of the International Consortium for Research on Governance of the Health Workforce (ICR-GHW), an international group of regulators, professionals and researchers established with the assistance of the WHO. It builds on a comparative study of systems of medical regulation undertaken by Allsop and Jones (2006) for the Chief Medical Officer in the UK, and on work undertaken by the research team and colleagues in the ICR-GHW (Adelman and Klass 2006, Ilyas 2006, Palmer and Short 2010, Short, Toneva and Hadjiev 2007, Thabrany 2004).

Before describing our methods, two points must be made to explain and clarify the project's scope. First, our study focused on the medical workforce. This emphasis was determined collaboratively by the study's Indonesian authors, and considered timely in light of both the introduction of a new medical law and the June 2007 admission at a hearing of the Constitutional Court of Indonesia by the Indonesian Medical Doctors Association that there was an absence of 'standards for the medical doctor profession' (Thabrany 2007). Second, our study fits within a move amongst researchers and policy makers from discussing medical *regulation* to discussing medical *governance*. This recognizes both the need for greater transparency and accountability and the greater range of stakeholders involved (Iredale 2009).

Methods

The methodological approach adopted for the project had three important features. First, it involved multiple methods, including document analysis, semi-structured interviews and key stakeholder workshops. This allowed for the emergence, testing and development of ideas, with preliminary findings from each stage of the research process informing subsequent stages. Second, it was overseen by a working group in Indonesia. This enabled input and collaboration from key stakeholders and the involvement of young scholars. Third, involvement of important and varied stakeholders through several phases of the research strengthened the collection of evidence and ideas to inform recommendations, but also meant that support for those recommendations was garnered as a result of the research process itself. The Ministry of Health, Indonesian Medical Council, Indonesian Medical Association, hospital directors, specialist associations, private health insurers, consumer organizations and researchers contributed to the research process. Thus the findings and recommendations have relevance for a range of academic, governmental, professional, community and private organizations.

The study was conducted in six stages during 2008. In the first stage, meetings were held in Jakarta to discuss research design and analysis of relevant national and sub-national legislative and policy documents. This provided an overview of the regulatory context for medical workforce governance (see Table 5.2) and background information for the interviews and key stakeholder workshops. Stage two was a planning workshop conducted in Jakarta. The research team, representatives from four provinces (Bali, Jakarta, South Kalimantan and North Sumatra) and key stakeholders came together to develop the interview schedule and select interviewees. In the third stage, the Indonesian team conducted semi-structured interviews with government decision-makers, public officials, medical professionals and researchers (n=25) in several districts in Indonesia. These identified strengths and limitations of the current governance system in Indonesia and proposals for reform. Analysis of findings and interim results were presented at a key stakeholder workshop as the fourth stage. Researchers, national experts and participants from four provinces attended. A policy paper was drafted and circulated to workshop participants for comments. In the penultimate stage, findings were presented at meetings of the ICR-GHW and the International Association of Medical Regulatory Authorities in Capetown (Short, Thabrany, Hadjiev et al. 2008), the Annual Conference of the Doctors' Reform Society in Australia (Short 2008) and the health governance research network, HealthGov. The last stage involved the finalization of the policy paper and synopsis. These were presented at the AusAID Policy Research Forum, Jakarta in December 2008 and disseminated in English and Bahasa-Indonesian versions to interviewees and national and sub-national Indonesian policy makers (Short, Thabrany, Ilyas et al. 2008).

The Indonesian Context

The Republic of Indonesia is the world's largest archipelago and fourth most populous country, with some 238 million people inhabiting approximately 950 of its 17,500 islands. About 60 per cent of the population lives on the island of Java, which includes the capital city, Jakarta (World Health Organization 2010). Indonesia is a 'middle economy', reflected in its membership of the G-20 (Group of Twenty). The GDP (gross domestic product) per capita in 2010 was USD $3,040, and over half of the population lives on less than $2 a day (AusAID 2006: 8; Central Bank Indonesia 2011).

Indonesia is divided into 33 provinces, each of which has its own political legislature and governor. The provinces are subdivided into districts and municipalities, of which there were 465 and 95 respectively in 2009, and in turn these are constituted by sub-districts (more than 6,000) and villages (more than 65,000) (World Health Organization 2010).

In 2001, government functions, staff and financing were devolved from the national centre to district governments in a rapid process of decentralization. This was intended, in health as in other areas of government activity, to enable policy makers to devise and implement locally-relevant policies and make use of local resources and expertise (McDonald et al. 2009). Within a year, more than 70 per cent of central government civil servants and most facilities had been transferred to local governments, although many of these staff continued to be paid, and hence controlled, by the centre (Heywood and Harahap 2009). In practice, the dynamic context of decentralization presents particular challenges and complexities for medical governance. First, delineation of roles and responsibilities remains unclear. Second, collection of adequate information about health human resources, necessary for effective planning, has become more problematic, with the central government having little information about locally contracted staff. And third, ongoing reliance by the districts on limited central government funding, often tied to national-level priorities, also limits actual regional autonomy (Heywood and Harahap 2009, McDonald et al. 2009).

The Indonesian health system includes both a public and private sector. The public system is the responsibility of the Ministry of Health and sub-national governments. Public facilities include public hospitals, community health centres at sub-district level (*puskesmas*), community health sub-centres (*pustu*), mobile health centres, and integrated health posts (*posyandu*) (a programme of village-based monthly health outreach and promotion meetings involving community volunteers). By 2005 there were 7,700 *puskesmas* (of which 27 per cent included beds), 22,200 sub-centres and 5,800 mobile health centres (World Bank 2008: 30). Private hospitals are located at the district level or associated with particular sectors (for example, police); there are also district-level private hospitals for women and for women and children, along with private maternity clinics and private medical practices (Heywood and Harahap 2009).

In July 2007, some 72,000 doctors, including 15,500 specialists, were registered and hence potentially able to practise in Indonesia (World Bank 2009: 13). Estimates of the number of general practitioners, calculated using different sources (some not nationwide) range from 28,000 to 55,000 in 2006/2007. These figures equate to between 0.18 and 0.25 general practitioners per 1,000 people in the population (World Bank 2009: 14). These figures are low by international standards. For instance, the global average is 1.3 doctors per 1,000 population, and the ASEAN average is 0.5 per 1,000, with Indonesia's doctor density figure the second lowest (to Cambodia) amongst the 10 ASEAN countries. This is in line with a reported overall shortage of health workers (also including nurses and midwives) in Indonesia, with more than 83,000 additional health workers needed to meet the WHO threshold of 2.28 health workers per 1,000 population (Kanchanachitra et al. 2011: 3).

In addition to internationally low doctor densities, there are stark inequities in distribution both between provinces and between urban, rural and remote areas. For instance, some provinces have less than 0.1 general practitioners per 1,000 population (for example, West Kalimantan, East Nusa Tenggara) while others have more than 0.4 (for example, North Sulawesi) (World Bank 2009: 14). The *Potensi Desa* provides census data, obtained through interviews with *desa* (village) and *kelurahan* (city block) leaders, including the number of general practitioners living within village boundaries. Figures are presented in Table 5.1. They reveal that densities of doctors in urban areas are consistently at least five times those in rural and remote areas (World Bank 2009: 12, 14–15).

There are very limited data on the number and distribution of specialists, with the best (and highest) estimate indicating that there are approximately 15,000 registered specialists, or only 0.07 per 1,000 in the population across the country. The large majority (over 10,000) are located in the five provinces of Jakarta, Yogyakarta, West, Central and East Java, with a density of 0.42 specialists per 1,000 population in Jakarta (World Bank 2009: 15–16).

According to the World Bank, Indonesia has 52 medical schools and an additional 12 schools awaiting accreditation. Of these, 27 (52 per cent) are private – the category which has contributed most to the 40 per cent growth since 2001. In addition clinical teaching occurs in 70 hospitals, of which only just over half (37) are legally qualified as teaching hospitals (World Bank 2009: 32). As is reported in our findings, the quality of graduates remains a problem. The average annual production of medical graduates is 5,500, which compared to other ASEAN countries is high in absolute terms, but not in relation to population. There are two medical graduates per 100,000 population in Indonesia, compared to highs of eight per 100,000 in Singapore and Malaysia and lows of one per 100,000 in Laos and Myanmar (Kanchanachitra et al. 2011: 3). Further, not all trained health professionals in Indonesia are able to gain employment: for instance, in the case of nurses, only half of Indonesian graduates are employed (Kanchanachitra et al. 2011: 5).

Table 5.1 Number and density of general practitioners by region, 2006

Region	Number	Ratio per 100,000 population	Number of people per GP[†]
Java/Bali	**23,944**	**18.5**	**5,400**
Urban	20,896	34.1	2,900
Rural	3,048	4.5	22,200
Outside Java/	**15,740**	**18.1**	**5,500**
Bali	11,187	40.9	2,400
Urban	3,141	8.3	12,000
Rural	1,412	6.6	15,200
Remote			

Note: [†] Figures are calculated by authors and rounded to nearest 100

Source: Adapted from World Bank (2009, Table 2–2)

Findings

Existing Regulatory Framework

Table 5.2 sets out the key legislative acts and regulations governing health and the medical workforce in Indonesia to 2007.

The majority of key informants agreed that, in general, existing acts and regulations for the governance of the medical profession in Indonesia were adequate for the existing health care system (some suggestions of additional regulations were nonetheless proposed, discussed below). However, problems reported included a shortage of doctors, quality standards, lack of financing and inconsistent, heterogeneous implementation of the regulations. They pointed to significant arbitrariness in the application of regulations by all levels of government. The health system did not work as a system; rather the quality of medical governance depended on the quality of leadership at particular institutions.

Table 5.2 Existing acts and regulations in Indonesia (to 2007)

Year	Name	Main function
1945	National Constitution	Guarantees the right of the people to health services.
1974	Instruction of the President (Inpres)	Mandates that all new medical graduates serve in health centre for one to three years, depending on remoteness of the location.
1991	Presidential Regulation No. 37	Regulates the recruitment of doctors as temporary employees for the government.
1992	Health Act No. 23	Regulates health personnel education and training as conducted by government and private sector institutions.
1996	Government Regulation No. 32	Regulates types of health personnel, including doctors, dentists, nurses, pharmacists, public health personnel, nutritionists, physical therapists and medical technicians.
1997	Ministry of Health Regulation No. 916	Regulates licensing of medical practitioners.
2002	Ministry of Health Regulation No. 1540	Regulates the placement of doctors during service period.
2004	Ministry of Health Regulation No. 1199	Guidance for recruitment of health personnel who will be posted in the government health facility. Used by Governor, Head of District/City or the Head of Government Health Facility Organization.
2004	Medical Practitioner Act No. 29	Regulates that every doctor and dentist has to ensure quality services and cost containment. Establishment of the Indonesian Medical Council.
2004	Local Government Authority Act No. 32	With decentralization each local government has authority to recruit their own medical personnel as local government employees.
2005	Ministry of Health Regulation No. 1419	Regulates the conduct of medical and dental practice.

The issues that emerged most frequently during discussions with health sector stakeholders can be grouped into six concerns and suggestions under the headings of distribution and quality:

Distribution

1. Policy and planning for medical workforce distribution.
2. Adequate public health financing and recruitment of doctors as government employees.
3. Local leadership and solutions to address distribution and access.

Quality

4. Medical education standards to improve quality of care.
5. Career planning for doctors.
6. Quality control.

One feature to note is that matters of distribution and quality are interrelated. This is seen in the finding of Barber, Gertler and Harimurti's (2007) study of public health care provision in Indonesia, that 'quality depends on the availability, type, and number of health workers, which, in turn, is affected by public policies'.

1. Policy and planning for medical workforce distribution Informants identified the need for a new policy on the distribution of doctors that is both clearer and able to be more consistently applied. This was seen as important to address the serious maldistribution of doctors between rural and urban areas highlighted in the 'Indonesian context' section of this chapter. A related concern was the absence of a clear planning process to determine the number of medical doctors needed by every district each year. These concerns can be seen in the context of a health system which previously had strong tools available for distributing doctors to remote areas and a current environment which favours urban employment.

In 1974, Indonesia began distributing doctors to all sub-districts, with the aim of ensuring that all people have access to medical care, in a programme popularly known as *Inpres* (Instruction of the President). *Inpres* mandated that all new graduates of medical schools be deployed to serve in sub-districts with populations of between 10,000 and 30,000 people, for a period of up to three years, as a condition of civil service employment. Under the scheme, those willing to accept postings in more remote areas served fewer years (Heywood and Harahap 2009). Following this service, doctors were eligible for permanent civil service employment (PNS) in the same location or elsewhere, providing access to lifetime job security, including monthly income following retirement. Initially the programme applied only for general practitioners, but it was later expanded to deploy specialists, in particular internists, paediatricians, surgeons and obstetricians/gynaecologists, to district-level hospitals. The programme successfully achieved a wider distribution of doctors (Barber, Gertler and Harimurti 2007) and significantly reduced infant mortality (Bappenas 2010).

However, financial constraints led to a reduced emphasis on PNS in the 1990s, and after the Asian financial crisis of 1997 and end of the authoritarian Suharto regime, mandatory service was challenged as violating the rights of doctors to choose their jobs. Instead, new medical graduates could volunteer to perform their three years of temporary central contract service (PTT) in remote areas, with salary supplements rewarding those working in remote areas (Heywood and Harahap 2009).

In the first decade of the twenty-first century, the demand for medical care, and the capacity of some sectors of the community to pay for it through out of pocket payments, has increased, especially in urban areas. The lure of better financial opportunities, combined with the discontinuation of the mandatory *Inpres* scheme, has contributed to a concentration of medical doctors in large cities. Increasing demand for medical care and ability of some patients to pay has further influenced the behaviour of doctors and hospitals towards maximizing profit.

Nonetheless, informants reported current initiatives that may prove useful. Realizing that provinces with fewer resources are unable to create programmes to attract doctors, the Ministry of Health is developing initiatives to provide placement-related fellowships for young doctors to pursue specialist training. Under this programme, a doctor may apply for a fellowship (covering educational costs and living allowances during four to five years of specialist training) conditional on the doctor signing a contract that after graduation they will serve in a smaller district for a stated number of years. The more remote and less developed the district, the shorter the period of required service in that district. Past evidence from the placement of general practitioners shows that doctors are more likely to consider remote postings when an adequate incentive scheme is in place, indicating that financial incentives can be an effective mechanism for achieving a more even distribution of doctors.

2. Adequate public health financing and recruitment of doctors as government employees Informants suggested that the biggest constraint facing health care in Indonesia is that over the last three decades, the government has allocated less than 2 per cent of its national budget for health care. According to World Bank (2008: 42) figures, national public health expenditure increased modestly from 0.5 per cent of GDP and 2.6 per cent of total national public expenditure in 2001, to 0.7 per cent of GDP and 3.5 per cent of total national public expenditure in 2005. World Health Organization (2011: 130–131) figures indicate that total (not just public) expenditure on health was 2 per cent of GDP in 2000 and 2.3 per cent in 2008. Within total health expenditure, the balance has shifted in favour of general government expenditure (36.6 per cent of total health expenditure in 2000; 54.4 per cent in 2008) and away from private expenditure (63.4 per cent in 2000; 45.6 per cent in 2008), most of which is from out of pocket payments (70.3 per cent of private expenditure in 2008). Indonesia's expenditure on health is low compared to the region, where for most other countries total health expenditure is more than 3 per cent of GDP (World Bank 2008: 43).

This low level of financing reflects and reinforces undervaluing of the medical profession. Complaints about insufficient remuneration for doctors employed by the government are universal. The low government salary drives many doctors working in public health centres, medical schools, public hospitals and other health offices to supplement their income through work in several private practices or hospitals (the Medical Practice law now limits doctors to practising in a maximum of three locations). It is estimated that between 60 and 70 per cent of public health care workers (including nurses and midwives) also practise privately. For *puskesmas* staff engaged in dual practice, less than half their income comes from public employment (World Bank 2008: 33, 2009: 19–20). Government-employed doctors are anecdotally seen as working for the public sector in the morning and the private sector in the afternoon, but 'the afternoons are starting earlier'. This is also evident in a survey finding that absenteeism rates for health staff in Indonesia (40 per cent) were highest amongst surveyed countries (cited in Heywood and Harahap 2009).

This practice has implications for both distribution and quality. The private practices are concentrated in urban areas where they are most profitable, taking advantage of a growing divide between rich and poor. This contributes to the unequal distribution of doctors between urban and rural/remote areas. In addition, when doctors work in many different places, they necessarily neglect some patients, compromising patient safety. Informants suggested the ideal for patients is that doctors work full-time in one venue to maximize their availability for patients.

The mushrooming of private hospitals in Indonesia and an inadequate pool of specialists were seen as other constraints to ensuring an adequate patient-centred public health care system. Currently, efforts are being made to improve quality and reduce medical errors by promoting a policy of 'put patient first', but the continuing trend of medical practitioners running multiple practices may compromise capacity to achieve high quality public medical services.

Globalization and the ASEAN Framework Agreement on Services, under which Indonesia must open its door for foreign doctors from 2010, also pose particular challenges in a climate with inadequate funding of the health care system and concerns about the quality of care by local doctors. Current flows of medical tourists, including Indonesians travelling overseas to pay for medical treatments, have some negative implications for Indonesia's public health sector. According to the Indonesian Medical Association of North Sumatra, North Sumatran people spend more than one trillion Rupiahs each year on health care in Malaysia. Significantly, many high income people in Indonesia trust doctors in Malaysia and Singapore more than they do Indonesian doctors, and they are willing to pay higher fees for doctors overseas.

Informants reported that the salaries of Indonesian doctors employed in the public sector are considerably lower than those in Malaysia and Singapore. This also contributes to the phenomenon of doctors working in multiple private practices or hospitals, discussed above, limiting their time to improve their knowledge and skills via continuing medical education. This further undermines attempts to improve the quality of medical services and encourages those with sufficient resources to continue to seek health care overseas (see Kanchanachitra et al. 2011 for discussion on the international flow of health care workers and patients in Southeast Asia; and Chapter 2 in this volume on global migration of health professionals).

3. Local leadership and solutions to address distribution and access A common theme amongst stakeholders was that lack of effective leadership in medical institutions was exacerbating maldistribution problems by leading to poor governance of currently available medical resources. As a corollary, strong leadership in provincial and district health offices and health institutions has the capacity to strengthen governance.

For example, informants suggested the Tabanan Hospital in Bali provided an example where good leadership led to good medical governance. There, the hospital director sought to introduce greater discipline in the prescription of medications. He addressed this through an integrated policy of basing doctors' salaries on the medications which they prescribed. Doctors who prescribed non cost-effective medications (that is, those not agreed by the Medical Council) suffered salary penalties. While there was some scepticism about whether doctors would adhere to this policy, in practice they did, resulting in benefits to hospital and patients of prescription of appropriate, cost-effective medications.

Similarly, provincial and district health offices are developing local initatives to improve patient access and address the inequitable distribution of doctors due to the imbalance of economic capacities and public facilities. For example, the concept of 'Family Physician', where a doctor is paid using a capitation payment system to take care of a family rather than an individual sick patient, is being piloted in East Kalimantan and West Sumatra. Given limited health workforce resources, this is a rational approach to structuring provision of health services. It increases access to medical care, with costlier specialists only used when necessary. This approach is consistent with the WHO's emphasis on primary care (World Health Organization 2008) and supported by Barber, Gertler and Harimurti's (2007: w177) finding that in health centres, 'moving from no physicians to one appeared to provide an important capacity as measured by significantly increased quality, separate from the presence and number of other staff'. And in Jimbaran, Bali, the local government has pooled resources to give general practitioners contracts to treat both the 'poor' (who are entitled to the national *askeskin* health insurance scheme for the poor) and the 'near-poor' for the same price. Such local initiatives, designed to anticipate and address difficulties in managing the supply and distribution of doctors, make a significant contribution to the development of effective health sector governance.

4. Medical education standards to improve quality of care The absence of a national standard of medical education leads to a variation in the quality of doctors produced. Often there is no match between the content of medical degree courses and the competencies required to be a doctor. Indonesia is experiencing a rapid growth in the number of medical schools, with new licences granted by the Ministry of Education each year. The World Bank (2009) reported 52 existing medical schools plus 12 awaiting accreditation; 67 were reported by an official during our Research Workshop; and at the beginning of 2011 there are 84. However, they vary greatly in terms of the quality of their medical training. There was a perceived need for greater cooperation between stakeholders, including the Medical Council, Medical Schools Association, Ministry of Education and Ministry of Health, to determine the national competency standards required by medical graduates and to monitor and control the process of medical education.

One of the important elements in enforcing high standards is the adequacy of medical equipment and the professional competence of academics in medical schools. The recent mushrooming of new medical schools, public and private, has raised concerns by experts that the quality of medical education is being sacrificed. Almost all informants acknowledged that the quality of medical graduates in Indonesia varies widely. This is due to weak accreditation, lack of equipment in some teaching hospitals, variability in the quality of teaching staff and sometimes high ratios of students to lecturers/professors. Many medical schools lack appropriate and up-to-date medical equipment, such as medical resonance imaging (MRI) machines, required for teaching. Participants suggested that in future, private hospitals and medical schools should take more responsiblity in workforce planning for medical professionals.

5. Career planning for doctors Informants suggested that the quality of medical practice could be enhanced by developing a comprehensive career planning system for doctors. Currently, professional career paths for doctors are not clearly articulated. It was considered that a new regulation that allows for three career options – civil employment, military and police employment, and private sector employment – could be beneficial.

6. Quality control In 2004, the *Medical Practitioner Act* (Law No. 29/2004) was passed, with lobbying in support by the Indonesian Medical Association. Informants observed that there was an escalating incidence of medical malpractice in the late 1990s, possibly linked to a profit-seeking orientation (associated with the high cost of medical education and access to wealthier patients in cities) and the 'asymmetry of information' attached to medical services, especially expensive procedures. Attempts by the Indonesian Medical Association to take disciplinary action were ineffective, due to a combination of factors including: lack of legal authority; no effective financial penalty; difficulties in proving malpractice; and weak organization. The commencement, in 2004, of the *Medical Practitioner Law* and formation of the Medical Council were supported by the Medical Association as a way to improve the quality of medical care and improve trust in doctors.

The Medical Council has two chambers: medical and dental. The Council registers doctors and dentists and stipulates competency levels for them. Although the Council is very young, road maps for governing medical and dental professionals, equivalent with those in more industrialized countries, have been developed. Procedures for screening the quality of inputs, process of education, accreditation, licensing and continuing medical education have been laid out. The 'Swiss Cheese' model (Reason 2000) of continuous screening to ensure consistent quality assurance at various levels of training and licensing has been adopted by the Council. However, enforcing legal sanctions for those who violate standard procedures remains a challenge (Thabrany 2007).

The study found that ensuring adequate continuing medical education for all practising doctors as a specific measure to maintain quality is a task confronting Indonesian authorities. Although the current licensing mechanism requires a degree and the accumulation of credits for continuing medical education, accreditation mechanisms for ensuring that specific medical competencies are acquired and updated by doctors have not been implemented. Without rigorous quality improvement, medical doctors in Indonesia will not be able to compete with incoming foreign doctors, will continue to lose patients to overseas health services, and will also be prone to malpractice suits.

More broadly, the lack of strict accreditation processes for institutions is a problem for the medical profession in Indonesia. Structural accreditation (based on input measures, such as having standard administrative operating procedures) and clinical audits in hospitals had not been implemented (by the end of 2010, only about 30 per cent of hospitals were structurally audited). This lack of effective quality assurance in overall medical practice, especially in hospitals, might be one factor in the increased prevalence of malpractice cases. It is acknowledged that the Indonesian health care system is facing the difficult task of balancing strict quality control with inadequate financing.

Strengthening Medical Workforce Governance in Indonesia

Having identified the major challenges and opportunities concerning medical workforce distribution and quality for Indonesia outlined above, the key stakeholder workshop provided the opportunity for development of recommendations for an overall mechanism and process for addressing these challenges. Broadly, the study recommended establishment by the Ministry of Health of a Medical Governance Task Force (MGTF) to develop, implement, monitor and evaluate a National Plan of Operation of Medical Care System. The details of the five recommendations appear in Table 5.3.

Table 5.3 Recommendations

1. Develop comprehensive and integrated medical governance

- That the Ministry of Health establish a Medical Governance Task Force (MGTF) at the national level to develop a comprehensive and solid medical governance scheme in Indonesia.
- This Task Force should be initiated and chaired by the Minister of Health as ex-officio and involve all key stakeholders in medical care such as Indonesian Medical Association, Indonesian Public Health Association, Medical Council, Medical School Association, Parliament, Consumer organization, Hospital Association, Health Insurance Association, etc.
- Appointment of the members of this Task Force should be based on their knowledge and expertise in medical and health care and should be appointed by a Letter of Decree of the President.
- The MGTF should be designed to work closely with the newly established Indonesian Medical Council, with a focus on medical professional governance rather than policy-making, which is the jurisdiction of the Medical Council.

2. Develop National Plan of Action

- The main task of the Medical Governance Task Force is to develop a National Plan of Operation of Medical Care System, covering medical practitioners, and addressing health care financing considerations.
- This National Action Plan should clearly stipulate the role and functions of the government, private sector and medical practitioners. This system should cover public and private sectors.
- This Action Plan should be developed with reference to all existing medical and health laws and regulations.
- If necessary, new laws and regulations should be developed during the course of the system development.

3. Define and clearly delineate the role and responsibilities of each institution

- The Plan should clearly define and delineate the roles and responsibilities of the relevant institutions in medical governance (including training, qualifying, certifying, licensing, monitoring and sanctioning) in order to define where the authority of one institution or organization starts and ends, as well as in cases of overlapping authority. These institutions include the Ministry of Health, Local Health Offices, Medical Council, Indonesian Medical Associations, and Medical Collegiums on Specialty, etc., at the national and local level.
- Special attention should be given to the District level due to the decentralization policy for practical reasons.
- The system should be based on experiences and lessons learned in medical governance from other countries, especially in Southeast Asia, as well as the experiences of regions within Indonesia.

4. Conduct special seminars, workshops and applied studies

- Seminars and workshops should be conducted by the Task Force during the development of the Plan of Operation. The participants should include experts and practitioners from relevant institutions to give their comments and inputs to the Plan. International experts should also be invited to contribute.
- Small applied or operations research could be conducted where necessary, to support the development of the Plan.

5. Implementation of the Plan

- Implementation of the Plan of Action should be executed with flexibility, in stages and with careful monitoring and evaluation of the progress.
- Implementation should start in regions that are more ready to implement the Plan, and then replicated in other regions.

Conclusions

Strengthening medical workforce governance in Indonesia is a difficult and complex task. Our research found that the problem is not simply one of insufficient regulation: rather, significant challenges include a shortage of doctors, lack of quality standards, lack of financing, inadequate payment and salary systems, and inconsistent implementation of existing regulations. Two key, related themes raised by our informants concerned distribution and quality of the medical workforce. Medical workforce maldistribution could be addressed through: a new post-*Inpres* policy and clearer planning process; adequate public health financing and greater support for recruitment of doctors as government employees; and development of strong leadership in provincial and district health offices and institutions to support effective local governance and solutions. Enhancing and regularizing the quality of medical education, doctors and medical care requires: development of appropriate medical education standards; establishment of a clear career paths for doctors; and implementation of consistent quality control and accreditation processes across all areas of medical training and practice.

This project developed a mechanism for medical workforce governance that will improve the capacity of policy makers and regulators to address the above concerns and implement reform. The recommendations were collaboratively developed, drawing on an integral feature of our research approach – the participation of key health sector stakeholders, including the Ministry of Health, Indonesian Medical Council, Indonesian Medical Association, hospital directors, specialist associations, public and private health insurers, consumer organizations and researchers. This encouraged recommendations that are culturally sensitive, policy-relevant, and have strategic support within the sector in Indonesia. Implementation of the recommendations would address the challenges facing medical workforce governance in Indonesia and bring improvements along the health workforce governance continuum: access to health care, patient safety and good regulatory practices.

Acknowledgements

This chapter is based on research conducted with support from AusAID under the Australia-Indonesia Governance Research Partnership. The authors would like to thank the key informants, researchers and young scholars involved in the project.

References

Adelman, H. and Klass, D. 2006. Governance of physicians in a globalized world: developing a transnational research program for medical regulation. Paper to the International Association of Medical Regulatory Authorities (IAMRA) 7th International Conference on Medical Regulation, Wellington, New Zealand, November 2006.

Allsop, J. and Jones, K. 2006. Quality assurance in medical regulation in an international context. Project report [Online]. Lincoln: University of Lincoln. Available at: http:// eprints.lincoln.ac.uk/769/ [Accessed: April 2011].

AusAID (Australian Agency for International Development). 2006. Australian aid: promoting growth and stability. A White Paper on the Australian Government's aid program [Online]. Commonwealth of Australia. Available at: http://www.ausaid.gov.au/publications/pdf/whitepaper.pdf [Accessed: April 2011].

Bappenas. 2010. Report on the achievement of the millennium development goals Indonesia 2010. Jakarta.

Barber, S.L., Gertler, P.J. and Harimurti, P. 2007. The contribution of human resources for health to the quality of care in Indonesia. *Health Affairs* [Online]. DOI 10.1377/hlthaff.26.3.w367. Available at: http://content.healthaffairs.org/content/early/2007/03/27/hlthaff.26.3.w367.citation [Accessed: May 2011].

Central Bank Indonesia. 2011. 2010 annual report. Jakarta.

Department of Health (United Kingdom). 2006. Good doctors, safer patients: proposals to strengthen the system to assure and improve the performance of doctors and to protect the safety of patients. Report by the Chief Medical Officer [Online]. Available at: http://www.dh.gov.uk/en/Publicationsandstatistics/Publications/PublicationsPolicyAndGuidance/DH_4137232 [Accessed: August 2009].

Esmail, A. 2005. Failure to act on good intentions. *British Medical Journal*, 330(7500), 1144–7.

Heywood, P.F. and Harahap, N.P. 2009. Human resources for health at the district level in Indonesia: the smoke and mirrors of decentralization. *Human Resources for Health* [Online]. 7(6). Available at: http://www.human-resources-health.com/content/7/1/6 [Accessed: May 2011].

Ilyas, Y. 2006. Determinan distribusi dokter spesialis di kota/kabupaten Indonesia (Determinant factors of doctors' distribution in city/district Indonesia). *Jurnal Manajemen Pelayanan Kesehatan*, 9(3), 146–55.

Iredale, R. 2009. Luring overseas trained doctors to Australia: issues of training, regulating and trading. *International Migration*, 47(4), 31–65.

Joint Learning Initiative. 2004. *Human Resources for Health: Overcoming the Crisis*. Cambridge: Harvard University Global Equity Initiative.

Kanchanachitra, S., Lindelow, M., Johnston, T., Hanvoravongchai, P., Lorenzo, F.M., Huong, N.L., Wilopo, S.A. and dela Rosa, J.F. 2011. Human resources for health in southeast Asia: shortages, distributional challenges, and international trade in health services. *The Lancet*, 377(9767), 769–81.

Lieberman, S. and Marzoeki, P. 2002. Health strategy in a post crisis, decentralizing Indonesia. Health, nutrition and population (HNP) discussion paper. Washington DC: International Bank for Reconstruction and Development/The World Bank.

McDonald, F., Yoganingrum, A., Purwaningrum, F., Ariani, D., Short, S.D. 2009. Evidence-based decision-making to strengthen local governance: nutritional health interventions in Bantul and Gunungkidul [Online]. Australia Indonesia Governance Research Partnership, Policy Brief 10. Canberra: Crawford School of Economics and Government, ANU College of Asia and the Pacific, The Australian National University. Available at: http://www.aigrp.anu.edu.au/docs/projects/1029/McDonald_Yoganingrum_brief.pdf [Accessed: April 2011].

Ministry of Health. 1999. Health development plan towards healthy Indonesia 2010 [Online]. Republic of Indonesia, Jakarta. Available at: http://perpustakaan.depkes.go.id:8180/bitstream//123456789/1383/1/BK1999-Okt37.pdf [Accessed: August 2009].

O'Brien, P. and Gostin, L.O. 2008/2009. Health worker shortages and inequalities: the reform of United States policy. *Global Health Governance* [Online], II(2). Available at: http://www.ghgj.org/obrien2.2healthworkershortages.htm [Accessed: May 2011].

Palmer, G.R. and Short, S.D. 2010. *Health Care and Public Policy: An Australian Analysis*, 4th edition. Melbourne: Macmillan.

Reason, J.T. 2000. Human error: models and management. *British Medical Journal*, 320(7237), 768–70.

Short, S.D. 2008. Good doctors, safer patients, improved access: an international approach to health workforce governance. Paper to the Doctors' Reform Society Annual Conference. Griffith University, the Gold Coast, October 2008.

Short, S.D., Thabrany, H., Hadjiev, H., Iredale, R., Ilyas, Y. and Lubis, F. 2008. Strengthening medical workforce governance in Indonesia: a collaborative multidisciplinary approach. Paper to the International Association of Medical Regulatory Authorities (IAMRA) 8th International Conference on Medical Regulation. Cape Town. October.

Short, S.D., Thabrany, H., Ilyas, Y., Lubis, F., Iredale, R. and Hadjiev, V.D. 2008. Managing the medical workforce (Pendayagunaan tenaga kesehatan) [Online]. Australia Indonesia Governance Research Partnership, Policy Brief 10. Canberra: Crawford School of Economics and Government, ANU. College of Asia and the Pacific, The Australian National University. Available in English and Bahasa Indonesian at: http://www.aigrp.anu.edu.au/docs/projects/1020/short_brief.pdf [Accessed: April 2011].

Short, S.D., Toneva, Z.D. and Hadjiev, V.D. 2007. On the inequitable impact of universal health insurance: the experience of Bulgaria in transition. *Health Sociology Review*, 16(2), 130–45.

Sridhar, D., Khagram, S. and Pang, T. 2008/2009. Are existing governance structures equipped to deal with today's global health challenges: towards systematic coherence in scaling up. *Global Health Governance* [Online], II(2).

Available at: http://www.ghgj.org/Sridhar%20Khagram%20and%20Pang_Are%20Existing%20Governance.pdf [Accessed: April 2011].

Thabrany, H. 2004. Akuntabilitas rumah sakit daerah. [Accountability of local hospitals]. *Jurnal Manajemen dan Administrasi Rumah Sakit*, 5(3).

Thabrany, H. 2007. Uji materi UU praktik kedokteran: untuk siapa? [Judicial review of medical practice law: to whom?]. *Maj Kedokt Indon*, 57(4).

World Bank. 2008. *Investing in Indonesia's Health: Challenges and Opportunities for Future Public Spending. Health Public Expenditure Review 2008*. Jakarta and Washington: World Bank.

World Bank. 2009. *Indonesia's Doctors, Midwives and Nurses: Current Stock, Increasing Needs, Future Challenges and Options*. Jakarta, Indonesia: World Bank.

World Health Organization. 2006. *The World Health Report 2006: Working Together for Health*. Geneva: WHO Press.

World Health Organization. 2008. *The World Health Report 2008: Primary Health Care (Now More Than Ever)*. Geneva: WHO Press.

World Health Organization. 2010. *WHO Indonesia: Indonesia Profile* [Online]. Available at: http://www.ino.searo.who.int/en/Section3.htm [Accessed: May 2011].

World Health Organization. 2011. *World Health Statistics 2011*. Geneva: WHO Press.

PART II
Good Regulatory Practice

Chapter 6

Challenging the Regulatory Trinity: Global Trends in Health Professional Regulation

Fiona McDonald

Introduction

Traditionally, health professionals have been regulated through the use of a trinity of regulatory tools: civil, criminal and government-sanctioned self-regulation. Prospectively, health professionals have been regulated through government-sanctioned self-regulation (although this also incorporated a retrospective element of discipline) (Kuhlmann and Saks 2008, Walshe 2009). Retrospectively, health professionals have been regulated through the mechanisms of civil litigation and, more rarely, criminal prosecution.

Development of the trinity of regulatory instruments used to regulate health professionals pre-dated modern health systems. When these health systems were created, and especially when a public health system was formed, governments had to reach an accommodation with the medical profession to ensure the system's successful operation, at least in countries such as Britain, Canada, Australia and New Zealand (McDonald 2010b). This accommodation had as an implicit condition the maintenance of professional autonomy. As a consequence there was a reluctance to employ additional regulatory tools, other than the accepted regulatory trinity, to govern health professionals. Over the last 25 years many of the traditional forms of regulation have attracted much critical scrutiny. This has led to some of the mechanisms being significantly reformed to accord less deference to the professions as arbitrators of acceptable standards, to increase the accountability of professions to the public, and to ensure that regulators were acting in the public interest to ensure patient safety. Other regulatory instruments were introduced in some jurisdictions to improve the health system. These instruments were designed to integrate health professionals into the health system and hence to strengthen the governance of that system.

The first section of this chapter discusses some of the significant changes to the trinity of tools used for health professional regulation that have occurred over the last 25 years. The second section of this paper analyses the different approaches to determining which, if any, occupations in the health sector should be regulated and how this might occur. The third section evaluates the previous reliance on the regulatory trinity and examines why additional regulatory tools are increasingly being used in parallel to the existent regulatory trinity to increase the control a broader range of regulatory actors have over the practices of health professionals. The regulatory trinity is no longer the dominant mode of regulation in a number of jurisdictions and health professionals are increasingly being enveloped in a regulatory framework that recognizes they are part of a broader, complex system that provides care and treatment.

Changes within the Regulatory Trinity

Two of the three traditional mechanisms for the regulation of health professionals – civil liability and government-sanctioned self-regulation – have attracted a great deal of scrutiny over the last 25 years. This is attributed to a multitude of factors, including the impact of scandal (see Chapter 12), changing public expectations in respect of participation in health care practice and governance (Allsop et al. 2004) and an increasing public desire for increased transparency (see Chapter 11) and greater accountability (Emanuel and Emanuel 1996, McDonald 2010b).

The standards applied in civil liability have been criticized as being too deferential to the professions (Woolf 2001). Progressively, the test used to determine negligence has been modified, at least to some extent, throughout common-law jurisdictions. It has moved, in most jurisdictions, from the *Bolam* test – 'acted in accordance with a practice accepted as proper by a responsible body of medical men skilled in that particular art …' (*Bolam v Friern Hospital Management Committee* per McNair J 586) – where the standard of care was to be determined by the professions, to the standard of care being determined by the courts (although with some consideration given to the profession in determining standards) (*Rogers v Whittaker* (1992) 175 CLR 479, *ter Neuzen v Korn* [1995] S.C.J. No. 79, 127 D.L.R. (4th) 577 (S.C.C.)).

Government-sanctioned self-regulation attracted a number of criticisms about its operation and function (Allsop and Jones 2006, Healy 2011, McDonald 2010b, Walshe 2009). The first was that regulators were insufficiently attentive to ensuring that health professionals maintained competence to practise (they did not achieve the prospective part of their mandate to manage the level of risk to the public). The second was that regulators were not sufficiently responsive when concerns were raised about a health professional's competence or conduct (they were not successful in retrospectively managing risks that had manifested in the practice of an individual health professional). In other words, regulators did not act, were slow to act or took ineffectual action to manage an evident risk to the safety of the public and patients associated with the competence or conduct of an individual health professional. Third, the regulators did not, or were slow to, recognize changing social or professional norms and issue appropriate guidance to the professions (for example, see discussion in Chapter 12 about sexual misconduct). All of these criticisms encompass an overarching concern about regulatory capture: that the regulators' interests were too closely influenced by the interests of the regulated, at the expense of the public interest. Priest (1997–1998: 273) thus describes government-sanctioned self-regulation as tantamount to 'putting the fox to guard the henhouse'.

In order to address the perceived weaknesses in the framework for government-sanctioned self-regulation of health professionals, the health professions and governments internationally undertook a variety of reforms to regulatory processes. The pace and priority of reforms differed by jurisdiction, not unexpectedly given the different histories of the professions, the legal and policy frameworks surrounding the health system, and policy priorities in each country (McDonald 2010b, Walshe 2009). These reforms have been well-described elsewhere and so will only be briefly described here (Allsop and Jones 2006, 2008, Freckelton 2009, Healy 2011, Walshe 2009).

In terms of regulating individual health professionals these reforms include the introduction of forms of recertification or revalidation of health professionals at regular intervals. Recertification requires health professionals to provide information about matters including complaints, any recently imposed limitations on practice, and any impairment that may affect the safety of a health professional's professional practice. As such, recertification is intended to remedy the information gap that resulted in some regulators being unaware of serious criminal convictions, restrictions on the ability to prescribe medications, and the like in relation to a registrant. It may alert regulators to potential problems. Revalidation, on the other hand, enables an assessment of a health professional's clinical practices and may provide some assurance of ongoing competence. As such both of these mechanisms provide a strengthening of the prospective regulation capabilities of government-sanctioned self-regulation.

In addition, reforms also saw the introduction of non-disciplinary pathways for practitioners with health related impairments and performance issues. These pathways were created to support the remediation of practitioners while ensuring patient safety (Freckelton 2009), recognizing a public interest in keeping health professionals in situ because of the demand for their skills and expertise and the social investment they represent (McDonald 2010a). In respect of discipline, the disciplinary gaze (Foucault 1995) was broadened to encompass matters of competence, whereas previously discipline had been predominantly concerned with addressing actions that brought the profession into disrepute (for example, criminal activity, fraud, disparaging another professional, sexual misconduct) and gross misconduct (Irvine 2006, Parry and Parry 1976, Walshe 2009). This widening of the disciplinary gaze is in accordance with community values requiring both accountability or justice and some assurance that the public will be protected from significant risks of harm.

The perceived, if not actual, conflict of interest raised by regulators investigating, prosecuting and disciplining those who were perceived to be 'their own' was another area for reform. In New Zealand and Australia, independent health complaints agencies were established to receive complaints about health services from the public. Their form and functions vary, with different requirements in respect of how closely they should work with health professions regulators, but in some jurisdictions, notably, New South Wales and New Zealand, these bodies have a prosecutorial as well as investigatory function (*Health Care Complaints Act 1993* (NSW); *Health and Disability Commissioner Act 1994* (NZ)).

There is also a trend towards the adjudication function moving from the regulatory bodies to independent adjudicatory bodies (Allsop and Jones 2008, McDonald 2010b, Walshe 2009). The rationale for this is quite clear. Administrative law principles require a fair hearing, untainted by allegations or perceptions of bias because of conflicts of interest. Conflicts of interest are readily apparent if there is no separation between investigatory and disciplinary functions. A conflict of interest can also arise if complainants and the public perceive that the process is overly dominated by professional interests at the expense of the public interest. Courts have raised concerns about the fairness of an adjudicatory process where an investigator becomes an adjudicator. As an example, from October 2000, when it came into force, the British *Human Rights Act 1998* led to greater judicial scrutiny of the processes for government-sanctioned self-regulation than were then in place. Prior to its enactment, the European Commission on Human Rights had expressed concern about fair processes and procedures in health professional regulatory bodies, especially the General Medical Council (GMC) (for example, *Stefan v United Kingdom*, *Wickramsinghe v United Kingdom*). After the enactment of the *Human Rights Act 1998* in Britain, the procedures of regulatory bodies in respect of disciplinary activities were examined and criticized by domestic courts (Glynn and Gomez 2005, *Priess v General Dental Council*, *Tehrani v United Kingdom Central Council for Nursing Midwifery and Health Visiting*). These legal judgements have emphasized the need for separation between policy and investigatory functions of the regulatory body and the adjudication function to avoid a perception of a conflict of interest. Tribunals have either developed specifically in respect of health professionals (for example, New Zealand's Health Practitioners Disciplinary Tribunal) or general adjudicatory bodies (for example, in Australia the use of each state's Civil and Administrative Tribunals to adjudicate disciplinary matters). The implications of this are not just that adjudication is now independent but that there is potential for it to increasingly be dominated by legal rather than professional norms.

Significant changes also flowed at the level of the governance of the health professional regulatory bodies. A trend has been to increase the participation of the public in the governance of the regulatory agency, by creating an increased representation of lay persons as members of the regulatory boards and/or though increasing their involvement in various processes associated with regulating individual registrants (for example, lay assessors) (see discussion in Chapter 8). Additionally, more oversight mechanisms were created, generally through increased formal accountability requirements to government (for example, requirements to report more frequently and in more detail to the Minister) and/or the creation of oversight bodies with varying responsibilities for regulating the regulators or at least scrutinizing them. The level and extent of these changes have constituted significant reforms in the manner in which health professions self-regulate with government sanction. The reforms to government-sanctioned self-regulation and civil liability highlight how the public became increasingly concerned about the degree of accountability the health professions and health professionals should have to the public and the level of transparency as to how the professional regulators exercise their legislatively conferred powers. These reforms strengthen the degree of accountability of health professionals to their patients, and the health professions to the public and, at least to some extent, manage some aspects of the risks associated with the activities of health professions. Questions remain about whether all occupations that provide a form of health services should be subject to government-sanctioned self-regulation and/or whether the use of other forms of regulation is required to effectively regulate the health system, which includes as a crucial component the activities of health professionals.

Which Health Professions Should be Regulated?

While changes to the way in which health professions self-regulate have occurred, as discussed above, a variety of approaches are being taken to the ambit of government-sanctioned self-regulation. Doctors were the first profession to achieve government sanction, with regulation in Britain first used in 1511 (*An Act for the Appointing of Physicians and Surgeons, 1511* (Eng.) 3 Hen. VIII., c. 11). Other professions, such as nurses and dentists, were also regulated from the late nineteenth and early twentieth centuries. The regulatory reach of government-sanctioned self-regulation has gradually extended to encompass a variety of health occupations, but more occupational groups, both inside and outside of the health sector, continue to seek regulation (Walshe 2009). Although there are a number of occupational groups providing health services, not all are recognized as 'officially' constituting a profession by being regulated through legislation. Health professional status is not necessary for health occupations to function or to provide care, but this status is seen to confer a number of benefits on the occupational group, particularly in regard to the sense of legitimacy granted to the profession through the state sanctioning or affirming its professionalism (Walshe 2009). Regulation also can confer economic benefits, in that the profession may be able to control who can do the work, or at least who can claim a title to do certain forms of work (Walshe 2009). Demand for government-sanctioned self-regulatory status to be conferred continues to increase for a number of reasons. The most obvious is that occupational groups are increasingly requesting it. But also there are a wider range of occupational groups that are potentially eligible for regulation as society conceives of health in a more expansive way, moving beyond a dependence on allopathic norms to accept alternative and complimentary modalities. Equally, processes of innovation continue within the health sector resulting in the creation of new professions and new professional roles.

The correlative question is what benefits do the regulation of health occupations confer upon the public? The general answer to that is said to be a measure of assurance that registered professionals are qualified and have the appropriate skills and experience that, in theory, should result in services of a certain quality being delivered (McDonald 2010a, Walshe 2009). It also creates an accountability mechanism (in addition to civil liability) that can hold individual health professionals to account and protect the public from any ongoing harm as a result of that professional continuing in practice.

Traditionally, the decision to regulate new health professions has been done in an ad hoc manner, usually as a result of sustained lobbying by the occupation in question. However, some jurisdictions are adopting a more planned approach to the admission of occupations into the professional fold. There are essentially two models that have been used in respect of this approach. The first is an advisory body led process where a general legislative provision authorizes an advisory body to review applications from occupations or to act on its own initiative to review whether a health occupation should be regulated by government. The second is a ministerial-led process where a general legislative provision authorizes the Minister of Health (or equivalent) to decide whether to regulate health occupations. The first model, an advisory body led process, is perhaps the most common. In the Canadian provinces of Alberta and Ontario, review is undertaken by a specialist standing advisory and/or regulatory body. For example, in Alberta applications are made to the Minister who refers the matter to the Health Professions Advisory Board for evaluation if the Minister is satisfied such a matter is in the public interest (*Health Professions Act*, R.S.A. 2000, c.H-7). The Health Professions Regulatory Advisory Council performs a similar function in Ontario (*Regulated Health Professions Act* S.O. 1991 c.18). In New Zealand (section 115(1) of the *Health Professions Competence Assurance Act 2003*), and the Canadian province of British Columbia (section 7 of the *Health Professions Act* R.S.B.C. 1996, c. 183) a ministerial led process is in place.

Whether a jurisdiction uses a ministerial or advisory commission focus appears to be more a matter of whether they already had an advisory body in place tasked with providing advice on health professional regulation. New Zealand and British Columbia did not have established advisory bodies to provide advice on the regulation of health professions so the decision to use a ministerial led process could reflect necessity or choice. There is no evidence to suggest that one process is any better than another, and the decision on which model to use may come down to whether the creation of a standing advisory body is the best use of resources.

Whether these jurisdictions use an advisory body led process or the ministerial led process, the criteria for the circumstances in which a health profession should be regulated are readily available. In terms of the criteria that guide the Minister's or advisory body's decision-making there are some significant differences between jurisdictions but some general themes include risk perception, regulatory necessity, manageability, and benefits exceeding disadvantages.

Risk

The degree of the risk to the public is generally a critical component in the decision whether or not to regulate, which is not surprising. This is particularly so given both that the primary objective of health professional regulation is to protect the public and that there are suggestions that we now live in a risk society – a society where regulation is preoccupied with controlling risk (Beck et al. 1994). The focus is on the extent of the risk of harm to the health and safety of the public caused by the activities of that occupation. In short, is it necessary to regulate the profession manage the risk?

Regulatory Necessity

A second common component of the criteria to determine whether a health occupation should be regulated is an assessment of regulatory necessity. Namely: is the occupation operating in a health related context or is it more appropriately regulated by another ministry? Are there existing regulatory mechanisms that could or should be used? Do the individuals whose occupation is being considered for registration currently practise under the supervision of other registered health professionals? In short, is there another way?

Manageability

A third common criterion is a concern about manageability – or is it possible and practicable to regulate the occupation? Attention is paid in the criteria, and in practice, to issues such as whether there is a recognized, distinct and identifiable occupation; a recognized body of knowledge for the occupation; agreed upon qualifications, standards, scopes of practice, and competencies; leadership or organization; and a commitment to professionalism, that is, a register, fitness to practise processes, continuing professional development and so on. In short, can it be done?

Benefits Exceed Disadvantages

A fourth, less common, criterion is whether the benefits of regulation exceed any disadvantages. Matters to be considered include costs, issues around access and availability, and whether there are possible improvements in quality associated with government-sanctioned self-regulation. In short, should it be done?

These general themes can be seen in the criteria set out in section 25(4) of the *Health Professions Act*, R.S.A. 2000, c.H–7. The Albertan Advisory Board, in determining whether a health profession should be regulated, may as part of its evaluation:

(a) evaluate the risk to the physical and psychological health and safety of the public from incompetent, unethical or impaired practice of the profession;

(b) ascertain what constitutes the practice of the profession, whether persons practising the profession should be authorized to provide restricted activities and the conditions, if any, that should apply to the practice of the profession or the provision of restricted activities;

(c) evaluate and make recommendations on the services normally provided by a person practising the profession, including the complexity of the services and how they are carried out;

(d) consider whether the services normally provided by persons practising the profession are regulated by an enactment;

(e) consider whether the profession is a distinct and identifiable profession;

(f) consider whether the proposed protected title is appropriately descriptive and whether it is likely to cause public confusion;

(g) consider the potential costs and benefits of regulating the profession, including the expected effect on practitioner availability and on education and training programs, the expected effect on enhancement of quality of service and the expected effect on prices, access and service efficiency;

(h) ascertain the qualifications and minimum standards of competence that are required for a person applying to practise the profession and how the continuing competence of practitioners is to be maintained, ascertain what education programs are available and evaluate the available education programs;

(i) ascertain the ability of the proposed college of the profession to carry out its powers and duties under this Act or consider whether they could be carried out by an existing college;

(j) evaluate the effect, if any, that there would be on any agreements on trade and mobility to which Canada or Alberta is a signatory if the profession would become a regulated profession;

(k) on the request of the Minister, consider any other matter.

Sub-sections 25(4)(a)–(c) focus on evaluating the level of risk to the public's health and safety from problematic health professionals or from the nature of the services that they provided. Sub-section 25(4)(d) examines the concept of necessity – does the health profession need to be regulated? Are there already mechanisms in place that regulate the types of services that the profession provides? Manageability is considered in subsections 25(4)(e)–(f) and (h)–(i) and benefits versus disadvantageous in subsections (g) and (j) both in relation to the profession's operations and in relation to broader economic questions about trade and mobility.

The question of whether to regulate or not is not considered solely by reference to the health context. For example, in New Zealand the Cabinet created a policy framework in respect of regulating occupations (in general, not specific to health) (Cabinet Office Circular 99(6) cited in Ministry of Health 2003). An application to regulate a health occupation must be consistent with this broader policy. The policy includes that government should only regulate an occupation when there is a problem or potential problem that is either unlikely to be solved in any other way or is inefficient or ineffective to solve any other way. In addition, the level of intervention into the occupation should be the minimum required to solve the problem and the benefits of any intervention must exceed its costs.

In general, explicit criteria for decision-making may create clear parameters for applicants. The publication of the forms of criteria may reduce the possibility of arbitrary decisions, increase transparency, and slow down the admission process to prevent a wholesale explosion of regulation (Castonguay 1978). One problem is that the criteria are open to subjective interpretation (Castonguay 1978, Dussault 1978), especially if lobbying occurs. In respect of the Québec system Dussault noted: 'in reality, the *Code* by itself does not enable one to set the limits, to determine the threshold beyond which a given activity is sufficiently "professional" to warrant regrouping in a corporation those persons engaged in that activity' (1978: 102).

Britain has in 2011 taken the first steps towards another approach. Until 2011 the Health Professions Council was responsible for assessing applications for health occupations to be regulated and for advising the government, pursuant to article 3(17) of the *Health Professions Order 2001*. However, it has ceased assessing applications after the government revisited this process. The Department of Health noted:

> Compulsory blanket statutory regulation of the health and social care workforce in England has too often been seen as the first resort, rather than the last, in deciding how best to assure safe, effective and respectful care … In general terms, the Government does not believe that the extension of statutory regulation to all workers in the health sector across the UK and the social care sector in England would be a proportionate response (Department of Health 2011: 16).

The Department has indicated that it prefers the development of a system of 'assured voluntary registration' for occupational groups not subject to statutory regulation (Department of Health 2011: 16). This requires the establishment of voluntary registers through which members of occupational groups may choose to be registered. The processes through which registration occurs for these groups is to be accredited by the Council for Healthcare Regulatory Excellence to provide some assurance to the public about the skills and training of those registered. Regulation of occupational groups is argued to be the responsibility of employers. The British government is essentially advancing an argument that the disadvantages of regulating hitherto unregulated health occupations outweigh any possible benefits to the public, are not proportionate to the degree of risk involved and place a significant regulatory burden on the regulated – many of whom are poorly paid and who would find it difficult to pay registration fees. It notes that 1.4 million staff in 31 professional and occupational groups are currently regulated with the potential for an additional 1.2 million who could be regulated – a significant extension of the ambit of health professional regulation.

The divergence in approaches indicates the difficulties faced by governments in making a decision whether or not to regulate a health occupation. It raises complex questions about to what end we choose to use law to sanction a profession's functions and operations. To manage risk is an apparent answer, but risk is a permeable concept: almost anything can be characterized as being 'risky'. There are also risks associated with rushing to regulate – as government-led regulation is not a cost-neutral process and carries with it a significant regulatory burden for the regulated and for the state. Perhaps more saliently, in the rush to manage risk, perspective can be lost about the extent of that risk and whether other regulatory strategies can be employed instead of government-sanctioned self-regulation. It is after all questionable whether government-sanctioned self-regulation has been particularly successful, at least to judge by the numbers of changes within the traditional regulatory trinity that are described in the next section.

Challenging the Trinity

One of the ongoing trends in the regulation of health professionals is the recognition that the trinity of regulatory instruments traditionally used to regulate the activities of health professions may be insufficient in modern health systems (McDonald 2010b). The roots of the regulatory trinity pre-date modern health systems and indeed also pre-date modern regulatory systems. The trinity is premised on an autonomous professional who is either competent and/or ethical or not competent and/or unethical (McDonald 2008). However, as McDonald (2008) notes, the present reality is that most health professionals are embedded in highly complex modern health systems, with multiple interacting health care providers and treatments, caring for patients with multiple co-morbidities, at times using advanced technology, in a highly pressured environment.

Modern health systems were generally formed on the basis of governments reaching accommodations with the medical profession. These accommodations generally privileged clinical and professional autonomy (Tuohy 1999). As such, there was a reluctance to use any other forms of regulation that impinged too greatly on clinical autonomy. This perception that clinical and professional autonomy should be privileged has been subject to challenge on at least three fronts.

First, it is clear that government-sanctioned professional self-regulation has not, in some circumstances, been successful at achieving the public protection ends claimed for it (Allsop and Jones 2006, McDonald 2010a, 2010b, Walshe 2009). In part, this is because of the perception that some regulators had been ineffectual in prospectively managing potential risks and some regulators seemed unwilling or unable to respond retrospectively to actual threats in a manner sufficient to safeguard the public. As discussed in Chapter 12, there has also been a perception, in some jurisdictions, that governance failures have occurred within the professions.

Second, recent research into patient safety has illustrated that healthcare carries inherent risks of iatrogenic harms (harms resulting from medical treatment) (for example, Institute of Medicine 2000) and these risks have been illustrated to the public in the types of scandals discussed in Chapter 12. However, while it is attractive and easy to blame a 'bad apple' the findings of research into the psychology of error are that the focus should be not purely or solely on health professionals as the cause of errors, but on factors inherent to the complex system within which they work (Reason 1990). Health professionals cannot be artificially divorced from the places and systems within which they work for the purposes of regulation. Therefore other regulatory tools are required to supplement or even supplant the more traditional tools.

Third, in some jurisdictions the New Public Management (NPM) has profoundly affected conceptions of how health systems and services should be regulated (McDonald 2010b). The embrace of the tenets of NPM saw a transformation in regulatory practices with a focus on clear prospective and retrospective accountabilities and control from the centre exercised by a variety of monitoring bodies (Dunleavy and Hood 1994, Pollit 1995). Ideologically, the NPM encapsulated a profound distrust of policy and regulatory actors, suspecting that these bodies were likely to be subject to capture by vested interests (Dunleavy and Hood 1994, Pollit 1995). As Aucoin (1995: 3) notes, '[c]hanges in public management are not merely changes to administrative processes and practices; they are also changes to governance itself'. It has been suggested in the context of Britain that the commitment to mechanisms of audit and accountability has resulted in the emergence of what Power (1997) calls an 'audit society' where the regulatory preoccupation is to monitor performance and increase resources devoted to audit and accountability.

Other factors that may be contributing to the widening of the ambit of regulation that is extended explicitly or implicitly to health professionals include: increasing evidence of what works in clinical practice accompanied by a widespread variations in clinical practice and outcomes; the emergence of data systems that enabled closer monitoring of performance; and the need of governments to contain costs (Davies and Mannion 2000). Davies (2000: 447) suggests that it 'is the cost factor that explains the shift from a self-regulatory paradigm to an interventionalist, managerial one'.

The impact of all of these factors on the regulation of health professionals can be seen in the development in some jurisdictions, notably Britain, New Zealand and Australia, of a suite of regulatory instruments that directly or indirectly regulate health professionals through mechanisms outside the traditional regulatory trinity (McDonald 2010b, Walshe 2009). One focus has been strengthening the accountability mechanisms implicit in employment relationships and/or the granting of clinical privileges (including strengthening the credentialing of health professionals). In Britain the perceived inability of the National Health Service (NHS), as well as professional regulators, to address concerns about doctors resulted in a strengthening of employment related mechanisms (McDonald 2010b) and in Australia the Patel scandal resulted in the development or the strengthening of credentialing processes across the states (McDonald 2010a; see also Chapter 9). The development of regulated standards for hospitals and other organizations that deliver treatment and care is another trend (McDonald 2010b). In order for organizations to comply with these standards health professionals working within those organizations must be involved. The introduction of limits on the hours worked by health professionals through legislation, collective bargaining or associational self-regulation is another regulatory initiative through which, to some degree, the practices of health professionals can be regulated (McDonald 2008). Other regulatory instruments include the promotion of audit and risk management within health systems and organizations; introduction of clinical guidelines; a focus on performance management processes in contracts between health professionals and organizations or systems; requirements for the publication of report cards providing information about a health professional's practice (Clarke and Oakley 2007); and other similar mechanisms. All these regulatory instruments go beyond the regulatory trinity and supplement and extend the regulatory reach of governments in relation to the health workforce.

Conclusion

The use of other forms of regulatory tools to regulate health professionals in some jurisdictions speaks to an increased tendency to question the effectiveness, efficacy, manageability and legitimacy of traditional forms of regulation. The traditional forms of regulation focus on the individual health professional divorced to a great extent from the broader context. They do not or cannot focus on the individual as a part of a system that provides health services. The symbiosis between the professional and the system is increasingly said to require the use of regulatory tools with a broader ambit and a systemic focus to compliment or occasionally supplant government-sanctioned self-regulation.

Determinations about whether to confer upon a health occupation government-sanctioned self-regulatory status illustrate a broader challenge about the most appropriate ways to regulate occupations, particularly occupations that work within complex organizational systems. There is growing recognition that individual health professionals cannot be divorced from the context within which they practise and of the essential interdependency between the activities of health professionals and of the organizations and systems that provide health services. This is increasingly leading to the use of a 'dense mosaic' (Salamon 2002) of regulatory tools, supplanting the traditional reliance on the regulatory trinity and particularly on government-sanctioned self-regulation. This is indicative of an approach that is less concerned about the maintenance of professional privileges, such as professional and clinical autonomy, and more focused on the management of risks, including to patient safety but also risks associated with management and regulatory practices, within complex systems.

References

Allsop, J., Jones, K. and Baggott, R. 2004. Health consumer groups in the UK: a new social movement? *Sociology of Health and Illness*, 26(6), 737–56.

Allsop, J. and Jones, K. 2006. *Quality Assurance in Medical Regulation in an International Context: Report for the Department of Health England*. London: University of Lincoln.

Allsop, J. and Jones, K. 2008. Protecting patients: international trends in medical governance, in *Rethinking Professional Governance: International Directions in Healthcare*, edited by E. Kuhlmann and M. Saks. Bristol: Policy Press, 15–27.

An Act for the Appointing of Physicians and Surgeons, 1511 (Eng.) 3 Hen. VIII., c. 11.

Aucoin, P. 1995. *The New Public Management: Canada in Comparative Perspective*. Montreal: Institute for Research on Public Policy.

Beck, U., Giddens, A. and Lash, S., (eds) 1994. *Reflexive Modernization: Politics, Tradition and Aesthetics in the Modern Social Order*. Cambridge: Polity Press.

Bolam v Friern Hospital Management Committee [1957] 1 WLR 582.

Castonguay, C. 1978. The future of self-regulation: a view from Québec, in *The Professions and Public Policy*, edited by P. Slayton and M. Trebilcock. Toronto: University of Toronto Press, 61–76.

Clarke, S. and Oakley, P. 2007. *Informed Consent and Clinician Accountability: The Ethics of Report Cards on Surgical Performance*. Cambridge: Cambridge University Press.

Davies, A. 2000. Don't trust me, I'm a doctor: medical regulation and the 1999 NHS reforms. *Oxford Journal of Legal Studies*, 20(3), 437–56.

Davies, H. and Mannion, R. 2000. Clinical governance: striking a balance between checking and trusting, in *Reforming Markets in Health Care: An Economic Perspective*, edited by P. Smith. Buckingham: Open University Press, 246–67.

Department of Health. 2011. *Enabling Excellence: Autonomy and Accountability for Healthcare Workers, Social Workers and Social Care Workers*. (Cmnd. 8008), London: Department of Health.

Dunleavy, P. and Hood, C. 1994. From old public administration to new public management. *Public Money & Management*, 14(3), 9–16.

Dussault, R. 1978. The Office des Professions du Québec in the context of the development of professionalism. The future of self-regulation: a view from Québec, in *The Professions and Public Policy*, edited by P. Slayton and M. Trebilcock. Toronto: University of Toronto Press, 101–10.

Emanuel, E. and Emanuel, L. 1996. What is accountability in health care? *Annals of Internal Medicine*, 124(2), 229–39.

Foucault, M. 1995. *Discipline and Punish: The Birth of a Prison*. London: Vintage Books.

Freckelton, I. 2009. Non-disciplinary pathways in health practitioner regulation, in *Patient Safety First: Responsive Regulation in Health Care*, edited by J. Healy and P. Dugdale. Sydney: Allen & Unwin, 167–191.

Glynn, J. and Gomez, D. 2005. *Fitness to Practise: Health Care Regulatory Law, Principle and Process*. London: Thomson.

Health Care Complaints Act 1993 (NSW).

Health and Disability Commissioner Act 1994 (NZ).

Health Professions Act, R.S.A. 2000, c.H–7.

Health Professions Act R.S.B.C. 1996, c. 183.

Health Professions Competence Assurance Act 2003 (NZ).

Health Professions Order 2001 (U.K.) S.I. 2002/254.

Healy, J. 2011. *Improving Health Care Safety and Quality: Reluctant Regulators*. Farnham: Ashgate.

Institute of Medicine. 2000. *To Err is Human: Building a Safer Health System*. Washington, D.C.: National Academy Press.

Irvine, D. 2006. A short history of the general medical council. *Medical Education*, 40(3), 202-211.

Jost, T. 1997. *Regulation of Healthcare Professions*. Chicago: Health Administration Press.

Kuhlmann, E. and Saks, M., (eds) 2008. *Rethinking Professional Governance: International Directions in Healthcare*. Bristol: Policy Press.

McDonald, F. 2008. The criminalisation of medical mistakes in Canada: a review. *Health Law Journal*, 16, 1–26.

McDonald, F. 2010a. The regulation of health professionals, in *Health Law in Australia*, edited by B. White, et al. Sydney: Thomson, 509–55.

McDonald, F. 2010b. Patient safety law: regulatory change in Britain and Canada. JSD thesis. Halifax: Dalhousie University.

Ministry of Health (N.Z.). 2003. New professions under the health practitioners competence assurance Act 2003: criteria for assessing applications for Inclusion in the Act [Online: Ministry of Health]. Available at: www.moh.govt.nz/moh.nsf/pagesmh/6425/$File/newprofessions-hpca.pdf [accessed: 1 August 2011].

Parry, N. and Parry, J. 1976. *The Rise of the Medical Profession*. London: Croom Helm.

Pollitt, C. 1995. Justification by works or faith? Evaluating the new public management. *Evaluation*, 1(2), 133–54.

Power, M. 1997. *The Audit Society: Rituals of Verification*. Oxford: Oxford University Press.

Priess v General Dental Council [2001] 1 W.L.R. 1926.

Priest, M. 1997–1998. The privatization of regulation: five models of self-regulation. *Ottawa Law Review*, 29, 233–302.

Reason, J. 1990. *Human Error*. New York: Cambridge University Press.

Rogers v Whittaker [1992] 175 CLR 479.

Regulated Health Professions Act S.O. 1991 c.18

Salamon, L. 2002. The new governance and the tools of public action: an introduction, in *The Tools of Government: A Guide to the New Governance*, edited by L. Salamon. New York: Oxford University Press, 1–12.

Stacey, M. 1992. *Regulating British Medicine: The General Medical Council*. Chichester: Wiley.

Stefan v United Kingdom [1998] 25 E.H.R.R. CD 130.

Tehrani v United Kingdom Central Council for Nursing Midwifery and Health Visiting [2001] S.L.T. 879 (Court of Session).

ter Neuzen v Korn [1995] S.C.J. No. 79, 127 D.L.R. (4th) 577 (S.C.C.).

Tuohy, C. 1999. *Accidental Logics: The Dynamics of Change in the Health Care Arena in the United States, Britain and Canada*. New York: Oxford University Press.

Walshe, K. (2009) Regulating health professionals, in *Patient Safety First: Responsive Regulation in Health Care*, edited by J. Healy and P. Dugdale. Crows Nest, NSW: Allen & Unwin, 144–66.

Wickramsinghe v United Kingdom [1998] E.H.R.L.R. 338.

Woolf, H. 2001. Are the courts excessively deferential to the medical profession? *Medical Law Review*, 9(1), 1–16.

Chapter 7

Interprofessionalism and Collaborative Self-regulation in the Health Professions: Two Variations on an Emerging Canadian Theme

William Lahey[1]

Introduction

Interprofessional collaboration among regulated health care professionals has received significant attention in Canadian health policy literature (Barrett 2005, Bosco 2005, Canadian Health Services Research Foundation 2006, Côté et al. 2008, Health Council of Canada 2009). This reflects widespread confidence that interprofessional collaborative care, or team-based care, will contribute to a wide range of interrelated and escalating benefits for patients, providers and the broader health care system. Notwithstanding the doubts of some (Cameron 2011, Greenfield et al. 2011), these benefits are thought to include expanded access (and choice of access) to necessary services; enhanced clinical quality and safety; reduced burdens on the members of some professions and expanded opportunities for the members of others; and a health care system that becomes more responsive to patient needs while simultaneously becoming more sustainable by making better, fuller and more flexible use of the competencies of all providers.

Much of the attention to interprofessional collaboration has focused on clinical collaboration and on collaboration in the education of health professions. Less attention has been given to interprofessional regulatory collaboration: that is, to collaboration among the regulatory bodies, generally called colleges or associations in Canada, which regulate the health professions that are typically self-regulating in Canada and in other countries (HPRAC 2008a). This neglect

1 The author wishes to note that he has been a facilitator and advisor (with the valuable assistance of Leah Hutt and Alison Hopkins) to the Nova Scotia Working Group on Collaborative Self-Regulation and that he was consulted by those who advised the Ontario Health Professions Regulatory Advisory Council on its *Critical Links* report. The author wishes to acknowledge all he has learned about interprofessional collaboration and health professions regulation more broadly, from Working Group members Dennis Holland, Dr. Cameron Little, Donna Denney, Bev Zwicker, Ann Mann, Gayle Salsman, Michelle Brennan, Michelle MacDonald and Marjorie Hickey. He also wishes to gratefully acknowledge the research assistance on this chapter of Jacqui Shaw.

is somewhat puzzling given that the literature on interprofessional collaboration identifies health professions regulation as a significant barrier to the collaboration that is desired in the clinical sphere (Davies 2007). Given the confidence that is placed in interprofessional collaboration to overcome the other kinds of barriers that it faces, it is perhaps surprising that more attention has not been given to the role that it might play in better aligning health professions regulation with interprofessional collaborative care.

The lack of attention to interprofessional collaboration in regulation is also interesting given the *prima facie* relevance of such collaboration to the challenges that health professions regulation faces in protecting patients from harm and in supporting their access to quality care. Among these challenges is the tension between a system of regulation that is segmented into multiple distinct processes defined by professional boundaries and a health care system that depends on coordinated and integrated effort (whether collaborative or not) from providers that come from two or more regulated professions. In such circumstances, the capacity of regulation to deal with the systemic factors that determine much of the risk of harm to patients must be as limited by its wide allocation among many regulators as it is by the tendency to leniency by individual self-regulators that receives so much attention.

This chapter is about Canadian initiatives to improve health professions regulation through application of interprofessional collaboration to regulatory work. Since health professions regulation (and the delivery of health care generally) are provincial matters, it is primarily about initiatives taking place at the provincial level, specifically in Ontario (the largest province) and Nova Scotia (one of the smallest). But the chapter is also about the broader national process of health care reform and governance that informs these initiatives and that might support them in the future.

The chapter is divided into three main parts. Part 1 situates the work taking place in Ontario and in Nova Scotia on collaborative regulation within their respective legislative frameworks for health professions regulation: while the framework in Ontario is built upon 'umbrella legislation' that applies to all self-regulating health professions and the statutes specific to each profession, the framework in Nova Scotia consists solely of the individual statutes of each self-regulating profession. Part 1 also situates the work of Ontario and Nova Scotia on collaborative health professions regulation in a national Canadian health care policy discourse that tends to view health professions regulation as a constraint on the capacity of the health care system to improve accessibility, quality and affordability. It then explores how the focus that two national Health Accords (and ensuing policy research commissioned by Health Canada) placed on the importance of interprofessional collaboration to a broad range of health care objectives, particularly in primary care, contributed to calls for a new paradigm of self-regulation based on interprofessional collaboration, dubbed 'collaborative self-regulation'. The expectations were that this new paradigm would not only enable interprofessional collaboration but also enhance the capacity of professions regulators to protect patients and the broader public interest in safe, competent, and ethical care.

Part 2 deals with the initiatives unfolding on the ground in Ontario and Nova Scotia respectively. It shows how each process is informed by an understanding of the relevance of collaboration to regulation that largely aligns with the call for a new 'paradigm' of self-regulation based on interprofessional collaboration. It also shows that the two processes differ markedly, both in terms of their process and their outputs, on a key question: whether collaboration is best achieved by making regulatory bodies accountable for collaborating, or instead by making it available to regulatory bodies as a tool to be used when and if they determine that it is necessary or helpful to the achievement of their mandates. In Ontario the process has been a 'top down' one that emphasizes the obligation of regulatory bodies to collaborate, subject to oversight. In Nova Scotia the process has been a 'bottom up' process, run by the regulatory bodies themselves, that emphasizes voluntary collaboration where regulators determine it is needed or helpful.

In Part 3, the broader significance of these differences is considered. It is suggested that the differences should be viewed as giving rise to fundamental questions that need to be answered if collaborative self-regulation is not only to happen but is to produce real and sustainable improvements in health professions regulation. One source of perspective on these questions may come from the debate taking place in multiple regulatory fields about whether systemic challenges and opportunities that cut across the mandate of individual regulators are best addressed through institutional consolidation or coordinated effort. Answering the questions requires evaluation from multiple perspectives, including that of national health care reform. More broadly, such evaluation would help to ensure that decision-makers in Ontario and Nova Scotia and in other provinces have full opportunity to know about and to act upon the lessons that can be learned from their respective initiatives in regulatory interprofessional collaboration.

Part 1: Health Care Policy and Health Professions Regulation in Canada

Relevance of Health Professions Regulation to Core Concerns of Canadian Health Care Policy

In Canada, health professions regulation is rarely, if ever, a leading health care policy issue. The dominant concern of citizens, governments and the policy community is the productivity and the fiscal and political sustainability of Medicare – the programme through which governments in every province and territory (with federal subsidization) fund the single-payer system that provides universal access to physician and hospital services under the 'iconic' (Romanow 2002) *Canada Health Act* (R.S.C. 1985, c. C-6). The related concern of comparable salience is that of access to other services (such as home care and prescription drugs) that are not universally funded with taxpayer dollars.

Much of the attention that is devoted to health professions regulation is ancillary to the pervasive preoccupation with the health of Medicare and the possible expansion of its principles to other health care services: it concentrates on the role that health professions regulation plays (or is thought to play) in limiting the delivery system's flexibility and responsiveness or in complicating efforts to enhance affordability through rational allocation of work to the least expensive competent provider (Romanow 2002, SSCSAST 2002).

This perspective on health professions regulation is hardly unique to Canada. But what may distinguish Canada is the extent of the emphasis on this aspect of health professions regulation – what might be called its collateral consequences – as compared to the attention that gets placed in other jurisdictions, particularly in recent years, on the internal effectiveness of health professions regulation, especially in the rigour and independence of disciplinary processes and on the accountability of regulators for patient safety (McDonald 2010). Such concerns do of course attract attention in Canada as elsewhere, particularly in the immediate aftermath of patient safety scandals (Cameron 2009, Creaghan 2008). But they do not often capture a lasting place in the wider realm of health care policy. Instead, the abiding preoccupation has been the obstacles that a fragmented regulatory system built around a multiplicity of colliding 'scopes of practice' creates for the achievement of broader health system policy objectives such as the reform of primary care, the optimal deployment of health human resources, the achievement of seamless continua of care, and the management of costs. This comes through in official reviews of the health care system (Romanow 2002, SSCSAST 2002) and in official reviews of health professions legislation (Health Professions Legislation Review 1989, B.C. Health Professions Council 2001, HPRAC 2001).

No doubt there are multiple explanations for this. One self-evident one is surely the legislative framework that structures health professions regulation in Canada. This legislative framework is found at the provincial level, since the delivery of health care services (as opposed to public funding of health care services) and the regulation of occupations are largely matters of exclusive provincial competency (Jackman 2000). Across the provinces, legislatures have, one statute at a time, instituted a system of health professions regulation that is largely synonymous with self-regulation for each regulated profession, including those that are regulated together as part of the 'health professions' in other countries (Epps 2011). In most Canadian provinces, this means upwards of 20 independently self-regulating health professions. This is true for small provinces like Nova Scotia (population *c.*900,000) and for large provinces like Ontario (population *c.*13,000,000).

In addition to distributing regulatory authority widely, the Pan-Canadian legislative model gives high autonomy and a wide mandate to each self-regulating profession. For example, no equivalent of the United Kingdom's Council for Healthcare Regulatory Excellence (CHRE) (CHRE 2011a) oversees the functioning of regulatory bodies in any Canadian province. Similarly, Canadian self-regulators typically enjoy comprehensive authority for professions regulation. In contrast, for example, to the choice of New Zealand to largely transfer disciplinary functions to state agencies that have jurisdiction over all regulated professions (Collins 2006), the Canadian pattern is to give each self-regulating profession exclusive jurisdiction over a regulatory mandate that is comprehensive and exclusive.

These common legislative features hold true for provinces (like Ontario) that have 'umbrella legislation' and for provinces (like Nova Scotia) that do not. The legislative framework for health professions regulation in the four Atlantic Provinces (which include Nova Scotia) and in Saskatchewan is a single-layer framework consisting of the distinct statutes of each self-regulating group or, in the case of Newfoundland and Labrador, single professions or those regulated under the Health Professions Act (*Health Professions Act*, S.N.L., 2010, c. H-1.02). In the rest of the provinces, now including Manitoba (*Health Professions Act*, S.M., 2009, c. 15), each regulatory body is also subject to its own statute (or regulation). But each regulatory body is also subject to an umbrella statute that applies to all regulated health professions (and in Quebec to all regulated professions). This umbrella statute establishes legislative uniformity on matters that are regarded as either requiring or being amendable to uniformity (HPRAC 2008a). It establishes (or recognizes) governmental responsibility for determining policy of general significance to the regulatory system as a whole. It typically institutes an advisory council that is accountable to the Minister of Health for advice on these matters of general policy. It abandons the idea of giving each profession a scope of practice that excludes all others except those in that profession from performing all activities encompassed by that scope of practice. It substitutes a legislative structure in which each scope of practice is merely descriptive and in which everyone (whether regulated or not) is only precluded from performing a limited list of 'controlled' or 'reserved' acts except where they belong to a regulated profession that is expressly authorized *by the Minister* to perform one or more of those acts.

Later, it will be suggested that Ontario's approach to interprofessional regulation, in comparison to that of Nova Scotia, can be traced to the ways in which umbrella legislation changes self-regulation. It layers a level of state governance upon the self-governance that legislation otherwise delegates to each self-regulating profession. This strengthens the authority of the state by making that authority more explicit and by instituting statutory mechanisms for its exercise. For now however, the point is how little is changed by umbrella legislation, especially in comparison to the kinds of changes to self-regulation that have been made in recent years in other countries. It does not consolidate professions regulators. It does not reassign regulatory functions to state regulators. It does not make regulatory bodies subject to operational oversight by a central 'regulator of the regulators'. Instead, it leaves the essential and common characteristics of the Canadian approach to health professions regulation intact: each regulated profession is given broad autonomy to discharge the full range of regulatory functions with respect to its own members. Indeed, given how hard governments have had to work to overcome resistance to the passage and implementation of umbrella legislation in most of the provinces that have adopted it, one might say that it does more to confirm than to challenge the strength of the traditional Canadian self-regulatory model.

Thus in provinces with and without umbrella legislation, a highly decentralized system of health professions regulation coexists with a system of health system governance that is, under the influence of Medicare, significantly centralized. This does not fully explain the tendency of Canadian health care policy to pay attention to health professions regulation mostly as a real or perceived obstacle to the performance of Medicare. The distinct and overriding preoccupation with Medicare as a core national institution is an important independent influence. But the tension between how the country has allocated and structured responsibility for health professions regulation and how it has structured the governance of the broader health care system is almost certainly a distinct and important part of the explanation.

Health Care Reform, Interprofessional Collaboration and Health Professions Regulation

The idea that the accessibility, quality and safety of clinical care can be improved through interprofessional collaboration has been around for many years. In Canada, it has gained elevated policy momentum through the Health Accords that the provinces (and territories) negotiated with the federal government in 2003 and again in 2004 (First Ministers' Meeting 2003, 2004). In general terms, both Accords committed the federal government to substantially increasing health care funding to the provinces in exchange for provincial commitments to make improvements in health care system functioning by, for example: improving access to primary care; expanding prescription drug coverage (for patients facing catastrophic drug costs); expanding public funding for home care (to include more acute care, palliative care and mental health care); reducing waiting times for specified diagnostic and surgical procedures; and accelerating the development and implementation of electronic health records (Lahey 2011). For present purposes, the commitment that matters most was that of the provinces in the 2003 Accord (in effect until 2008) to make primary care through multidisciplinary teams available to 50 per cent of Canadians. In the 2004 Accord, which remains in place until 2014, this commitment was extended and scheduled for completion in 2011.

One of the influences shaping both deals was the analysis of the Commission on the Future of Medicare (Romanow 2002). Its 2002 report to the federal government expressed great confidence in the role that flexible, collaborative and multidisciplinary teams could play in 'fixing' primary care, arguably the weakest part of the Canadian health care system. This confidence aligned with one of the report's underlying themes, that improved health system performance required more collaboration, not the greater competition that some advocated. Collaboration (and the mechanisms that would enable it) was the needed remedy at all levels of governance, including between governments, between governments and the health care system, between sectors of the system, and between categories of providers. To make it possible between providers, the Commission (like the contemporaneous review of the 'Kirby Committee') observed that health professions would have to stop fighting over their 'scopes of practice' and occupational turf and start working together to provide 'patient-centered care' in accordance with Medicare's underlying values (Romanow 2002: 93, 106, 107, 113, 119, 151–2, SSCSAST 2002: 87–8, 199).

To enable this transition, considerable effort was invested after the Accords into the identification and understanding of both the enablers of and barriers to interprofessional collaboration. For example, Health Canada sponsored a series of papers primarily on the role of education in interprofessional collaboration that included one by Lahey and Currie on 'Medico-legal and Regulatory Barriers to Interprofessional Practice' (Lahey and Currie 2005). This reflected the importance that law was thought to have for the prospects for collaborative practice. It also reflected the basic assumption that law (including health professions regulation legislation) was primarily if not exclusively relevant as a barrier to the sharing, flexibility, cooperation and coordination that was vital to collaborative practice.

Lahey and Currie (2005) argued for caution in basing policy on such assumptions. They argued that alignment between professional self-regulation and collaborative care should be possible because of their shared objectives – the delivery of safe and quality care to patients. They further argued that to the extent that such alignment was not possible, the value to be gained through wider adoption of collaborative care had to be weighed against the value gained from professional self-regulation (as opposed to more unitary alternatives). One aspect of this value was the importance of professional self-regulation as a relatively independent process of governance in a health care system that concentrates as much power as the Canadian system arguably does in governments, regionalized health care bureaucracies and unions. Another was the function it performed (or might perform) in encouraging the provision of care under a professional ethos that emphasizes ethical obligations and altruistic motivations.

More fundamentally, Lahey and Currie argued that care had to be taken to ensure that the removal of regulatory obstacles to collaborative care did not also weaken regulation as a barrier to harmful conduct, including inappropriate collaborative arrangements. Finally, they suggested that regulatory barriers might be less important than other factors, such as professional cultures, methods of payment, education, workplace rules, and the internal structure and management of health care organizations, in preventing the wider adoption of interprofessional collaboration.

The conclusion was that some of the changes to health professions regulation that might be made to facilitate collaborative care might prove irrelevant, unnecessary or disproportionate to the objective. Meanwhile, these changes could compromise the functionality of professional regulation in protecting quality and patient safety. Accordingly, Lahey and Currie (2005) suggested an approach that sought to align self-regulation and collaborative practice through a programme of proportionate and calibrated reform within self-regulation that would evolve with improved understanding of collaborative practice and its actual interactions with health professions regulation. Such an approach would depend as much on how self-regulation was practised as it would on how self-regulation was legislatively structured (or restructured). It would thereby create opportunities for regulators to model the behaviour that collaborative care requires of regulated professionals. It could also create opportunities for those with governance responsibilities across the broader system to leverage the influence that regulatory bodies enjoy as self-regulators with those they regulate. To facilitate this leveraging, Lahey and Currie (2005) recommended that regulatory bodies be mandated to facilitate interprofessional collaboration and assisted in doing so through the creation of enabling institutions.

The underlying idea was that more might be possible than the elimination or reduction of barriers. Health professions regulation might be reconceived as a key enabler of interprofessional collaboration. This idea was developed by the Conference Board of Canada (2007) in their follow up to Lahey and Currie. The Board elaborated on the practical actions that could be taken to make legislative frameworks for professions regulation and for clinical practice more enabling of collaboration. For example, it called for mechanisms for continuous review and updating of scopes of practice; for institutions (like England's CHRE) that would pull individual regulators into a tighter and more coordinated system of integrated regulation; and for legislation that would make interprofessional collaboration in regulation mandatory. It also elaborated on the specific actions that regulators could take to provide professional providers with the tools and other support they needed not only to collaborate but to collaborate efficiently and effectively. Further, it argued that such collaboration could produce general improvement in health professions regulation by enabling regulators to combine their capacities to improve critical regulatory functions, such as the investigation of patient complaints.

The broader thrust was that something more than improved self-regulation was both needed and possible. This was essentially a new approach to professions regulation which was neither self-regulation as traditionally conceived nor the traditionally listed alternatives to self-regulation, such as regulation by government appointed agency. Called 'collaborative self-regulation', this new 'paradigm' would be built on a regulatory culture 'measured by its success in the creation, continuing development and support of collaborative, interdisciplinary, patient-centred health-care team practice' (Conference Board of Canada 2007: 15–16). The implication was that alignment between professions regulation and collaborative care required a transformation of regulatory governance, practice and culture that was like the transformation that collaborative care called for in clinical governance and practice.

It would be going too far to suggest that collaborative self-regulation has become the new paradigm of health professions regulation that the Conference Board said it had to be for health professions regulation to deliver on its potential both in encouraging interprofessional collaboration and enhancing public protection. But it is now typical for the policy literature to view professions regulation in a more balanced way. While the emphasis on its role as barrier remains, there is more optimism that the barriers can be overcome. Moreover, professions regulation is now sometimes viewed as a potential enabler of collaborative care (Barrett et al. 2007, Interprofessional Care Steering Committee 2007). And as will be seen from the work underway in Ontario and Nova Scotia, the view that collaborative self-regulation can improve health professions regulation in ways that go beyond the contribution it might make to interprofessional collaborative care is also gaining wider acceptance.

Part 2: Implementation: the Differing Approaches of Ontario and Nova Scotia

Although more detailed, the Conference Board (2007) was, like Lahey and Currie (2005), still essentially conceptual. As such, it left many important questions unanswered. Why would self-regulators collaborate to such an extent as to transform independent and self-interested self-regulation (the perceived problem) into 'collaborative self-regulation' (the envisaged solution)? How could governments or other decision-makers, including regulators, overcome the resistance, scepticism or inertia that might stand in the way of collaborative self-regulation? What were the legislative, institutional and administrative measures needed to make collaborative self-regulation feasible and effective?

Ontario: Pushing Collaboration from Above

The interaction between professions regulation and interprofessional collaborative care seems to have received more attention from policy-makers in Ontario than anywhere else in Canada. Much of this attention comes from the Health Professions Regulatory Advisory Council (HPRAC), the agency established by the *Regulated Health Professions Act* (*RHPA*) – Ontario's 'umbrella legislation' – to provide advice on the regulation of the health professions to Ontario's Minister of Health and Long-term Care (1991, S.O., c. 18.). In 2006, HPRAC concluded that multidisciplinary and collaborative practices were among the key changes in health care delivery that a modernized system of health professions regulation needed to address. As stated by HPRAC:

> … Significant changes have occurred since the *RHPA* was first introduced in Ontario in 1991, including a shift to multidisciplinary and collaborative care. Facilitating this trend, through provisions in health professions regulation is essential. It is also vital that our professionals have the flexibility to provide treatment and patient care to the fullest extent of their qualifications and training … (HPRAC 2006: 7).

HPRAC concluded, 'the health professions regulatory environment should be structured to encourage and support this kind of positive development and innovation in the delivery of health care' (HPRAC 2006: 13). This required changes in the legislative framework for health professions regulation to ensure it was supportive and enabling of collaboration while maintaining clear regulatory accountability. Among the changes needed were ones that would: determine when and how the performance of controlled acts was to be delegated between professions; otherwise assist professional health care workers in exploiting the opportunity to collaborate that was created by descriptive and overlapping scopes of practice under Ontario's controlled acts model of regulation; facilitate the sharing of information between regulated providers or their regulatory bodies; meet the need for collaboration among regulatory bodies on standards of practice for professionals involved in multidisciplinary teams; address the importance of adequate liability insurance for all members of multidisciplinary teams; and improve the handling of complaints, investigations and discipline in the context of multidisciplinary practice (HPRAC 2006: 25).

On this basis, HPRAC recommended amendment of the procedural code that applies to all regulatory bodies (Schedule 2 of the *RHPA*) 'to give the colleges the flexibility to deal with multidisciplinary practice and to send a signal encouraging colleges to cooperate and share information' (HPRAC 2006: 25). The 'signal' was to be sent by making the promotion of 'interdisciplinary collaboration on matters such as common scopes of practice, joint investigations and quality programmes' into one of the objects that colleges would be expected, by law, to fulfil (HPRAC 2006: 25). For HPRAC, this would mean that each college would be responsible, 'To promote interprofessional collaboration with other Colleges as it relates to matters affecting two or more health professions', including on 'standards of qualification, knowledge and skill', on 'programs and standards of practice' to assure quality, on 'programs to promote continuous evaluation, competence and improvement' for the performance of shared or similar controlled acts, and on, 'joint investigations of regulated health professionals practicing in multidisciplinary environments' (HPRAC 2006: 94).

The Ontario government quickly acted to add new objects to the statutory mandate of all colleges that were similar to those proposed by the Council. In the *Health System Improvement Act, 2007* (2007, S.O., c. 10.) it amended the procedural code to make each college responsible for:

> promoting and enhancing relations between the College and its members, other health profession colleges, key stakeholders, and the public; promoting interprofessional collaboration with other health profession colleges; and developing, establishing, and maintaining standards and programs to promote the ability of members to respond to changes in practice environments, advances in technology and other emerging issues.

Shortly thereafter, Ontario's Minister of Health and Long-term Care asked HPRAC for 'Recommendations on mechanisms to facilitate and support interprofessional collaboration between health colleges', including in relation to the development of 'standards of practice and professional practice guidelines' where regulated professions shared authority to perform 'the same or similar controlled acts' (HPRAC 2008b: 1). This produced three substantial reports from HPRAC – two interim reports in 2008 and the *Critical Links* report of 2009, which called for far-reaching changes in Ontario's system of professions regulation that would make interprofessional collaboration a core concern of professions regulators and a core feature of Ontario's system of health professions regulation.

HPRAC approached its task in two parts. First it undertook detailed reviews of the scopes of practice 'of professions whose work fundamentally demands interprofessional relationships', including dentistry, nursing, optometry, pharmacy, midwifery, dietetics, and physiotherapy (HPRAC 2008c, 2009). In general terms, the goal of these reviews was to better align scopes of practice with competencies, thereby permitting more professions to perform more tasks independently, while at the same time creating wider opportunities for collaborative arrangements that more flexibly exploit the full competencies of all professions.

Second, HPRAC asked how the *RHPA* should evolve to more generally enable and support interprofessional collaborative care. In this connection, HPRAC envisaged a legislative framework that would be more enabling of interprofessional collaborative care by giving new authority to all colleges (including those with expanded jurisdiction in consequence of the reviews of scopes of practice) to make binding 'standards of practice', including in areas of interprofessional overlap (HPRAC 2008c). At the same time, it contemplated an obligation on colleges to establish these standards of practice through multidisciplinary Professional Standards Committees. These would include members from, 'those health professions who share the same or similar or controlled acts, and those who engage in collaborative practice'. In broad strokes, the balance was between wider distribution of clinical and regulatory authority among self-regulating professions and a new accountability to establish rules for the exercise of this more widely distributed authority through a process that was 'multidisciplinary' (that is, interprofessional).

HPRAC elaborated on these elements of its proposed 'enabling framework' most extensively in its Critical Links report (HPRAC 2009). It emphasized the greater autonomy and flexibility that colleges would enjoy once they had the authority to make binding practice standards instead of having to seek government approval for regulatory changes. It also emphasized that the role of the proposed Interprofessional Standards Committees in the process for making binding standards was to be advisory only (HPRAC 2009). The report also extended the logic of interprofessional consultation on the 'rules of the game' on matters (such as conflict of interest rules, codes of ethics and common advertising rules) that would continue to be addressed in government regulations because they were amendable to common rules for all regulated professions. It recommended that such regulations be developed through a consultative process that involved all regulatory bodies. This was because such a process would, 'in and of itself, begin to enhance interprofessional collaboration' (HPRAC 2009: 42).

At the same time, *Critical Links* stressed the accountability that colleges would have to use expanded clinical and regulatory authority to promote collaboration and to generally enhance health professions regulation. In addition to recommending a specific statutory duty to collaborate in the development of binding practice standards, HPRAC recommended the creation of a new agency – the Council on Health Professions Regulatory Excellence (CHPRE) (HPRAC 2009: 20–21, 34–7, 42–51). As conceived, this agency would replace HPRAC and assume responsibility for its mandate of providing health professions regulation policy advice to Ontario's Minister of Health. But it would also have far-reaching responsibilities to both support and oversee the functioning of regulatory bodies and their collaborative activities and to report on the functioning of regulatory bodies and of the broader system of health professions regulation to the Minister and the public. Specifically, CHPRE would monitor the implementation by colleges of their new obligations to facilitate interprofessional collaboration. It would monitor, provide assistance and resolve disputes in the collaborative development of standards of practice. It would keep the interprofessional development of regulations to be made by government on common matters 'on task'. More broadly, the new agency would ensure that colleges discharged their mandates with 'regulatory rigour' and that the regulatory system generally was strengthened through 'an increased focus on accountability'.

The rationale provided for CHPRE wove together two distinct strands of thinking. One strand was the idea that the contribution of interprofessional collaboration in regulation to interprofessional collaboration in clinical practice depends on a transformation – a 'fundamental shift' – in how health professions regulation is carried out. In words that echoed the call of the Conference Board of Canada for a new paradigm of self-regulation, HPRAC suggested that the transformation required would involve not only more collaboration in regulation but 'a new type of interprofessional regulation' (HPRAC 2009: 47). It therefore required a level and quality of change that needed external oversight and accountability if it was actually to occur – or so HPRAC concluded.

The second strand of thinking in HPRAC's analysis was the idea that regulatory performance in general can be improved in self-regulatory systems through external oversight and accountability or, in other words, through a system of regulated self-regulation. Here, HPRAC (2009: 24–33) relied heavily on the specific example of England's CHRE and on broader trends in regulatory governance, particularly as tracked and interpreted by the OECD (2007) and by academics, including Ayers and Braithwaite (1992), Braithwaite et al. (2005), Gunningham and Grabosky (1998), Sparrow (2000) and Doern et al. (1999, 2006). From these sources, HPRAC concluded that a regulatory system with 26 self-regulating professions needed centralized coordination, technical assistance and oversight to meet the challenges facing health professions regulation in the twenty-first century. Moreover, it concluded that such coordination, technical assistance and oversight could be instituted in ways that respected and indeed enhanced professional self-regulation.

Perhaps the most intriguing aspect of HPRAC's analysis was the linkages it drew, largely implicitly, between these two distinct rationales for a new oversight agency. At one level, the linkage was that the need for interprofessional regulatory collaboration that enabled and facilitated interprofessional clinical collaboration was one of the challenges that the new agency could help regulatory bodies to meet. But at another level, the linkage was the role that interprofessional regulatory collaboration needed to play in improving regulatory performance as an end in itself. Thus, while working with colleges to enhance regulatory interprofessional collaboration was one of the three goals that the new agency would pursue, interprofessional regulatory collaboration would also be a significant component of the work of the agency in pursuing its other goals of 'Regulatory Rigour and Excellence' and 'Accountability, Transparency and Public Interest'. The basic idea here seems to have been that in a health care system based on integrated effort among members of many separately regulated professions, regulatory performance in general is likely to depend increasingly on a parallel level of integration among the regulators of those professions.

In 2009 the Ontario legislature passed Bill 179, the *Regulated Health Professions Statute Law Amendment Act* (2009, S.O., c.26) shortly after the completion of the *Critical Links* report. It implemented many of the scopes of practice expansions recommended by HPRAC. Bill 179 also included a new collaboration duty that was more specific than those given to colleges in 2007. For controlled acts shared with other colleges, each college is now required in consultation with those colleges to develop standards of knowledge, skill and judgement relating to the performance of those acts. However, Bill 179 stopped short of adopting HPRAC's recommendations that interprofessional consultations should take place through a formally structured 'Interprofessional Standards Committee' and that resulting standards should have statutory force.

What Bill 179 did not do was create the proposed CHPRE. Indeed, it made the existing oversight mandate of HPRAC in relation to the patient relations programmes of colleges conditional on the Minister asking for such a review to be done. In place of the proposed Council, Bill 179 gave wide ranging powers of oversight directly to Ontario's Minister of Health and Long-term Care, together with the power (though the provincial cabinet) to appoint a supervisor to govern a college in place of its governing council where the Minister considered it appropriate, taking account of: the 'quality of administration'; the administration of the *Regulated Health Professions Act* or the Act of the regulated profession; the performance of 'other duties and powers imposed on the College'; and whatever other considerations the Minister deemed relevant. This suggests that the government shared the view of HPRAC that regulatory collaboration and regulatory performance more generally required stronger oversight. Clearly, however, it thought this oversight should come directly from government, not from a new layer of arms-length regulation. Whereas such oversight is likely to be less continuous than that which would have been applied by the proposed CHPRE, it is also potentially much more fundamentally at odds with the traditional Canadian concept of self-regulation.

Nova Scotia: Nurturing Collaboration from Below

Nova Scotia's system of health professions regulation has no equivalent to HPRAC. There is no overarching legislative framework equivalent to Ontario's *RHPA* that applies to all of the province's 22 regulated health professions. With the exception of legislation recently adopted to establish common standards and a centralized review process for the registration function of regulatory bodies – the *Fair Registration Practices Act* (2008, S.N.S, c.38) – each regulated profession is governed exclusively by its own legislation.

Nova Scotia's government, like that of Ontario, has launched initiatives that are designed to enable, facilitate and support interprofessional collaboration among health care providers (Tomblin Murphy et al. 2010). As in Ontario, these initiatives fall broadly within the distinct but overlapping policy domains of health human resource planning and the restructuring of primary health care, with a particular connection to alleviating reliance on hospital emergency rooms, especially in rural Nova Scotia (Ross 2010). But unlike Ontario, Nova Scotia's government has not made reform of health professions regulation a high profile part of its focus on interprofessional collaboration.

Instead, interprofessional regulatory collaboration has been taken up by the regulators themselves. Specifically, with encouragement and support from the Department of Health and Wellness, it has been taken up by the Nova Scotia Health Professions Regulatory Network (now called the Nova Scotia Regulated Health Professions Network). This is a voluntary organization for discussion of issues of mutual interest among health professions regulators. In 2008, it formed a Working Group, with participation from the Department of Health, to explore the concept of 'collaborative self-regulation' (Lahey, 2009).

Although the Working Group decided to concentrate on the role that collaboration could play in the investigation of patient complaints, it did so recognizing that collaboration was potentially applicable and worthwhile across the spectrum of regulatory functions, including: managing the interaction of scopes of practice (which are designed to be mutually exclusive in Nova Scotia); the development and implementation of policies, standards and codes of practice; the identification and sharing of regulatory best practices; and the design and delivery of continuing education programming (Lahey 2009: 7).

This broad agenda reflected the understanding of the Working Group that 'a range of challenges and opportunities facing the health care system called for greater collaboration among health professions regulators', including 'the growing reliance of the system on interprofessional teams to deliver patient-centered care', and 'the priority being placed on improved quality of care and better protection of patient safety' (Lahey 2009: 6). More broadly still, the Working Group concluded that a range of Nova Scotia's health system objectives – including improved quality and safety, greater responsiveness to patient needs, better resource allocation, fuller utilization of the skills and competencies of all providers, and enhanced professional fulfilment and improved workplace conditions – 'either depend upon or stand to be benefited by increased collaboration between self-regulating health professions and their members, both at the regulatory and the practice level' (Lahey 2009: 6).

On investigations, the Working Group saw opportunities in two scenarios: where one or more complaints cut across the jurisdiction of two or more regulatory bodies and where complaints, whether or not they were 'interprofessional', were beyond the capacity of the regulator who received them. To address these problems, the Working Group considered the merits of a collaborative model – under which legislation would enable but not prescribe a joint investigation where one or more complaints raised interprofessional dimensions or capacity concerns – against alternatives that would consolidate investigative responsibility either by consolidating regulators or by assigning investigative responsibility to a specialized investigative agency, such as New Zealand's Health and Disability Commissioner. In arguing for the former, the Working Group (Lahey 2009: 12–24) questioned the proportionality of the solutions provided by the alternative models to the problems at issue: the lack of alignment between clinical and investigative structures where complaints involved services received from teams and the vulnerability of all regulators to receiving complaints that were beyond their individual capacity. It questioned the level of institutional overhead involved in some of the alternatives and the feasibility of these models for a small jurisdiction like Nova Scotia. It questioned the extent of the reliance on one agency or official in alternative models that might, like New Zealand's model, be feasible because they concentrated authority in a single all-purpose investigative agency.

But the core reason for a model that built the option of voluntary collaboration into the existing investigative system was the view that it would retain the relative strengths of self-regulation while addressing its institutional and structural limitations. At one level, these relative strengths were the expertise built into self-regulatory processes as opposed to consolidated or externalized systems of regulation. At another level, they consisted of the greater influence that self-regulators should have with those they regulate relative to external regulators that might be required to place greater reliance on enforced compliance with rules. Here the Working Group worried about moving to a system, 'that may result in an emphasis on external accountability that displaces or minimizes internal responsibility' and that might reduce the legitimacy of the regulatory system in the eyes of the regulated (Lahey 2009: 26).

The Working Group also worried that the implication to be drawn from solutions that removed investigative responsibility from self-regulating professions was that self-regulation 'cannot be reformed from within but must be reformed from outside' (Lahey 2009: 26). This could mean the loss of opportunities 'for regulatory reform to harness the credibility of regulated professionals to the reform process and its outcomes'; resistance and limited buy-in to changes; and to 'outcomes that are stronger on paper than they are likely to be on the ground' (Lahey 2009:26). It could also mean that the reform process would provide less encouragement for collaboration in other parts of the regulatory process than might otherwise be the case. Another possible outcome would be the loss of opportunities to enlist regulators in modelling the collaborative behaviour that the changes to health professions regulation are expected to enable among regulated professionals.

The exploration of collaborative self-regulation in Nova Scotia has entered 'Phase 2', with continuing support from the Department of Health. One deliverable is more detailed understanding of the legislative changes needed to enable collaborative investigations. This will mean answering questions about: who actually does collaborative investigations; the mechanisms and processes that would ensure efficient organization and oversight of these investigations; and the options for interconnecting 22 separate statutes and the distinct investigative processes and legislative limits on the sharing of information that they specify. Other deliverables of Phase 2 include an evaluation of the potential for worthwhile collaboration in other regulatory functions and options for a structure and mandate of the Nova Scotia Regulated Health Professions Network that would reflect the role it may have to play in a legislative framework of 22 (or more) interconnecting statutes. All of this work continues (Lahey et al. 2011).

Ontario and Nova Scotia Compared

On some levels, the processes that have unfolded in Ontario and Nova Scotia are not comparable. In Ontario, the analysis of interprofessional regulatory collaboration, although originally raised by HPRAC in a general review of the RHPA, has been mandated by government. It has unfolded within a legislative framework that was designed to limit the restrictiveness of health professions regulation and that was very recently amended to make interprofessional collaboration between regulatory bodies mandatory. It was comprehensive in its scope, in that it asked how Ontario's system of professions regulation as a whole could be improved to make it more conducive to interprofessional regulation. It has largely proceeded on the premise that interprofessional regulation was a good or even a necessary thing. It has therefore focused almost exclusively (after the *New Directions* report) on how it was to be accomplished.

The process in Nova Scotia has, in contrast, been led by Nova Scotia's regulatory bodies, acting through their own informal association. It has been supported by government and aligned with government priorities in broader health care reform but it has not been mandated by government. Its focus has not been the general concept of interprofessional collaboration. Rather, it has been the value and feasibility of collaboration in specific regulatory functions, as well as the mechanisms or structures necessary to facilitate collaboration in those regulatory functions. It has been as much about the merits of interprofessional collaboration in regulation as it has been about the ways and means of making it happen. It has been designed to be incremental rather than comprehensive.

Yet, the two processes can be meaningfully compared on other levels. Both were grounded in the idea that collaboration in the delivery of care between providers from multiple professions could be encouraged and enabled by changes in professions regulation. While both focused on changes to the legislative structure that would make it less of a barrier to interprofessional collaboration among providers, both processes also embraced the idea that collaboration among providers could be positively encouraged and modelled by collaboration among their regulators.

Both assumed that the changes that were needed in the legislative structure or formal processes of regulation could be accomplished within a system of regulation that continued to be based on self-regulation. Indeed, both processes ruled out options that each regarded as inconsistent with self-regulation. Even though self-regulation was not defined by the Working Group and defined only in general terms by HPRAC, it is clear that both thought that a commitment to self-regulation precluded consideration of options that would take regulatory responsibility and authority away from the regulatory body of each regulated profession. In these respects, both processes align with and to some extent validate the conceptual analysis of Lahey and Currie (2005) and of the Conference Board of Canada (2007).

In addition, both processes came close, if only implicitly, to embracing the call of the Conference Board of Canada (2007) for a new collaborative regulatory paradigm. Both looked beyond the value of regulatory collaboration to collaboration among regulated providers to the contribution that such collaboration might make to the effectiveness of professions regulation, independently of its contribution to interprofessional collaboration in the delivery of health care services. Thus in *Critical Links*, HPRAC's recommendation of a new agency to oversee regulatory collaboration rested as much on the conclusion that collaboration was needed to ensure the effectiveness of the regulatory system as it did on the conclusion that regulatory collaboration would support interprofessional collaboration among providers. In Nova Scotia, the Working Group decided to focus on investigative collaboration to ensure the effectiveness of the investigative process given the reality that more complaints could be expected to arise from team-based care and given the risk of misalignment between investigative requirements and capacity due to the wide distribution of Nova Scotia's limited investigative resources among many regulatory bodies. The role that investigative collaboration might play in enabling and supporting team based care, while important, was secondary.

Given these similarities, it is worth pondering the differences between the two processes from a more critical perspective. One of these differences is the obvious one that each focuses on a very different part of the legislative framework for professions regulation and of the regulatory process. Clearly, the focus for HPRAC was scopes of practice. More particularly, it was the parts of the regulatory process, including the allocation of authority among professions to perform various controlled acts, which define the clinical jurisdiction of each profession and the jurisdictional overlap between professions. This focus was largely a function of the emphasis on scopes of practice in the mandate given to HPRAC by Ontario's Minister of Health after HPRAC highlighted the need for regulatory collaboration in *New Directions* (2006). It is clear from *New Directions* that HPRAC itself saw regulatory collaboration as being needed in other parts of the regulatory process, including the investigation of complaints. Nevertheless, the subsequent focus of HPRAC on scopes of practice places its work on interprofessional regulation within the tradition of Canadian health policy to focus on the culpability of health professions regulation in causing or contributing to a rigid, inflexible and hierarchical distribution of clinical 'turf'.

Nova Scotia's Working Group noted the potential for a collaborative process for dealing with scope of practice disputes. But it concentrated initially on collaborative investigation of patient complaints. The choice shows that health professions regulators may have different priorities than governments (and the broader health reform process) in evaluating the potential for interprofessional collaboration in regulation. This could simply confirm that the reform of scopes of practice must be initiated from above due to the unwillingness or inability of regulated professions to relinquish or share jurisdictional turf. But it could also suggest that regulators understand that collaboration is needed in other parts of the regulatory process that go more directly and immediately to the capacity of regulation to protect patients.

Another key difference between the analysis of HPRAC and that of the Working Group is that HPRAC but not the Working Group concluded that regulatory collaboration would only happen if regulatory bodies were externally accountable for making it happen. Collaboration needed more than changes in the legislative framework that made it possible or easier. It needed legislation that placed a duty of collaboration upon regulatory bodies; that obligated each regulatory body to develop enforceable standards of practice that would be consistent among professions that shared clinical authority; and that obligated each profession to establish and to take advice on these standards of practice from an Interprofessional Standards Committee that included members from professions with overlapping clinical authority. Most dramatically, it required a strengthening of the intermediate level of governance put in place by Ontario's umbrella legislation to ensure more centralized oversight of the discharge by regulatory bodies of their regulatory responsibilities, including their newly acquired duties to collaborate.

The Working Group did not deal explicitly with the question of what was needed to ensure regulatory collaboration. But its general approach to 'collaborative self-regulation' and to investigative collaboration in particular implies the idea that collaboration would happen if it was appropriately enabled. On this view, it would happen because of its proven value in expanding the capacity of regulators to discharge their mandates. One corollary is that legislation that enabled but did not mandate collaboration would limit the risk of collaboration for the sake of collaboration and the diversion of resources from necessary regulatory work that such collaboration would entail. Another corollary is that collaboration which is voluntary is more likely to be genuine collaboration based on true commonality of interests and objectives. It is therefore (perhaps) more likely to yield the benefits in and beyond the regulation of professions that collaboration is said to promise. Finally, it is perhaps more likely to be collaboration that provides an example to regulated providers about the need for 'patient-centered' collaboration from them.

The thinking of the Working Group aligns with one of the leading criticisms levelled at the recommendations of HPRAC (and Ontario's obligations-based approach to regulatory collaboration more broadly) by Ontario's regulatory bodies: that real and meaningful collaboration cannot be legislated (College of Dieticians of Ontario 2008, Ontario College of Family Physicians 2008, College of Nurses of Ontario 2009). On the other hand, the Working Group can be said to have expressed questionable confidence in the willingness of regulatory bodies in a highly decentralized system of distributed governance to collaborate voluntarily. The general track record of Canadian health professions regulators is probably not encouraging in this regard. There is also the question of whether a purely voluntary system of regulatory collaboration is more plausible in a small jurisdiction like Nova Scotia than it is likely to be in a large jurisdiction like Ontario. From this perspective, the divergent approaches in Ontario and Nova Scotia may reflect underlying differences in policy dynamics between small and large provinces as well as between provinces that do and provinces that do not have umbrella legislation and the more formal and centralized policy development process that goes with it.

Part 3: Broader Perspectives

Regulating Systemic Problems: Consolidation vs. Collaboration

The different approaches being followed in Ontario and Nova Scotia give rise to a number of questions about how interprofessional regulatory collaboration can be achieved to produce meaningful and sustained improvement. Can regulatory collaboration (or collaboration more broadly) be legislatively mandated and enforced? Or is mandated and enforced collaboration a contradiction in terms that is capable at best of yielding the form but not the substance of collaboration? Alternatively, will enough collaboration happen to matter under a system that pits only voluntary opportunities for collaboration against all of the forces that encourage isolated regulation within exclusive professional domains? Does regulatory collaboration happen best when governments leave it largely to regulators and the regulatory process or is it an imperative that governments insist upon and enforce it? Do the answers to these questions suggest that either provinces with or provinces without umbrella legislation and the associated mechanisms of centralized policy-making have an advantage in making a meaningful transition to 'collaborative self-regulation'? Or is it more likely that the transition either can or must be pursued using different strategies in provinces that have and do not have umbrella legislation?

These questions are ultimately empirical questions to be answered on the basis of empirical evaluation, considered below. The point here is to suggest some of what may be at stake in that evaluation. It may not only be the matter of which approach is best suited to ensuring effective regulatory collaboration. It may also be the larger question of whether collaborative self-regulation means a combining of the strengths of regulation that is self-regulation and of regulation that is collaborative or whether it instead entails a trade-off or choice between the strengths it can draw from being collaborative and self-regulatory.

The basic idea of collaborative self-regulation is to address a range of challenges and opportunities that face health professions regulation but transcend the jurisdictional boundaries and the practical capacity of individual regulators. It is, therefore, a solution to a problem that arises in multiple fields of regulation, especially in the age of globalization: how to address systemic problems (like stability in financial markets, watershed governance, or climate change) that transcend the jurisdictional boundaries and practical capacity of multiple specialized regulatory agencies (Christie 2006, Ferran 2002–3, Haueber 1996, Markham 2002–3, Peel 2010).

One side of this debate advocates for regulatory integration through the creation of 'super regulators' that either replace or oversee some or all of the more narrowly mandated regulators who have authority over aspects of a given problem. This is said to facilitate more comprehensive approaches to regulation, greater cooperation among those involved in the regulatory process, improved capacity for evidence-based decision-making, more consistency and stability in the regulatory process, and reduced 'red tape'. Conversely, it is thought to be vulnerable to implementation problems, including those that arise from the gap between the legal authority and the practical capacity of super regulators to effectively control the large scale and multifaceted problems that are the rationale for their creation. Cautions are also raised that regulatory consolidation invites consistency where consistency is not warranted. Further, it concentrates power in relatively few hands, magnifying the consequences of failure when failure comes, as it can to any regulatory regime.

The alternative approach is a 'bottom up' one that emphasizes coordinated action between regulatory agencies based on agreements and voluntary initiatives. It seeks to avoid the implementation problems that are said to often beset solutions based on regulatory consolidation. It is also less dependent than regulatory consolidation is on politically difficult changes to legislation and institutions. More positively, it seeks to harness the greater potential that cooperative approaches have as 'laboratories' that can put integrative approaches to the test before they are applied on a wider scale. It is also thought to be good at nurturing the trust between regulatory players that optimal regulatory reform is said to require, whether or not it is pursued through top down regulatory consolidation or bottom up collaboration. Conversely, however, bottom up approaches may obviously involve more incrementalism than is consistent with effective regulatory governance. Meanwhile, their value as laboratories can be limited by transferability difficulties in applying experience and 'lessons learned' from one regulatory field or scale to another.

In health professions regulation, the choice between the two approaches is likely to involve a choice between regulatory modes as well as between regulators. Regulatory consolidation entails a move away from self-regulation and towards third party (or external) regulation (Jackson and Parker 2009). In many other regulatory fields, consolidation will more typically mean a move from multiple to one (or fewer) third-party regulators. Given the strong arguments that can be made for either the necessity or the superiority of self-regulation in the regulation of health professions (van der Burg 2009), it is to be expected that regulatory consolidation will be both difficult and questionable as a regulatory reform strategy in health professions regulation. Taken too far, it may deprive the regulatory enterprise of the special kind of influence that regulators who are the agents of professional self-regulation can enjoy with the providers that regulation must influence no matter how regulatory authority is allocated.

Yet it is a strong trend in the field. Canada became one of the early trend-setters when Quebec and Ontario adopted umbrella legislation that created a common legislative framework for health professions regulation (Health Professions Legislation Review 1989). The Ontario version of this model has now been adopted by three other provinces (Alberta, British Columbia and Manitoba) and has been under consideration in two others (Prince Edward Island and Newfoundland and Labrador) and one territory (North-West Territory). A stronger version of the strategy can be seen in England's decision to subject regulatory bodies to regulatory oversight through the CHRE (CHRE 2009, 2011b). The decisions taken in New Zealand, to transfer both the investigation and adjudication of complaints against regulated providers to state agencies that have jurisdiction over all regulated professions, represent an even stronger application of the strategy (Collins 2006).

These examples suggest that consolidation will likely always have limits in health professions regulation. It will encompass some but not all regulated health professions or some but not all regulatory functions. Regulatory consolidation can therefore be expected to reduce or minimize the tension between an integrated health care system and a decentralized regulatory system but not to eliminate it. Thus, with or without regulatory consolidation, improving health professions regulation may depend on interprofessional regulatory collaboration.

In Ontario, HPRAC concluded that the imperative of collaboration in regulation warranted another significant step towards regulatory consolidation. Regulatory collaboration was to be mandated and supervised by a new 'super regulator' that would assist and supervise regulatory collaboration and regulatory performance more broadly. Although the latter recommendation was not accepted, the overall thrust of Ontario's approach to interprofessional collaboration in regulation falls broadly within the trend toward regulatory consolidation. Health profession regulators in Ontario are now subject to a duty to collaborate with each other. Ontario's Minister of Health and Long-term Care now has statutory powers to oversee the work of regulatory bodies and to assume control of their governance when the Minister determines it is warranted. These powers exceed those that HPRAC proposed for the arms-length oversight body it recommended.

In contrast, regulatory collaboration is being developed in Nova Scotia as a process of tactical partnerships under legislation that would enable but not mandate such partnerships. In other words, regulatory collaboration is being envisaged and designed as a 'bottom up' mechanism developed through a process that is itself 'bottom up'.

Each approach strikes a different balance between the strength it seeks to gain through collaboration and the strength it seeks to retain through self-regulation. Clearly, striking this balance is a delicate task. On the one hand, regulatory collaboration must take place for it to be effective. This may require direction and oversight from outside of the regulatory community (and especially from government) that dilutes the self-regulatory quality of the regulatory system. On the other hand, collaboration is more likely to be effective if it is embraced by the regulatory community as a beneficial or necessary process for discharging regulatory mandates. This may be more likely to occur where regulatory collaboration evolves from within the regulatory community as an enhancement to self-regulation.

This balancing act is at the core of the different approaches being followed in Ontario and Nova Scotia. In Ontario, regulatory collaboration has been framed by government as a statutory obligation of regulators that is part of a larger governmental policy focus on the health care work force. (Interprofessional Care Steering Committee 2007, Interprofessional Care Strategic Planning Committee 2010). In contrast, it has developed in Nova Scotia largely as an in internal regulatory improvement initiative of regulatory bodies. What remains to be seen is which approach enjoys the greater success in improving health professions regulation through collaboration, both in respect of the contribution of regulation to interprofessional collaboration in the delivery of health care and more broadly.

Evaluation and the Continuing Relevance of National Health Care Governance

We cannot conclude on the basis of the processes unfolding in Ontario and Nova Scotia that 'collaborative self-regulation' has been achieved or validated as a new paradigm for the regulation of health professions in Canada. Ontario and Nova Scotia are only two of ten provinces. The impact of each process in facilitating collaboration remains uncertain. This is especially so in Nova Scotia, where the process is at a pre-legislative stage.

Nevertheless, the two processes mean that collaborative self-regulation in Canada is no longer just an idea to be evaluated on the basis of conceptual plausibility. Actions are now being taken on the ground in two provinces to make it into functioning reality. Evaluation of the idea on the basis of what it accomplishes in application can now begin. More specifically, given the different approaches being followed in Ontario and Nova Scotia, the idea can be evaluated for what it accomplishes when applied using different approaches and strategies under different legislative frameworks and in different provincial and/or health policy settings. The outcome of such evaluation is unlikely to be a clear-cut conclusion in favour of one or the other. More likely are conclusions about the relative strengths and weaknesses of each approach in their respective jurisdictional, legislative and health care system contexts. But the evaluation would still be worthwhile, particularly for the success factors it might identify as important for either approach, or for both approaches, or for provinces that have and for provinces that do not have umbrella legislation, or for all provinces.

Such evaluation would deepen our understanding of the potential for interprofessional collaboration in health professions regulation and of the benefits that it might yield both to regulatory efficacy and to interprofessional collaboration in professional practice. In the process, it might also advance our understanding of the relative strengths and weaknesses of Canada's two types of legislative frameworks for making and evaluating systemic changes in health professions regulation. These understandings could inform future policy discussions, both about the internal efficacy of health professions regulation and its consequences for the broader health care system. More specifically, to the extent that the processes in Ontario and Nova Scotia generate 'lessons learned' that might be applicable to initiatives on regulatory interprofessionalism in other provinces, evaluation will help to make those lessons available to decision-makers in those provinces, be they government officials or the members, governance bodies or professional staff of the self-regulating professions.

So far, the Nova Scotia process has not dealt with the question of how the effectiveness and value of legislative changes made to enable collaboration might be evaluated. In Ontario, evaluation would have been a core mandate of the oversight Council which HPRAC recommended to take its place under the *RHPA*. This evaluation mandate would, however, have come with an oversight function. It is this part of the proposal that may have been a bridge too far for the Ontario government. The decision to give the Minister the authority to place colleges under external supervision gives the Minister responsibility for evaluating the performance of colleges but only in the most global of terms. It is not likely to be the kind of evaluation that will advance understanding of the strengths and weakness of Ontario's framework for interprofessional regulatory collaboration. This may, however, be one of the tasks that Ministers of Health ask HPRAC to undertake in the future.

It is a concern that neither the Ontario nor the Nova Scotia process has dealt adequately with the question of evaluation. In any event, evaluation should not be left solely to these processes. It should also be undertaken independently to ensure objective comparative evaluation. This suggests a role for scholars and a role for research funding agencies. It suggests the value in continuing evaluation from a national perspective, if not of collaborative self-regulation as such, then more broadly of actions being taken to extend interprofessionalism to the regulatory domain and to otherwise improve professions regulation and align it with health system performance objectives. The Health Council of Canada was paying some attention to enabling changes in professions regulation as part of its general mandate to monitor implementation of the 2003 and 2004 Health Accords (Health Council of Canada 2005, 2009), but its continuing mandate or interest in this area is unclear. The Canadian Interprofessional Health Collaborative (CIHC 2011), the Canadian Mental Health Commission and the Canadian Patient Safety Institute might all have a contribution to make.

This national layer of evaluation may have particular value in facilitating inter-provincial learning between the processes unfolding in Ontario and Nova Scotia and those that have been or might be launched in other provinces. Although Canada's decentralized federalism is often portrayed as a significant barrier to better health care governance in Canada, it is also said to allow for more policy variation, experimentation and innovation than might be possible under a more centralized model (Adams 2001, Maioni 2002, Pelletier 2004). Given the country's social, economic, and geographic diversity, some would suggest that the policy consistency that emerges gradually through provinces adopting proven approaches from each other is likely to be preferable to the greater policy consistency that centralized governance might try to impose.

Increasingly, those who hold (or accept) this glass-is-half-full view also believe that this process of experimentation and emulation needs to be facilitated, supported and encouraged at a national level. They argue for national (not necessarily federal) institutions and processes that can play the role of policy clearing houses and otherwise 'nudge' reform at the provincial level. This was very much the thinking adopted by the Romanow Commission. It is the thinking that, more or less, underpins the 2003 and 2004 Health Accords, the general mandate to monitor Accord implementation given to the Health Council of Canada (2008) and the more specific mandate to track waiting times given to the Canadian Institute for Health Information (2011). More to the point here, it is also the thinking that aligns with the role that Health Canada played in the aftermath of the accords in stimulating research and discussion on collaborative interprofessional care and therefore on professions regulation.

It cannot be said that the work being done on regulatory collaboration in Ontario and Nova Scotia is being done because of the focus that the Accords (and the Romanow Commission) placed on what the Accords called 'multidisciplinary teams', or because of the role played by Health Canada in sponsoring research that culminated in a call for a new collaborative paradigm for health professions regulation. But it can be said that the Ontario and Nova Scotia processes have been informed by these influences from the national level and by the impetus they have created for action in the broad realm of interprofessionalism by provincial governments and provincial health care systems. From this it can perhaps be concluded that continuing national engagement with collaborative self-regulation might be important and even necessary to the continuing evolution of the concept into a functioning reality in, and beyond, Ontario and Nova Scotia.

Conclusion

Like other Canadian reforms to health professions regulation, the concept of collaborative self-regulation emerged from an anxiety in health policy forums that the structures and processes of professions regulation would inhibit health care reform, specifically, the transition of the health care system to interprofessional collaboration. It proposes to make self-regulation an enabler of provider collaboration while improving regulation in its internal functioning. In other words, collaborative self-regulation emerged as a mechanism for making an occupationally inclusive system of professional self-regulation compatible with a health care reform agenda that prioritizes integration, seamlessness, and shared responsibility and accountability. In this way, collaborative self-regulation has been posited as a Canadian alternative to the choice that might otherwise be necessary between self-regulation and a widely shared vision of health care reform that places considerable faith in interprofessional collaboration in the delivery of health care services.

Ontario and Nova Scotia are two provinces that have sought, in very different ways, to implement collaborative self-regulation. In combination, their efforts are pushing the development of the concept into the realm of regulatory practice. This transition has been shown to raise many hard questions about how collaborative regulation can be operationalized and optimized. One of these questions relates to the fundamental balance to be struck between the collaboration that probably must come from the choices that must be made by regulators and the collaboration that might have to come from the obligation of regulators to be externally accountable.

Getting this balance right depends on many factors, including the similarity and differences between provinces and the particular combination of policy opportunities and constraints that each faces. One of these factors may be whether the evolution of collaborative self-regulation continues to be connected, including through evaluation, to the evolving national health care reform processes that largely account for its origination.

References

Adams, D. 2001. Canadian federalism and the development of national health goals and objectives, in *Federalism, Democracy and Health Policy in Canada*, edited by D. Adams. Kingston: McGill-Queens Press, 61–105.

Ayers, I. and Braithwaite, J. 1992. *Responsive Regulation: Transcending the Deregulation Debate*. New York: Oxford University Press.

Barrett, J. et al. 2007. *CHSRF Synthesis: Interprofessional Collaboration and Quality Primary Health Care*. [Online]. Ottawa: Canadian Health Research Foundation. Available at: http://www.healthcouncilcanada.ca/docs/rpts/2008/Synthesis%20Report_E_FINAL%20%282%29.pdf. [Accessed: 6 August 2011].

Bosco, C. 2005. *Health Human Resources in Collaborative Mental Health Care*. Mississauga, ON: Canadian Collaborative Mental Health Initiative.

Braithwaite, J. et al. 2005. *The Governance of Health Safety and Quality*. Canberra: Commonwealth of Australia.

Cameron, Hon. Margaret A. 2009. *Commission of Inquiry on Hormone Receptor Testing*. St John's: Commission of Inquiry on Hormone Receptor Inquiry.

Cameron, A. 2011. Impermeable boundaries? Developments in professional and interprofessional practice. *Journal of Interprofessional Care*, 25(1), 53–8.

Canadian Institute of Health Information. 2011. *Wait Times in Canada – A Comparison by Province, 2011*. [Online]. Available at: http://secure.cihi.ca/cihiweb/products/Wait_times_tables_2011_en.pdf [Accessed: 13 September 2011].

CIHC (Canadian Interprofessional Health Collaborative). *Welcome to the CIHC Website*. [Online]. Available at http://www.cihc.ca/. [Accessed: 7 August 2011].

Christie, D.R. 2006. Implementing an ecosystem approach to ocean management: an assessment of current regional governance models. *Duke Env. Law and Pol. Forum*, 16(2), 117.

College of Dieticians of Ontario. 2008. *Nurturing Interprofessional Collaboration in Ontario*. [Online]. Available at: http://www.cdo.on.ca/en/pdf/Publications/Submissions/IPC%20CDO%20SUBMISSION%20TO%20HPRAC%20MAY%2030.pdf. [Accessed: 13 September 2011].

College of Nurses of Ontario. 2009. *Response to A Report to the Minister of Health and Long-Term Care on Mechanisms to Facilitate and Support Interprofessional Collaboration and a New Framework for the Prescribing and Use of Drugs by Non-Physician Regulated Health Professions*. [Online]. Available at: http://www.cno.org/Global/docs/policy/hprac_IPC_Drug_Response_Feb272009.pdf. [Accessed: 13 September 2011].

Collins, D. 2006. New Zealand's Health Practitioners Disciplinary Tribunal. *Med. Law*, 25(2), 249.

Conference Board of Canada. 2007. *Achieving Public Protection through Collaborative Self-Regulation: Reflections for a New Paradigm*. Ottawa: Conference Board of Canada.

Côté, G., et al. 2008. Environmental scan of interprofessional collaborative practice initiatives. *Journal of Interprofessional Care*, 22(5), 449–60.

CHRE (Council for Healthcare Regulatory Excellence). 2009. *Assuring Patient Safety through Regulation*. [Online]. London: Council for Healthcare Regulatory Excellence. Available at: http://www.chre.org.uk/_img/pics/library/090910_Assuring_patient_safety_through_regulation_1.pdf [Accessed: 7 August 2011].

CHRE (Council for Healthcare Regulatory Excellence). 2011a. *Welcome to CHRE*. [Online]. Available at: http://www.chre.org.uk/ [Accessed: 6 August 2011].

CHRE (Council for Healthcare Regulatory Excellence). 2011b. *Overseeing Regulators*. [Online]. Available at http://www.chre.org.uk/overseeingregulators/ [Accessed: 7 August 2011].

Creaghan, Hon. Mr Justice P.S. 2009. *A Report with Recommendations of a Commission of Inquiry into Pathology Services at the Miramichi Regional Health Authority*. [Online]. Fredericton, N.B.: Department of Health. Available at: http://www.gnb.ca/0051/index-e.asp [Accessed: 6 August 2011].

Davies, C. 2007. The promise of twenty-first century professionalism: regulatory reform and integrated care. *Journal of Interprofessional Care*, 21(3), 233–9.

Doern, B., et al. eds. 1999. *Changing the Rules: Canada's Changing Regulatory Regimes and Institutions*. Toronto: University of Toronto Press.

Doern, B., et al. eds. 2006. *Rules, Rules, Rules, Rules: Multilevel Regulatory Governance*. Toronto: University of Toronto Press.

Epps, T. 2011. The regulation of health care professionals, in *Canadian Health Law and Policy*, 4th edition, edited by Jocelyn Downie, Timothy Caulfield and Colleen M. Flood. Toronto: LexisNexis, 75–113.

Ferran, E. 2002–3. Examining the United Kingdom's experience in adopting the single financial regulator model. *Brook. J. Int. Law*, 28, 257.

Fair Registration Practices Act 2008, S.N.S, c.38.

First Ministers' Meeting. 2003. *First Ministers' Meeting on Health Care Renewal, 5 February 2003, Doc. 800–039*. Ottawa: First Ministers Meeting.

First Ministers' Meeting. 2004. *A Ten-Year Plan to Strengthen Health Care, 16 September 2004, Doc. 800–042*. Ottawa: First Ministers' Meeting.

Greenfield, D., et al. 2011. Factors that shape the development of interprofessional improvement initiatives in health organizations. *BMJ. Qual. Saf.*, 20, 322–37.

Gunningham, N. and Grabosky, P. 1998. *Smart Regulation: Designing Environmental Policy*. Oxford: Clarendon Press.

Haueber, R. 1996. Setting the environmental policy agenda: the case of ecosystem management. *Nat. Resources J*, 36(1), 1.

Health and Disability Commissioner. 2011. *Health and Disability Commissioner*. [Online]. Available at: http://www.hdc.org.nz/. [Accessed: 6 August 2011].

Health Council of Canada. 2005. *Modernizing the Management of Health Human Resources in Canada: Identifying Areas for Accelerated Change*. Toronto: Health Council of Canada.

Health Council of Canada. 2008. *Rekindling Reform: Health Care Renewal in Canada, 2003–2008*. [Online]. Available at: http://www.homecareontario.ca/public/docs/news/2008/June/rekindling-reform-health-care-renewal-in-canada-03–08-summary-june-08.pdf [Accessed: 13 September 2011].

Health Council of Canada. 2009. *Teams in Action: Primary Care Teams for Canadians*. [Online]. Available at: http://www.healthcouncilcanada.ca/teamsinaction.pdf [Accessed: 13 September 2011].

Health Professions Act, S.N.L. 2010, c. H–1.02

(B.C.) Health Professions Council. 2001 *Safe Choices: A New Model for Regulating Health Professionals in British Columbia.* Victoria: Health Professions Council.

Health Professions Legislation Review. 1989. *Striking a New Balance: a Blueprint for the Regulation of Ontario's Health Professions*. Toronto: Health Professions Legislation Review.

HPRAC (Health Professions Regulatory Advisory Council). 2001. *Adjusting the Balance: A Review of the Regulated Health Professions Act: Report to the Minister of Health and Long-Term Care.* Toronto: Province of Ontario.

HPRAC (Health Professions Regulatory Advisory Council). 2006. *Regulation of Health Professions in Ontario: New Directions.* Toronto: Province of Ontario.

HPRAC (Health Professions Regulatory Advisory Council). 2008a. *Interprofessional Collaboration: A Summary of Interprofessional Regulatory Collaboration in Other Jurisdictions.* Toronto: Province of Ontario.

HPRAC (Health Professions Regulatory Advisory Council). 2008b. *An Interim Report to the Minister of Health and Long-Term Care on Mechanisms to Facilitate and Support Interprofessional Collaboration Among Health Colleges and Regulated Health Professionals.* Toronto: Province of Ontario.

HPRAC (Health Professions Regulatory Advisory Council). 2008c. *An Interim Report to the Minister of Health and Long-Term Care on Mechanisms to Facilitate and Support Interprofessional Collaboration Among Health Colleges and Regulated Health Professionals: Phase II, Part I.* Toronto: Province of Ontario.

HPRAC (Health Professions Regulatory Advisory Council). 2009. *Critical Links: Transforming and Supporting Patient Care.* Toronto: Province of Ontario.

Health Systems Improvement Act, 2007, S.O., c. 10.

Interprofessional Care Steering Committee. 2007. *Interprofessional Care: A Blueprint for Action in Ontario.* Toronto: Province of Ontario.

Interprofessional Care Strategic Implementation Committee. 2010. *Implementing Interprofessional Care in Ontario.* [Online]. Available at: http://www.healthforceontario.ca/upload/en/whatishfo/ipcproject/hfo %20ipcsic %20final %20reportengfinal.pdf. [Accessed: 13 September 2011].

Jackman, M. 2000. Constitutional jurisdiction over health in Canada. *Health L.J.*, 8, 95–

Jackson, K. and Parker, M. 2009. Full steam ahead on the SS 'External Regulator'? mandatory reporting, professional independence, self-regulation and patient harm. *Journal of Law & Medicine*, 17, 29.

Lahey, W. and Currie, R. 2005. Regulatory and medico-legal barriers to interdisciplinary practice. *Journal of Interprofessional Care*, 19 (Suppl), 197–223.

Lahey, W. 2009. *Collaborative Self-Regulation and Professional Accountability in Nova Scotia's Health Care System.* [Online]. Halifax: Dalhousie Health Law Institute. Available at: http://hli.law.dal.ca/Files/WG_Document_Nov_4_2009.pdf. [Accessed: 7 August 2011].

Lahey, W. 2011 Medicare and the law: contours of an evolving relationship, in *Canadian Health Law and Policy*. 4th edition, edited by J. Downie, T. Caulfield and C.M. Flood. Toronto: LexisNexis, 1, 61–5.

Lahey W. et al. 2011. *Improving Health Professions Regulation through Collaboration: An Emerging Nova Scotia Model*. Presentation to the Dalhousie Health Law Institute Seminar Series on Health Law and Policy, March 18.

McDonald, F. 2010. *Patient Safety Law: Regulatory Change in Britain and Canada*. Halifax, N.S.: Dalhousie University JSD Thesis.

Maioni, A. 2002. Federalism and health care in Canada, in *Health Policy and Federalism: A Comparative Perspective on Multi-Level Governance*, edited by K. Banting and S. Corbett. Kingston: McGill-Queens University Press, 174–99.

Markham, J.W. 2002–3. Super-regulator: a comparative analysis of securities and derivatives regulation in the United States, the United Kingdom and Japan. *Brook. J. Int. Law*, 28, 319.

Ministry of Health and Long-term Care. 4 June 2007. *Fact Sheet/Promoting Greater Patient Protection Through Amendments to the Regulated Health Professions Act*. [Online]. Toronto: Province of Ontario. Available at: http://www.health.gov.on.ca/english/public/legislation/hsib/hsib_mn.html [Accessed: 6 August 2011].

New Zealand Health Practitioners Disciplinary Tribunal. [Online] Available at: http://www.hpdt.org.nz/Default.aspx?tabid=1 [Accessed: 7 August 2011].

Ontario College of Family Physicians. 2008. *Interprofessional Collaborations amongst Health Colleges and Professionals*. [Online]. Available at: http://www.ocfp.on.ca/docs/publications/interprofessional-collaboration-amongst-health-colleges-and-professionals.pdf [Accessed: 13 September 2011].

Peel J. 2010. Climate change law: the emergence of a new discipline. *Melbourne U.L. Rev.*, 32(3), 922.

Pelletier, R. 2004. Intergovernmental cooperation mechanisms: factors for change?, in *The Romanow Papers: The Governance of Health Care in Canada*, edited by G.P. Marchildon et al. Toronto: University of Toronto Press. 127–68.

Regulated Health Professions Act, S.M., 2009, c. 15.

Regulated Health Professions Statute Law Amendment Act, 2009, S.O., c.26.

Romanow, Roy J. 2002. *Building on Values: The Future of Health Care in Canada – Final Report*. Ottawa: Commission on the Future of Health Care in Canada.

Ross, J. 2010. *The Patient Journey Through Emergency Care in Nova Scotia: A Prescription for New Medicine*. Halifax: Province of Nova Scotia.

Sparrow, M. 2000. *The Regulatory Craft*. Washington D.C.: The Brookings Institute.

SSCSAST (Senate Standing Committee on Social Affairs, Science and Technology). 2002. *The Health of Canadians – The Federal Role – Volume Six: Recommendations for Reform*. Ottawa: SSCSAST.

Tomblin Murphy, G., et al. 2010. *Model of Care Initiative in Nova Scotia (MOCINS) – Final Evaluation Report*. Halifax: Province of Nova Scotia.

Van der Burg, W. 2009. *The Regulation of Health Professionals. Two Perspectives*. Rotterdam: Erasmus Working Paper Series on Jurisprudence and Socio-Legal Studies. [Online]. Available at: http://ssrn.com/abstract=1456422. [Accessed: 8 August 2011].

Walshe, K. and Benson, L. 25 June 2005. GMC and the future of revalidation: time for radical reform. *BMJ*, 330, 1504.

Chapter 8

Saving Polly: Can Professional Self-regulation Play an Ongoing Role in the Delivery of Medical Care?

Daniel Klass

Introduction

In the last decade of the twentieth century and the first decade of the twenty-first, there has been widespread recognition that the self-regulation of the medical profession has been faltering, and the reactions to this perception of governments and professional bodies have begun to take effect. The recognition of failure of self-regulation in general is dramatically described by H.W. Arthurs, former Superior Court Justice, Province of Ontario, when, quoting Monty Python's famous Dead Parrot skit, he concluded:

> Professional self-regulation exhibits all the vital signs of a dead parrot: it is definitely deceased; it is pushing up the daisies, it has joined the choir invisible; it is bereft of life; it has met its maker; it is no more; it is bleeding demised (Arthurs 1995).

As health care is increasingly viewed as a societal right, governments and other health system owners or managers have encroached upon the traditional autonomy of medical professionals in the delivery of their defined services. In addition, legal authorities have come increasingly close to substituting their own judgments over those traditionally exercised by professionals when acting within their scope of expertise. Finally, the element of public trust in the profession, which is the cornerstone for the maintenance of professional self-regulation, has declined, and the expression 'Trust me, I'm a Doctor' is now used only in jest.

Some would argue that this encroachment is simply the filling of a void, and that the loss of trust is well deserved. With the staggering complexity of modern health care delivery, the willingness and/or ability of medical professionals to regulate themselves has withered, and the profession may have forfeited its right to even a degree of autonomy. This loss of public trust appears linked to the profession's failure to live up to the expectations of society.

While the ability of the profession to regulate its own affairs and to effectively maintain high standards of practice has been called into question, it would nonetheless be premature to declare medical self-regulation a dead issue. Vital signs are still present. This chapter begins with a brief rationale for a continuing role for professional self-regulation. Then follows a description of what appear to be the major and fundamental threats to its existence. The last section describes several concrete steps that the profession has already taken, or could take, which, by addressing the major difficulties in current regulatory regimens, can provide society at large with the confidence to maintain its support of self-regulation for the profession.

The Role of Professional Self-regulation

The current regimen of professional self-regulation, especially as it is known in the English-speaking world and in the far-flung remnants of the British Empire, traces its origins to medieval arrangements between rising workers' guilds and the royal authority in England. In essence, the original professional organizations of physicians and surgeons received legal protection to ply their trade independently and according to their own standards provided that they proved capable of maintaining professional discipline within their membership.

The core elements of self-regulation (Freidson 1970, Klass 1961) have traditionally included, and, to a large extent, include now, the rights to:

1. Define the turf, or scope, of protected professional practice.
2. Determine and control the educational and personal (mainly 'moral') qualifications for entry to practice, specialization within practice.
3. Set and maintain standards of practice.
4. Adjudicate public or professional complaints against practitioners, judge the competence of practitioners, in general or in specific instances, and act in the interest of the public to remove physicians from the profession, to discipline them or otherwise to modify the practice of physicians.
5. Establish acceptable terms and conditions for remuneration of medical practice.

The maintenance of autonomy with respect to some elements of self-regulation raises little public concern. For example, the educational mandate seems to be little at risk, except to the extent that health human resource demands for physicians sometimes temporarily run roughshod over educational standards of the profession. The definition of scope of practice, largely related to the claims of alternative health practitioners to autonomy in overlapping scopes of practice, is moderately at risk. In contrast, elements relating to the setting and adjudication of standards, especially in high-profile, contested situations, and the control of the terms and conditions of practice, appear to be in greatest jeopardy.

Despite these threats, the logic of the founding principles of autonomous professional status still resonates today. The first is the notion of expertise, which embraces the ideas of a collectively held body of specialized knowledge, that is, the theory of medicine, acquired in a scientific manner, a practical kind of experiential know-how (best practice) in complex matters, and the expectation that the special knowledge and its application in individual situations are subject to regular critical review by peers within the aegis of the profession. The rationales for most of the listed rights of self-regulation are contingent on the notion of a profession holding the keys to this specialized knowledge, and exercising their judgement and basing their actions upon this knowledge. But beyond the notion of expertise is the clear understanding that professionals enter into special ethical relationships with their patients to guarantee that their professional competence is mobilized in the interest of the patient. Finally, there is a powerful notion of discipline within the profession; that is, that the competence of each individual practitioner is assured by the profession as a whole.

Freidson (1994: 200) has described the content of professional endeavour as needing to be high stakes and highly valued, but inevitably clouded by uncertainty. Importantly, he stipulates that completion of the tasks of the practice require such unusual degrees of knowledge, experience, skill and judgement that the adjudication of claims of malpractice or incompetence cannot be properly undertaken from 'outside' the practising profession. This concept is at the heart of the profession's insistence on a high degree of autonomy.

The key roles of the self-regulating professional organization, then, are to define the scope of competence of the whole profession, and to ensure the competence of individual practitioners within the profession through a combination of processes that include: original selection of candidates, their education and maintenance of competence, assurance of the discipline of practitioners and the warrant that implementation of that competence serves the best interests of patients. To undertake self-regulation, the profession needs to take collective responsibility and demonstrate trustworthiness in its ability to ensure the discipline of its membership in the maintenance of the collective competence. From the perspective of individual practitioners, the critical requirements of self-regulation include the willingness and capacity to maintain their individual practice standards within the envelope of professional requirements and, especially in the age of patient rights and entitlement, to maintain the professional standards of care with respect for individual patient expectations.

What are the Threats to the Effectiveness of Self-regulation?

The fundamental threat to the maintenance of self-regulation lies in the widespread perception of a self-serving profession and consequential loss of trust. This perception is fed by concerns of a political nature; that the governance of the profession is weak, leaving observers to question 'Who is minding the store?' It is also propelled by the difficult task the profession faces in maintaining the validity and integrity of its collective judgements as well as those of its practitioners in difficult and uncertain clinical situations. In addition, in matters related to the determination of the appropriateness of medical services, the spectre of conflict of interest is difficult to counter.

These threats play out over a variety of situations, but there are common, underlying political or scientific elements in their causation. By addressing flaws in the governance of the profession, by capitalizing upon advances in the science of 'judgement' making, both at the governance and the clinical levels, and by changing important elements of the educational philosophy of the profession, some of the critical political and scientific threats to self-governance can begin to be addressed.

Loss of Trust in a Self-regulating Profession

Stresses derived from the context of health care delivery The origin of trust for the profession resided in the hallowed doctor-patient relationship, but the context of modern health care has threatened the validity of this interaction.

Health care delivery is moving from an uncomplicated, independent practice model within a poorly integrated system, to a highly complex systems-based model with far less independent provision of service. The consequences of this shift are manifold, but in particular the relationships of professionals to their patients, to colleagues, and to the institutions and systems in which they work all take on a complexity that is not anticipated in the traditional self-regulatory model. In fact there is an aura of unreality in the very use of the term 'self-regulation' in a system that has become so complex and interdependent (Fuchs 2011). Especially in an era where accountability and liability have become major determinants of action, the growing interdependence of professionals in care delivery has not been matched by a parallel evolution of accountability mechanisms. As a result, from the patients' perspectives, it is not clear who is controlling the process of care, nor with whom a trusting relationship can be developed. From the practitioners' perspectives, fear of liability in a variety of circumstances has become a barrier to establishing trusting relationships with patients and a certain wariness about being held liable can poison the working environment and add risk to an already difficult endeavour.

Within this newly complex environment, there is a broad challenge to society as a whole to redefine regulatory scope for all health professions. Any likely adaptations portend a relative decline in the autonomy of all of the professions, if only because there are so many competing partners in health care delivery.

Nonetheless, expectations of physician performance are high and there remains a clear sense that when things go wrong, it is physicians who are held accountable, not the system. Medical events that highlight the changes in public appreciation of medical professionalism have, for the most part, received abundant attention in the press, and are perceived as unmitigated disasters. Outstanding examples have included the deaths of babies in special surgical units through error, poor judgement or negligence (Bristol Royal Infirmary Inquiry: Final Report 2001,

Sinclair 2001), the poisoning of patients and colleagues by licensed practitioners (Shipman Inquiry 2001–2005, Stewart 1999) or the reflexive and unforgiveable cover-up of errors and omissions and malpractice that lead to death, disability and disappointment (Jacobs 2005: Chapter 6; see also Chapter 12 in this volume).

Protecting the integrity of professional judgement in the face of inevitable uncertainty: can experts be trusted? Professional regulation appears to be failing to meet public expectation. Whether it is also failing public *needs* is an important matter for debate. Long-held beliefs that professional activities can only be properly understood and dealt with by the experts themselves are being trumped by the perceived failure of the professions to put public interest above the interests of the professions. Rather than permitting professions to maintain their autonomy, governments, managers of health care systems and the courts are increasingly reluctant to defer contentious judgements to professional adjudication and are subsuming the decision-making to themselves or their appointees. Erosion of the cherished status of self-regulation is the inevitable result.

In order to make a convincing case for the maintenance of currently existing self-regulatory regimens, visible improvement must be made in the fundamental elements of objectivity and validity of judgement.

The quest for objectivity and freedom from bias and conflict of interest in regulation can be enhanced by concrete steps ensuring that discrete elements in the processes of judgement-making and adjudication are rendered immune to exercise of self-interest of the profession or of professionals. Even simple measures such as inclusive representation at committee levels, maintenance of commercial free environments and the enforcement of strict ethical standards regarding self-enrichment can go a long way to creating an environment that is hostile to self-serving behaviour on the part of professionals.

As part of the current *zeitgeist*, scepticism towards scientific reasoning and evidence seems to be rampant (Jacobs 2005: Chapter 4). Denial of climate change is a stark example. In the medical arena, unwillingness of significant groups in society to accept scientific views about the benefits of vaccination reveals the extent to which health policies can be modulated by a spectrum of beliefs, not all of them evidence based.

The validity of judgements is best assured if the content of judgement-making is, to as great an extent as possible, based upon evidence that is gathered, assembled and used systematically. Great strides have been made in developing the field of evidence-based medicine, which uses scientific data to support individual clinical judgements (Sacket et al. 1996). The parallel idea of using evidence-based regulation, that is, a formal evidentiary base to guide regulatory judgements, has not yet gained traction. Just like the practice of medicine before the late twentieth century, medical regulation has thrived on anecdote and personal or institutional wisdom. The systematic use of evidence provides a firm foundation for consistent decision-making and automatically provides transparency.

An important starting point toward building the evidentiary basis to regulate scientifically in the public interest would be detailed evaluation of the scope of regulatory activity in medicine, including an assessment of its overall effectiveness.

Failure in the Political and Moral Dimensions

Examination of the framework of self-regulation reveals some glaring soft spots in the implementation of sufficiently stringent disciplinary regimens. Of great concern are examples of regulatory lapses of a moral nature that create the suspicion of regulation in support of doctors', rather than patients', rights.

Despite the attention paid to dramatic events that make headlines, there is a growing sense that, above all, regulation of the day-to-day affairs of the profession has been ineffectual or worse, devoted to the preservation of professional prerogatives rather than to patient benefits. The contrast between the dramatic and the mundane is best seen in the matter of the infamous Dr Harold Shipman, a respected general practitioner in the United Kingdom, who, late in his career, was discovered to have been poisoning large numbers of his elderly patients. The horrific nature of Shipman's deeds led to, among other things, a judicial hearing, out of which arose two insights of relevance to this discussion. The first was that the nature of his crimes was so egregious that no reasonable extent of regulatory rigour could have been expected to detect and prevent them. The second observation was that in a number of instances in which Shipman's ordinary behaviour in his clinical practice had been brought under scrutiny, he was invariably granted the benefit of the doubt by his peers in the clinical governance process. So while the Judge's final opinion was that there was little in the way of preventive steps that could have stopped the psychopathic behaviour of Shipman, the greater crime was the unwillingness of his professional colleagues, within their everyday governance framework, to defend patients against his more ordinary failings, and on the contrary, their willingness to systematically cover them up (Shipman Inquiry 2001–2005).

The value of a profession derives from the benefits it provides to the whole society, not just to its members. Yet, the democratic structure of medical professional societies skews their attention toward benefits for members. For example, in direct elections, the choice of the governors of the profession seems likely to be made on the basis of platforms that promise immediate benefit for the profession and the individual practitioner, rather than the patient and society. Progressive regulatory policy that benefits the public more than the profession does in fact exist. Nonetheless, implementation and the actual uptake of these policies in the end depends largely upon individual professionals' views that the proposed change reflects the best wisdom of colleagues, and that it has been arrived at fairly and inclusively. This is the nature of a democratic organization. As a result, those details of progressive regulation, which might appear to protect the public at the expense of individual or collective physician autonomy, are hard to justify to the profession, and therefore are difficult to sustain. Thus within many professional self-regulatory authorities there resides an official opposition, usually comprising members of the profession who, more or less openly, though not officially, represent the branch of the profession which serves in the fashion of a professional union, with the interests of its membership as its primary objective.

In order to counter this paradoxical defect of democratic governance, a major trend among regulatory authorities has been to be more inclusive in the composition of their governing councils and working committees by adding to the power and numerical representation of lay (non-professional) members whose presence is intended to represent the public interest. Fundamentally, these authorities have recognized that any claim to act in the public interest rings hollow so long as that interest is not represented in the decision-making councils of the authority. As an example, the College of Physicians and Surgeons of Ontario, the regulatory authority for physicians in the Province of Ontario in Canada, pays strict attention to the substantial, though not majority, representation of lay members on both its governing Council and working committees. It also uses the orientation process for new members to ensure that the culture in group meetings empowers lay members to act freely in what they perceive to be the public interest and to avoid being co-opted by professional members.

Failures of a Scientific Nature

Beyond these issues at the political and moral level, there is also growing concern over evidence of systematic failure of the profession to perform at expected professional levels, even when those standards have substantial evidentiary basis (McGlynn et al. 2003). The increasing availability of professionally generated 'guidelines' have, for the first time, provided objective benchmarks for individual performance, and many studies reveal the extent to which professional actions fall short of the expected standards. A case can be made for the fuzziness of these guidelines, or the need for the exercise of discretion in their deployment, and, indeed, many professionals claim that individual circumstance precludes systematic adherence to many of the requirements. Nonetheless, these studies reveal that the most troubling deficiencies occur in rather straightforward circumstances in which individual variation should not be an issue; for example, the requirement of regular eye and foot examinations in diabetics.

There is some irony in the observation that despite the great strength that the practice of medicine has gained from its fundamental empirical grounding, it is only recently that an infrastructure for the application of evidence to individual clinical judgements has been established (Sacket 1996). To underscore the importance of this new framework of clinical decision-making, the systematic use of outcome data to guide clinical policy-making reveals that the competence of individual practitioners does in fact significantly influence important patient outcomes (McLeod et al. 1997, Weng et al. 2010). But at the same time, there is compelling evidence that medicine is not as competent (safe, effective and compassionate) as it should be, even when judged by its own standards.

Evidence of substandard medical performance has been found in large studies in the US, Canada and Australia. Wherever systematic studies of errors in medicine have been performed, evidence for performance deficiencies has been found (Baker et al. 2004). As a result of these accumulating revelations, doubt is being cast on the unquestioned competence of the profession as a whole, and by inference of large numbers of individual physicians.

Failures of a Relational Nature

For years, the oxymoronic concept of the competent doctor who is unable to communicate effectively with patients or colleagues has been accepted at face value. Consideration has recently turned to the requirement of the competent professional to be fully capable of engaging all dimensions of competence, including in the relational aspects of professional behaviour (Epstein and Hundert 2002). These include communication with patients and colleagues and full participation in the requirements for team performance in the current complex systems of health care delivery. The set of 'competent physicians' does not include those physicians who lack the ability to deal effectively and empathetically with patients and families under stress. Nonetheless the profession has much catching up to do in the objective of living up to a multidimensional concept of competence (Klass 2007).

Failures of Transparency and 'Owning Up'

It is worth pointing out that it is not only in the field of health care that the breakdown of trust in regulation is occurring (Jacobs 2007: 129); in financial arenas, public utilities, legal institutions, even the church, serious doubt has been cast on the trustworthiness of individuals and whole institutions who serve vulnerable individuals or institutions. And as in health care, anger over 'cover-ups' tops the list of egregious behaviours:

> … there is no quicker way for a profession to lose public respect than to cover up, institutionally, for members who have done arrant wrong. Since self regulation is based on trust, loss of respect is tantamount to loss of self-governing status (Jacobs 2007: 129).

According to Jacobs, if self-regulation is to be resuscitated and preserved, the profession must address this list of fundamental weaknesses: loss of trust, lack of transparency, conflict of interest, lack of relational skills/team capabilities, lack of accountability to science and public, failure to define and enforce standards, and failure to acknowledge, prevent or detect error and misjudgement.

The major question to be posed, in the context of Jacob's scathing indictment, is whether the effort to resuscitate the concept of professional self-regulation under a new set of expectations and requirements will be successful, or whether a dead horse is being flogged.

Self-regulation, by definition, implies a degree of control of issues of professional competence. At issue is not a power struggle over that control. What the public wants is assurance of regulation in the public interest. The key to 'Saving Polly' is recognition by the profession that commitment of regulation to the public interest is not negotiable. It is up to the professions to develop and implement new tools to maintain accountable self-regulation.

This author's contention is that in the specific areas described, a strengthening of the autonomous regulation of the profession may yet be engineered. No prediction is made that these issues actually will be tackled successfully; only that the defence of professionalism as we now know it can only be successful if these areas of great concern can be successfully addressed.

Promoting the Idea of Regulatory Competence

Regulatory competence is a multidimensional concept, and recognition of the spectrum of regulatory responsibility is the starting point for understanding the challenges faced to correct current deficiencies. In today's environment, the manifold relationships of the professions in health care must also be taken into account, so that regulatory competence means dealing in balance and being accountable for challenges to competence at levels of the individual, organizations and systems (Wenghofer et al. 2006).

Accountability for regulatory processes in the past has involved the notion of *retrospective accountability*. When questions are raised about regulatory decisions, recourse is limited to examination of legislative requirements and assurance of attendance to due process, with heavy dependence on credentialing as pro-forma evidence of competence.

But there are other routes to accountability; for example, the burgeoning field of performance assessment combined with the availability of systematic clinical management records allow for assurance of accountability based on a record of performance that falls within the sanctioned envelope of the profession. This form of prospective accountability should prove to be a more effective route to system competence that just 'doing current processes better'.

At the regulatory level, performance measures have become available to satisfy a panoply of accountability measures; they can assure validity and reliability of medical standards and judgements, and help to provide transparency. Administrative data derived from actual clinical performance and used to develop performance criteria can, among other things, spawn evidence-based risk management protocols, support studies of decision/judgement consistency, and demonstrate a consistency of judgements and freedom from bias.

These tools promise to provide a new scientific basis for the practice and discipline of medicine.

Figure 8.1 portrays the scope of the 'accountability framework' by which the medical profession regulates its activities. The portrayal here likens the process to

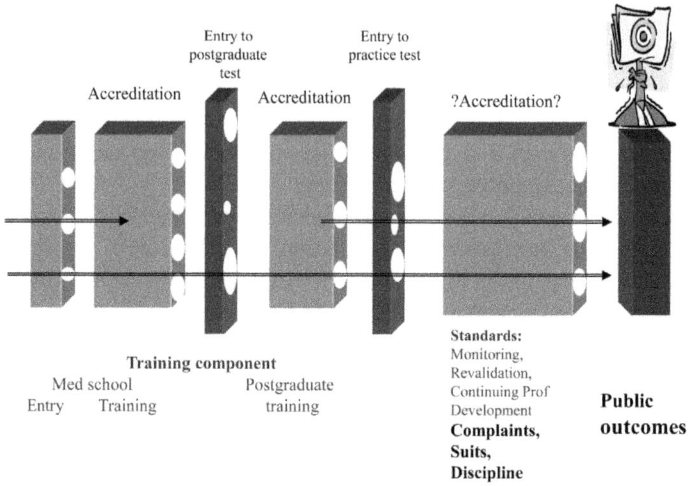

Figure 8.1 Scope of regulation for individual and system competence

James Reason's (1990) 'Swiss Cheese Model' of safety. The version depicted is the North American model. Its elements are likely to be present in most modern societies, though with different weightings and measures at the various critical barriers, such as assessments at exit from medical school, prior to licensing, and so on.

The ordinary focus, of regulators and students in particular, is on the dark vertical bars, which depict the barrier tests to entry, either to postgraduate training or to practice. But we should not forget the other cornerstones of the regulatory framework in which we all work; that is accredited education (either for medical students or residents in training) and the monitoring of performance that goes on in all of these educational frames. It is the combination of all of these factors that determines the overall accountability of our systems, and which determines how many 'bad apples', here depicted as arrows, can penetrate through all layers of the system to produce preventable bad events.

Recognizing and incorporating a systems approach to regulation is just beginning. Currently we in Canada are very active in the 'Monitoring in Practice' area, developing processes of 'Revalidation' that ensure an educational approach to practice that will be accountable to the public, but in other jurisdictions other parts of the system are receiving attention.

Priority Areas for the Revitalization of Self-regulation

The critical pathways through which the profession might re-establish its worthiness to maintain a self-regulatory regime need to address important deficiencies in the current regulatory regimens: first, political questions about who is involved in the governance of the regulatory process, and second, the need for both evidence-based medicine and regulation. The third pathway relates to the management of clinical information and medical judgement in the determination of clinical appropriateness, one of the most complex of judgemental tasks of the profession. Finally, a fourth pathway would see a dramatic realignment of educational philosophy and method within the profession, in which activity would focus on quality improvement rather than individual achievement, and the current form of educational assessment would be replaced by assessment in a framework of improvement.

1) Changing Professional Governance

a) Governance of or for the profession? In North America and other English speaking jurisdictions, governance of the profession is seen by the profession to require governance by the profession. In other words, the political view is often expressed that unless the profession itself remains in control of its domain, quality in all aspects of service will decline. Yet many critics of self-regulation argue that quality of service has already reached unacceptable levels, at least in part because the profession serves its own interests ahead of those of the public.

This paradoxical situation needs to be addressed. The social contract between society and the profession has traditionally been based upon the romantic notion of professionalism, referred to as 'the soul of professionalism' by Eliot Freidson (quoted in Relman 2003: 166), as a sufficient guarantor of the profession's placing the interests of society and patients above those of the profession and individual practitioners. While professional regulation is undoubtedly well intended, and incorporates many steps to ensure integrity of process and outcome, breakdown of professionalism occurs sufficiently frequently, and receives sufficient publicity, to ensure that the public will no longer accept uncritically the notion that 'the doctor knows best', whether in the contexts of the management of disease for individual patients or the governance of professional acts as a whole.

Many jurisdictions are exploring solutions to the traditional imbalance of power in the governance of the profession. In Canada, the tendency has been for provincial governments to expand their powers by enacting legislation that increasingly limits professional autonomy in many of the detailed rules and regulations found in medical acts. In particular, mandatory public representation is prescribed at the levels of governance, typically governing councils, and working committees.

It is too early to know much about the outcomes of this new combination of public representation and professional expertise in reaching balance and fairness in adjudicating complex issues. However, this social experiment has at least revealed that representatives of the public and members of a profession can, in fact, collaborate within a regulatory agency and come to agreement in difficult medical disputes without either obvious co-option of public members or decreased respect for the integrity of professional judgement.

In other jurisdictions (mainly Australia, New Zealand, the UK and Ireland) a different approach is being taken to the difficulty of vested professional interest in difficult clinical adjudications (Horsely and Thomas 2003). The remedy for the regulatory failures found in the Shipman case appeared to be the wresting from the hands of the profession regulatory authorities of the processes of disciplinary investigation and management.[1] Separate bureaucracies have been created under government mandate, with lay management, to carry out the traditional 'disciplinary' role for physicians. Much like ordinary administrative tribunals, physicians act in advisory and consultative roles, but do not have the opportunity to operate behind closed professional doors (Shipman Inquiry 2001–2005).

There is great need for careful research both to determine the utility of innovations of this kind, and to answer validity related questions, such as whether expert judgements made in isolation compare to those made in the context of a transparent and representative process. Of greatest concern to the profession, and of course ultimately to the public, is the question of whether something is lost if public interests are allowed to override valid scientific judgements.

b) Who is representative of the profession? A related governance issue, also of a political nature, concerns occasional efforts of professional associations or societies, (that is, groups representative of the profession and acting clearly in the interest of the profession) to dominate the political process of electing members to the governing councils of regulatory authorities. This is the flipside of the profession's fear that public gerrymandering will gain control of processes now in the profession's hands. This form of political control can be avoided if electoral processes can be employed to ensure that elections are free of organizational manipulation, but retain fair professional representation. An important area of research is in the arena of political science; are there electoral methods that can be applied to governing councils of professional organizations that could insulate these councils from blatantly 'political' manipulation, yet which could preserve the sense that 'the rank and file' of the profession maintains a strong voice in controlling scientific professional affairs?

---

1 Some detail of the UK Government response to the fallout from the Shipman Report and other contemporary inquiries includes the following:

- the councils that regulate health professionals have, as a minimum, parity of membership between lay and professional members, to ensure that purely professional concerns are not thought to dominate their work;
- the Government will agree arrangements to ensure that all councils become more accountable to Parliament, presenting annual reports to the UK Parliament and, for those councils that regulate professionals whose regulation is a devolved matter, to the Devolved Assembly legislatures;
- to dispel the perception that councils are overly sympathetic to the professionals they regulate, council members will be independently appointed (Secretary of State for Health 2007: 5).

2) *Accountability for Medical Judgements and Clinical Appropriateness*

Billing for services rendered has traditionally been an important clinical act; as much a part of the professionalism of doctors as is choosing the right diagnosis. For example, ethical doctors in unregulated systems have been expected to charge according to a patient's ability to pay, as well as to provide a certain amount of charity service for patients in difficult financial straits. There have been two related 'game changers': the movement of medical services from one-on-one medical care to ever greater dependence upon teams within systems of delivery; and changed billing for services, through various forms of insurance coverage, in such ways that the connection between patient and doctor is lost. Yet the obligation of the profession to ensure that the interest of patients is attended to even in the act of billing remains intact. So it is the collective responsibility of the profession to ensure that only 'appropriate' services are ordered, and that only reasonable and affordable billings be charged. At the same time, it is strongly felt within the profession that an important part of professionalism is the right to establish the terms and conditions of remuneration and to maintain a degree of fiscal autonomy in the workplace.

Today, rough estimates are that decision-making by the profession accounts for about 70 per cent of health care costs; this percentage, of course, is not all physician earnings. Most of it represents the 'add-on' costs, such as equipment, other health personnel, and care facilities. Yet in the current hot debates about the 'sustainability' of health care delivery due to rising costs, the responsibility of the profession to ensure appropriate use and billing is not often acknowledged (Fuchs 2011). Are there ways that the profession can overcome the obvious conflict of interest, represented for example, by the surgeon who is paid fee for service for diagnosing and providing a surgical service; or by a radiologist who owns an X-ray facility and benefits financially from ordering multiple examinations of dubious value?

In fact, a massive effort has been made by the profession for over 20 years to provide rigour to medical judgements through 'evidence based guidelines' designed to assist practitioners when making difficult clinical decisions. So far, the results of this exercise have not proven hugely successful; large studies reveal that in practice, less than 50 per cent of guidelines are successfully implemented by most practitioners under ordinary circumstances and for common disease conditions (McGlynn et al. 2003). It turns out that it is one thing to announce guidelines; it is another to assure their application in practice.

The attempt to effectively implement these guidelines in the United States has not proven politically feasible, even in large Health Maintenance Organizations (HMOs), where efforts to provide incentives for the right judgements (for instance, pay for performance) have provided only marginal benefits in early trials. So here is a strong challenge for the ability of an autonomous profession to demonstrate the kind of discipline required to regulate itself in the interest of the public.

Ongoing efforts to find solutions to these troubling problems are in progress. Proposals have been made to incorporate clinical guidelines as the measurement tools in programmes that assess the performance of physicians directly in clinical settings. These programmes have been resisted by the profession when they are administered by government or health system administrators, but in some Canadian Provinces, including Quebec and Ontario, evidence-based measures have been incorporated into peer assessment programmes that retain purely formative educational objectives. While results are not yet available for study, it is possible that this form of quality assurance measure will prove influential in doctors' decision-making habits. It will be critical for the profession to be part of some resolution of this thorny issue, since it is clear that the rising cost of medical services can no longer be tolerated by already overburdened health care budgets.

3) The Concept of Evidence-based Medical Regulation

It is not only the loss of public respect for the profession that is creating pressure for revision of medical self-regulation. The current global shortage of health professionals highlights the challenges faced in human resource components of professional regulation, and threatens disruption of traditional standards of governance. What are the minimum requirements for entry into practice? How can the abilities of internationally trained professionals be judged? How are exit standards from training programmes determined? How is accountability for care standards adjudicated in team care delivery settings?

Governance decisions of this kind are optimized and made most defensible when they are supported by empirical evidence, yet the culture of medical workforce governance remains unmoved by empirical approaches.

Figure 8.1 portrays the accountabilities of the profession. Regulatory authorities acting on behalf of the profession are accountable to prevent, detect, educate or correct non-professional acts over the broad spectrum of regulatory activity, from entry to professional education, through training, to practice including the maintenance of competence and corrective discipline in practice. This sweeping list is the 'scope' of regulation for individual and system competence; but it also can provide something of a template or score card for the success of the profession in maintaining 'discipline' among its practitioners.

The objective behind the idea of 'evidence-based regulation' is to commence the establishment of a vigorous research enterprise at a national or international level, designed to explore and improve the quality of the governance processes that control workforce deployment and regulate the competence of health professionals, including the whole scope of professional regulation.

Critical to the success of this objective would be the creation of a repository of databases so that targeted research can mobilize the wealth of data now sequestered in individual data banks. The problem for research in this area is not the lack of data; databases exist with credentials and performance information encompassing health professional careers in most developed countries. However, the capacity for linking and sharing is limited. The core problem is the fragmentation, inaccessibility and lack of organization of this data for research purposes. What would be needed for an enterprise of this scope would be database identifiers, accession protocols, and structures to sustain a linked repository in an accessible, yet extraordinarily secure, infrastructure. In their absence, research efforts are expensive and time consuming. Furthermore, because data is discontinuous across regions or jurisdictions, it is difficult to achieve generalizable outcomes. As a result, evidence to inform governance decisions is lacking, and policies for governance of the workforce lack the consistency and validity to meet accountability or psychometric standards for performance measurement.

There is a need to create, at nationally distributed university and/or research sites, special purpose facilities to house the equipment and personnel of a highly specialized and secure health workforce governance data repository. This is unexplored territory, so that software development would be a key investment to configure the network of data, and to develop the processes needed to organize, standardize and render researchable, data from a number of regulatory sources. Finally, the infrastructure would need to include technology to facilitate the translation of research findings into policy actions, through national communication tools and established relations with the regulators themselves.

The availability of such an infrastructure would surely catalyse systems-level inquiry into the determinants of quality in professional health workforces. Studies could examine the processes and outcomes of professional performance across the spectrum of education and practice to find areas of governance that can be rationalized and improved. Regulatory and educational databases could be linked to national and regional health service databases in a conceptual framework for research related to health outcomes. This approach would expand upon the current, narrower disease-focused analyses. The roles and performances of professionals could then be examined in the broader context of typical encounters with patients in characteristic practice settings as they are actually found in the environment of systems of practice (Laduca 1994).

The research framework would need to emphasize the structural elements of competency, accountability and workplace management. It could also focus upon topical crosscutting dimensions, such as scope of practice, quality and safety, inter-professionalism, and migration and professional mobility.

Creation of a network of this complexity and size would be groundbreaking in the fields of health education and regulation. But it is not without precedent. Analogous networks have been created in other areas of science, where scientists and policy makers have come to recognize the benefits of a robust, flexible and properly secured data infrastructure that meets broad information and decision support needs. A strong commitment to the concept of a research enterprise based upon this organized data is an important precondition for undertaking this scale of work. Governance leaders must be determined to ensure that their policy decisions be informed by reliable evidence to meet the rising standard of public accountability in professional spheres.

4) Transforming Medical Education: Assessment in a Quality Improvement Framework

The truism that 'assessment drives performance and learning' is well accepted in medical education. Typically, the evaluation of learners in clinical medicine has focused on end-of-course or end-of-programme 'capstone evaluations': that is, on summative decisions rather than ongoing formative processes to provide progress reports for promotion and feedback for self-improvement (Klass 2010). Current assessments are constructed as high-stakes events, with momentous, make-or-break implications for trainees. In turn, this has made the process conflicted for faculty, who would prefer to see their main task as teaching, not making life-changing pass/fail decisions, and intimidating for trainees. In general, once these assessment hurdles have been cleared, the resultant benefit is viewed as being 'good for life'. This author has previously described this concept as part of the failing 'ballistic model' of evaluating medical competence (Klass 2007). Fortunately, this model is yielding to a more contemporary expectation that practitioners must continually show competence and maintenance of certification, and that the concept of 'once in, good for life' is no longer supportable. Standards are important in education, but they can best serve as targets and milestones of training, not solely as cut-offs as they often do today.

Thus, a first injunction for sweeping change in the educational programme for the profession is the need to commit resources to ensure that the values of medical education conform to a progressive culture of assessment featuring regular evaluation and feedback and down-grading the typical end-of-programme testing. Assessment should be viewed as the ongoing critical evaluative component within a system of clinical quality improvement, rather than as the sharp edge of a summative academic exercise. The major purposes of assessment must be educational, or formative, not judgemental and summative.

No doubt occasional 'bad apples' must be excluded from any educational programme, but this should not be at the expense of devaluing an effective, improvement-oriented culture. In most medical education programmes, the valid objective of creating a culture of quality improvement among all graduates is sacrificed to the single objective of 'weeding out' occasional laggards.[2] This more positive attitude should serve as the framework for organizational efforts to make the ideas of quality improvement pervasive throughout the development and outcome of the education system. Educators need to recognize, just as most regulators have come to understand, that at the end of a purely summative process, students at all points on the educational continuum and at both extremes of the performance curve, are falsely imbued with a sense of accomplishment bordering

2 The sudden discovery of a failing student at the end of programme evaluation is as much an indictment of the programme's evaluation system as it is of the student. Who is failing whom?

on entitlement; having passed the test, they now feel themselves to be 'good for life'. Far better that all students learn the simple values of quality improvement.

Until recently, test methods emphasized in medical schools have concentrated on the concept of competence in the sense of 'being ready' for entry to practice. The alternative paradigm of assessment, much more aligned with quality improvement, examines physician trainees' action in context; it judges competence on the basis of completion of real-life performances in the workplace or in highly authentic simulations.

These assessment activities should now be seen as part of an educational process within a system of health care delivery, and are captured in the US-based Accreditation Council for Graduate Medical Education (ACGME) competency of 'practice-based learning and improvement'. Ultimately, this synthesis of quality improvement and performance assessment in an educational framework should become the educational standard of the profession.

Additional Frontiers and Challenges in Education for Accountability

Nearly one hundred years ago, the famous Flexner Report (Flexner 1910) commenced a process of change that brought some order and rigour to the previously chaotic education system for medical trainees in North America. These educational changes were not made in isolation. In fact, they were made as part of a larger effort of the North American establishment in medicine (including the regulatory authorities and the medical societies, aided by large philanthropic organizations (the Carnegie and Rockefeller Foundations) to raise the standards of the medical profession so that their regulatory independence could be defended against the challenges of other less well established healing groups identified by organized medicine as quacks (Starr 1982: 116–23). Educational reforms were supported at medical schools deemed successful by the Flexner ranking. But these reforms were accompanied by the introduction of systematic evaluation schemes for licensure, heralding the founding of the National Board of Medical Examiners in the United States and the Medical Council of Canada. At the same time, the requirements for licensure of defined postgraduate training were introduced. Analogous sweeping changes in medical education are again needed to enhance and strengthen the standards of education for medical professionals to meet society's demands and to maintain a degree of independence for the profession.

Accountability is the watchword of medical professionalism in the twenty-first century, and it is also a key to continuing trust for the profession. Indeed, assessment, in its many forms, is the 'tool' of accountability. To be deemed 'accountable' any educational programme in medicine, whether at medical school or for practising doctors, must have the outcome of its efforts clearly in its sights, and must be willing to take stock of, and be accountable for, the competence of its participants in their subsequent practice. Clinical assessments can no longer be limited to academic achievement and the accumulation of disaggregated competencies in individuals; rather, it needs to address the ability of individuals to perform competently in real world situations

To be accountable in this performance-based concept of competence, a test system must define the scope of medical practice to be served within a projected population, and it should allow feedback to ensure that the outcomes of health care delivery to that population validate the evaluation system. The elements of trainee assessment should be seen as prototypes for a more elaborate plan that could be devised by any educational institution to ensure that all its practitioners satisfy their accountability to the public they serve. Performance evaluation of the practising profession is a hot topic as a means of maintaining financial and professional accountability (Weng et al. 2010). Tools originally designed as performance measures for practicing physicians should, in due course be disseminated into training programmes.

The resulting new tradition and culture will link the assessments of competencies in trainees to equivalent quality-related measures for practicing physicians. The hope is that the philosophy behind these latter assessments – that of quality improvement – will also become the ethos of assessments in the teaching arena. That being the case, education will have proven itself a tool that strengthens the accountability and transparency of professional processes, and will add substantially to the credibility of the profession in the eyes of the public.

So one hundred years after Flexner, we may be witnessing a new revolution in medical education, one that, like Flexner's, strengthens the values of the medical profession and contributes to the sustainability of its independence in society.

References

Arthurs, H.W. 1995. The dead parrot: does professional self-regulation exhibit vital signs? *Alberta Law Review*, 33, 800–809.

Baker, G.R., Norton, P.G., Flintoft, V., Blais, R., Brown, A., Cox, J., Etchells, E., Ghali, W.A., Hébert, P., Majurndar, S.R., O'Beirne, M., Palacios-Derflingher, L., Reid, R.J., Sheps, S. and Tamblyn, R. 2004. The Canadian Adverse Events Study: the incidence of adverse events among hospital patients in Canada. *CMAJ*, 170(11), 1678–86.

Bristol Royal Infirmary Inquiry: Final Report. [Online]. 2001. Norwich: The Stationery Office Limited. Available at: www.bristol-inquiry.org.uk [Accessed: 30 September 2011].

Epstein, R.M. and Hundert, E.M. 2002. Defining and assessing professional competence. *JAMA*, 287, 226–35.

Flexner, A. 1910. Medical education in the United States and Canada: a report to the Carnegie Foundation for the Advancement of Teaching, *Bulletin No. 4*. New York City: The Carnegie Foundation for the Advancement of Teaching.

Freidson, E. 1970. *Profession of Medicine: A Study of the Sociology of Applied Knowledge*. New York: Harper Rowe.

Freidson, E. 1994. *Professionalism Reborn, Theory, Prophecy and Policy*. Chicago: University of Chicago Press.

Fuchs, V.R. 2011. The doctor's dilemma: what is 'appropriate' care? *N Engl* J Med, 365, 585–7.

Jacobs, J. 2005. *Dark Age Ahead*. Toronto: Vintage Canada.

Klass, A.A. 1961. What is a profession. *Canad. MAJ*. 85, 698–701.

Klass, D.A. 2007. Viewpoint: a performance-based conception of competence is changing the regulation of physicians' professional behaviour. *Acad Med*, 82(6), 529–35.

Klass, D.J. 2010. Developing a system for evaluation of learners, in *Leadership Careers in Medical Education*, edited by L. Pangaro. Philadelphia: ACP, 151–78.

Laduca, A. 1994. Validation of professional licensure examinations: professions theory, test design, and construct validity. *Eval Health Prof*, 17(2), 178–97.

McGlynn, E.A., Asch, S.M., Adams, J., Keesey, J., Hicks, J., DeCristofaro, A. and Kerr, E.A. 2003. The quality of health care delivered to adults in the United States. *N Engl* J Med 348, 2635–45.

McLeod, P.J., Tamblyn, R.M., Gayton, D., Grad, R., Snell, L., Berkson, L., Abrahamowicz, M. 1997. Use of standardized patients to assess between-physician variations in resource utilization. *JAMA*, 278(14): 1164–8.

Reason, J.T. 1990. *Human Error*. Cambridge: Cambridge University Press.

Relman, A.S. 2003. A physician's view of Freidson's analysis. *Journal of Health Politics, Policy and Law*, 28(1), 164–8.

Sacket, D.L., Rosenberg, M.C., Muir-Gray, J.A., Haynes, R.B., and Richardson, W.S. 1996. Evidence based medicine: what it is and what it isn't. *BMJ*, 312, 71–2.

Secretary of State for Health. 2007. *Trust, Assurance and Safety – The Regulation of Health Professionals in the 21st century*. [Online]. London: The Stationery Office. Available at: www.dh.gov.uk/prod consum_dh/groups/dh_digitalassets/@dh/@en/documents/digitalasset/dh_065947.pdf [Accessed: 30 September 2011].

Shipman Inquiry: Reports. [Online]. 2001–2005. Available at: www.shipman-inquiry.org.uk/reports.asp [Accessed: 30 September 2011].

Sinclair, C.M. 2001. The report of the Manitoba Pediatric Cardiac Surgery Inquest: An Inquiry into Twelve Deaths at the Winnipeg Health Sciences Centre in 1994. [Online]. Available at: www.pediatriccardiacinquest.mb.ca [Accessed: 30 September 2011].

Starr, P. 1982. *The Social Transformation of American Medicine*. New York, NY: Basic Books.

Stewart, J. 1999. *Blind Eye: How the Medical Establishment Let a Doctor Get Away With Murder*. New York: Simon & Schuster.

Weng, W., Hess, B.J., Holmboe, E.S., Lipner, R.S. 2010. Measuring physicians' performance in clinical practice: reliability, classification accuracy, and validity. *Eval Health Prof*, 33, 302–20.

Wenghofer, E., Williams, A.P., Klass, D.J., Faulkner, D. 2006. Physician-patient encounters: the structure of performance in family and general office practice. *J Cont Educ Health Prof*, 26, 285–93.

Chapter 9

A National Scheme for Health Practitioner Registration and Accreditation: the Case of Australia

Fiona Pacey, Kirsten Harley, Craig Veitch and Stephanie D. Short

The introduction of the National Registration and Accreditation Scheme (the Scheme) in Australia in 2010 was designed to deliver a best practice structure for health practitioner regulation in order to support the provision of safe health care to the community. The Scheme codifies arrangements for the registration and accreditation of health practitioners.[1] This new legislative framework provides a system intended to deliver consistency across the nation and across 10 of the largest health professional groups in Australia, a significant advance. Prior to the decision to introduce the Scheme there was a proliferation of regulatory regimes with each state and territory regulating health practitioners under different legislative instruments. This hampered many aspects of reform relating to the management and evolution of Australia's health workforce. As new technologies emerged and distances were effectively diminished, as health practitioners moved around Australia and across the globe, it became evident that existing regulatory arrangements were not able to keep pace with twenty-first century expectations. There was also a growing unease about the work of regulators in assessing health practitioners trained overseas and in the approach taken to identifying and managing underperforming or poorly behaving practitioners, informed by media coverage in Australia and elsewhere.

The Scheme commenced operation in the middle of 2010. While strands of its history go back for decades, much of the detailed work concerning its introduction occurred only in the two years prior to its establishment. Thus it is still too soon for research to have unravelled all the threads leading to the introduction and shape of the Scheme. However, this chapter is able to present a chronological overview of the Scheme's formation and introduction and identify and analyse some of the key factors contributing to its evolution, including developments at a macro policy level (economic and productivity reform), meso level (health workforce planning and management) and micro level (the assessment of overseas trained health practitioners) against the backdrop of a desire for national consistency. In

1 In this chapter we describe health professionals as practitioners to mirror the language of the legislation and national body.

moving from commentary to analysis, we use the framework used to assess policy processes developed by US political scientist, John W. Kingdon (2011).

The chapter begins with a chronological overview of the introduction of the Scheme, then outlines Kingdon's analytic framework. We then introduce the Australian political context, showing that constitutional and budgetary arrangements require intergovernmental collaboration to achieve national health workforce reform. In the next section we trace the emergence of health workforce as a problem on the national political agenda, including the relevance of broader economic and productivity concerns. Next we discuss the scandal surrounding overseas-trained surgeon Jayant Patel at Bundaberg Hospital, which highlighted failure of existing processes for registration of overseas trained health practitioners. Finally, we turn to analyse the decision-making required in the details of implementation.

Introduction of the National Registration and Accreditation Scheme: an Overview

The Scheme, introduced on 1 July 2010, provides a mechanism for registration of individual health practitioners and accreditation of related educational programmes. The national Scheme was established by generally consistent legislation passed in each state and territory of Australia.[2] A chronology of the major steps towards implementation of the Scheme appears in Table 9.1.

By the time the Scheme commenced, the somewhat organic development of the registration or licensing of health practitioners on a state by state basis meant that there were more than 85 bodies across the country involved in determining the standards required for inclusion on various registers. Almost inevitably, this gave rise to a situation where requirements were inconsistent, even across a single profession such as medicine or physiotherapy. A national regulatory scheme enabled a number of these pre-existing challenges to be addressed. These included consistently mapping the distribution of health practitioners, enabling a consistent process for the assessment of overseas-trained practitioners, and creating a national

2 There were two key variations from consistency in relation to the introduction and structure of the Scheme. First, legislation was not passed in all jurisdictions prior to commencement of the Scheme. Echoing a pattern demonstrated in the formation of the Commonwealth of Australia over one hundred years earlier, the Western Australian legislation commenced on 30 August 2010 (*Health Practitioner Regulation National Law (WA) Act 2010*), and subsequently Western Australian practitioners joined the Scheme on 18 October 2010 (Morauta 2011). Second, in one of the few substantive variations to the Scheme's application, the state of New South Wales retained existing arrangements to address 'notifications' in relation to practitioner conduct, health or performance (*Health Practitioner Regulation Act 2009 (NSW)).* This variation was managed through a provision within the national law (Morauta 2011).

process for determining approved courses of education to qualify individuals as eligible for registration.

The operational structure of the Scheme is now in the public domain and is of growing interest to those professions who are regulated under its auspices (for example, Bird 2010, James and Francis 2011). Our primary interest here is in tracing and illuminating the pathway that led to the establishment of the Scheme.

Table 9.1. Major steps towards implementation of the National Registration and Accreditation Scheme

1992	Legislation to support mutual recognition between the states and territories of professional qualifications (*Mutual Recognition Act 1992* (*Cwth*))
1995	Establishment of the Australian Medical Workforce Advisory Committee, an entity of Commonwealth and state/territory governments to monitor medical workforce
2000	Establishment of the Australian Health Workforce Advisory Committee, an entity of Commonwealth and state/territory governments to monitor health workforce
2002	Release of the first *Intergenerational Report,* issued by the Commonwealth Treasury to address the long term sustainability of government finances as the population ages
2004	Launch of the first national Health Workforce Strategic Framework (by Health Ministers) Ministers announce a decision to pursue a nationally consistent approach to medical registration
2005	Jayant Patel, 'Dr Death', who had been practising medicine in Bundaberg, Queensland since 2003, emerges into the public arena
2005	Three reports issued by the Productivity Commission (*Economic Implications of an Ageing Australia, Impacts of Advances in Medical Technology in Australia,* and *Australia's Health Workforce*) addressing issues of the relationship between economic development and health expenditure and workforce
July 2006	Council of Australian Governments (COAG) decides to move towards establishment of schemes for registration and accreditation for health professionals by July 2008
March 2008	COAG members sign *The National Partnership Agreement to Deliver a Seamless National Economy* and an *Intergovernmental Agreement for a National Registration and Accreditation Scheme for the Health Professions*
2009	Introduction of the Qld legislation (*Health Practitioner Regulation National Law Act 2009* (*Qld*))
1 July 2010	Introduction of the National Registration and Accreditation Scheme for Health Practitioners
October 2010	Western Australia joins the national scheme

An Analytical Frame

John Kingdon's (2011) influential work, *Agendas, Alternatives and Public Policies*, was first published in 1984. It presents a theoretical framework developed by tracing the progress and process of public policy agenda-setting and decision-making within health and transportation in the United States of America, and has been applied broadly in relation to policy evolutions (for example, Birkland 1998, De Voe 2003). In building on previous theory around decision-making (Cohen, March and Olsen 1972), Kingdon's framework recognizes a complexity of influences on agenda-setting and consequently decision-making in public policy.

As shown in Figure 9.1, Kingdon (2011: 19) articulates three 'streams' – problems, policies and politics – which play different but interconnected roles in shaping the formation of public policy. In the problem stream, Kingdon traces the ways in which certain problems are demonstrated to decision-makers as problems requiring policy solutions. This can be through regular forms of reporting or data, as well as through 'focusing events' or 'crises' (2011: 19). His policy stream incorporates the policy alternatives that float in a 'policy primeval soup' (2011: 20) and that may, at some juncture, resonate with broader policy concerns. The politics stream describes the shifting nature of political influence, and how who is in power generates opportunities and constraints for particular policies (2011: 145). A 'policy window' occurs when the streams line up – when the policy stream delivers solutions to problems that garner the necessary political support (2011: 166). The 'problems' we will be focusing on include enduring challenges in health workforce governance and management in Australia (of which regulation is the manifestation) and an event that may have hastened the Scheme's introduction

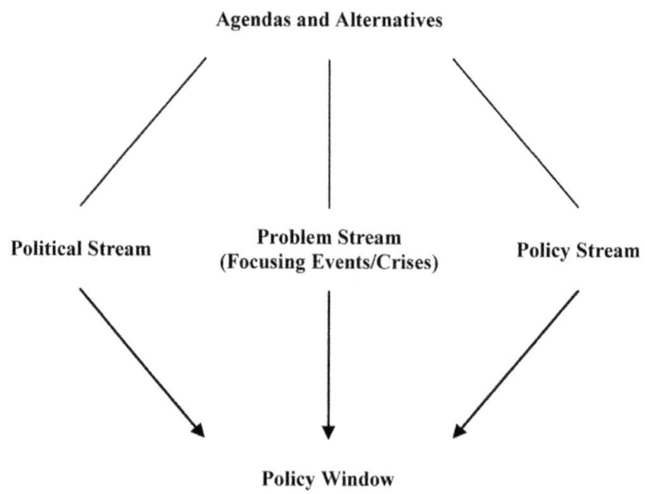

Figure 9.1 Kingdon's framework for analysing policy processes

and influenced parts of its design. The 'policy' stream will be recognized by noting economic and regulatory reform agendas to which the Scheme's development became attached, and the 'political' stream was informed by factors in the other two streams, and a shared political value in creating a Scheme that was national, bridging the interests and responsibilities of both the Commonwealth (federal) and state and territory level of governments. The drive towards efficiency and a more systemic, national approach to health practitioner regulation is a unique story influenced by the more specific history of political players, industry stakeholders and economic drivers. The chapter adopts Kingdon's streams to enhance an explanation of events, but does not use them as a means of formally structuring content. We turn now to an overview of the complex Australian political environment in which the scheme evolved.

The Australian Context

Australia is a country that occupies a single continent. It has six states and two major territories. The *Commonwealth of Australia Constitution Act 1900* that established the nation of Australia in 1901 provided for a federal system of government in which there are distinctive roles and responsibilities for the Commonwealth Government and the states and territories. Both tiers of government have responsibilities for components of the health care system in conjunction with individuals, for-profit and not-for-profit organizations.

Section 51 of the Constitution outlines those areas in which the Commonwealth government has the authority and responsibility to undertake law-making. Areas not included are considered to be residual powers that fall to the states. Because regulation of health practitioners is not specified in s.51, this responsibility rests with the state and territory governments. While the Commonwealth holds a critical interest in the effectiveness of regulatory regimes, given its role in overall economic management, it does not have the power to act unilaterally in regard to the registration and accreditation of health practitioners.[3] This means that any national approaches or solutions in this area of governance would require collaborative efforts.

The primary mechanism through which national (intergovernmental) policy solutions are driven is the Council of Australian Governments (COAG), the forum and organizational entity that formally brings together the Prime Minister, the Premiers of each state, and the Chief Ministers of each territory. Similar fora are operative across different areas of governmental activity, with the work of the Australian Health Ministers' Conference (AHMC) of particular relevance in this instance. The importance of the Scheme to governments is highlighted by the fact that the peak body, COAG, was the entity that formally initiated it in 2008.

3 See McDonald (2010) for more detailed discussion of the Constitution in relation to regulation of health practitioners, and specifically medical practitioners.

Health policy, including that concerning the health workforce, is a central and omnipresent concern to Australian governments. Health accounts for approximately a quarter of state/territory budgets (Government of South Australia 2010, Queensland Government 2010) and 16 per cent of the federal government budget (Australian Government 2010). Collectively, governments spend approximately two-thirds of their health budgets on payments or salaries to individual healthcare practitioners (Productivity Commission 2005).[4]

Australia's political structure then gave the Commonwealth, state and territory governments some incentive to work together to address health workforce regulation. Both levels of government had funding responsibilities and problems to address. And one of the key rationales for inception of the Scheme was the standardization of regulatory requirements across each of Australia's eight states and territories. Constitutional arrangements were such that these national reforms required collaborative efforts and decision-making on an intergovernmental stage to develop a solution. One of the initial challenges in the evolution of reform was a clear articulation and agreement of what problems these collaborative efforts should address.

Health Workforce – an Emerging 'Problem' on the Political Agenda

Discussions about health practitioner regulation were occurring for at least 20 years before introduction of the Scheme. In 1992, the Australian Institute of Health and Welfare (AIHW) reported that mutual recognition of professional qualifications was on the intergovernmental agenda, after being initiated as a form of micro-economic reform through Special Premiers' Conferences in 1991 and 1992 (AIHW 1992: 111). The introduction of mutual recognition registration was reported as a means of enhancing the mobility of health practitioners. However, it has been observed that despite the reporting of intergovernmental commitment to change, there were no significant changes at that juncture at a national level[5] (Palmer and Short 2010: 145) and the issue of workforce mobility remained effectively unresolved until the reforms contained within the Scheme were introduced.

The importance of coherent workforce planning informed by reliable data was not translated into substantive policy responses until the mid-late 1990s, with the establishment of the Australian Medical Workforce Advisory Committee (AMWAC) in 1995 by Health Ministers and the Australian Health Workforce Advisory Committee (AHWAC) in 2000. By 2002, health financing concerns and the related issue of health care practitioner availability were highly visible.

4 While the Commonwealth funds the majority of services delivered by doctors under the Medicare Benefits Scheme, the salaries of medical practitioners in public hospitals are paid by state and territory governments.

5 See Carlton (2005) for a more detailed review of regulatory reform undertaken at a jurisdictional level in Victoria.

Health Ministers recognized the importance of health workforce governance and management, but it came to attract the interest of a broader policy audience within the context of micro-economic reform addressing Australia's future economic security. In 2002 the Commonwealth government, through its Treasury department, issued the nation's first *Intergenerational Report* as part of the 2002–2003 Budget (Australian Government 2002). Its aim was to examine the long-term sustainability of government finances as the population aged. In terms of health expenditure, Treasury noted that while its modelling recognized the presence of demographic pressures, other challenges were forecast as having a more significant influence on expenditure. These were technological developments; the expectation of an increased use of existing services; and consumer-driven demand and desire for health care (Australian Government 2002). Each of these factors would create further pressure on the health workforce. It would concurrently be facing its own demographic challenge with workers characterized as 'baby-boomers', born in the decades following World War II, increasingly retiring from the workforce. In regard to the provision of health care, most technological advancements do not diminish the number of staff needed to deliver or manage the equipment and treat and care for those patients whose diseases or injuries might otherwise have gone undetected, or been untreatable.

In addition to release of the *Intergenerational Report*, negotiations were underway in 2002 for the 2003 to 2008 Australian Health Care Agreements. These agreements are the primary mechanism of hospital funding flowing from the Commonwealth to the states and territories, but also provide an opportunity for the Commonwealth to seek change in health service delivery by negotiated influence. To address the many challenges that had been identified across the health system as a whole, Australian Health Ministers formed nine reference groups, one of which was addressing collaboration across workforce, education and training (Reid 2002).

Although these agreements brought no explicit outcomes in respect of specific health workforce initiatives, the presence of a health workforce agenda was set and by 2004, a commitment to collaboration was clearly evident. The Health Ministers launched the first national Health Workforce Strategic Framework (AHMC 2004b) which echoes concerns that Treasury articulated in 2002. The April 2004 Ministerial Conference was a critical one in the timeline of events that ultimately led to the creation and introduction of the Scheme, with Ministers also addressing a direct question of workforce governance with a decision to pursue a nationally consistent approach to medical registration (AHMC 2004a). Furthermore, it was announced that the Australian Competition and Consumer Commission (ACCC) and the Australian Health Workforce Officials' Committee (AHWOC) would undertake a review of specialist medical college activities in relation to the selection and training of trainees and their assessment of overseas trained specialists. This followed a specific review of the practices of the Royal Australasian College of Surgeons, finalized in 2003, who sought authorization from the ACCC in relation to its processes for accrediting hospitals and training positions and assessing overseas trained surgeons (ACCC and AHWOC 2005).

These activities saw governments taking a more explicit interest in the regulatory arrangements around health practitioner training and the processes of assessing the qualification of overseas trained health practitioners.

So in 2004, health workforce matters (and a demonstrated appreciation of the interconnectivity between health workforce management and regulation) had emerged substantively through what Kingdon (2011: 117) describes as 'the primeval policy soup', from deliberation among health ministers onto the agenda of chief ministers. At the June 2004 meeting of COAG, it was decided that an extensive review of health workforce issues should be undertaken. In March 2005, the Commonwealth Treasurer, Peter Costello, formally requested the Government's independent economic research body, the Productivity Commission to undertake that work. The scope of the review was extensive, addressing demand and supply issues, workplace planning and reform and regulatory measures over a 10-year period. This action indicated that an initial mechanism to address structural challenges of health workforce development had been identified, with the nature of a Productivity Commission review being both deliberative and public.

The *Productivity Commission Act 1998 (Cth)* establishes the guiding principles for its activities and inquiries. These include the expectation that it considers the need to 'reduce regulation of industry (including regulation by the state, territory and local governments) where it is consistent with the social and economic goals of the Commonwealth' (Section 8 (1) b)). The Productivity Commission undertook three inquiries building on the initial concerns identified by the Intergenerational Report: *Economic Implications of an Ageing Australia* (2005a), *Impacts of Advances in Medical Technology in Australia* (2005b) and *Australia's Health Workforce* (2005c). While the first two reports contributed to the broader context of health care financing and delivery, the final report served to drive explicit consideration of the Australian health workforce. Regulatory concerns were recognized as both an impediment to and an opportunity for reform. In the final report, the Commission explicitly recommended regulatory streamlining of the health workforce. Specifically, it recommended establishment of a single national registration board with profession specific panels to manage issues around codes of practices, performance and discipline functions, and a single national board to undertake or manage the accreditation of health professional education (Productivity Commission 2005c).

The next COAG meeting, in July 2006, formally considered *Australia's Health Workforce* (Productivity Commission 2005c) and responded to its recommendations. It should be recognized that the process of reviewing and coming to agreed positions at this meeting represented significant work undertaken across the country, both between the federal and state/territories governments and within those governments across the departments and offices of ministers, premiers and first ministers. At this meeting, COAG (2006a, 2006b) agreed that following stakeholder consultation, national schemes for registration and for accreditation would be established within two years, by July 2008. The schemes would initially incorporate the nine health professions already regulated by legislation in all states and territories. The COAG meeting also agreed that: an Intergovernmental Agreement would be completed by mid 2007; both schemes would be self-funding once operational; and the estimated start-up costs of AUD$12.3 million for the registration scheme (COAG 2006a) and AUD$7.5 million for the accreditation scheme (COAG 2006b) would be met by the federal and all state and territory governments. The timelines that eventuated were longer than those initially envisaged, and the two schemes became combined as one, as the process of consultation among stakeholders ensued.

The Scheme was also linked to broader economic reform agendas concerning national consistency, seen in its inclusion as a component of a key instrument detailing COAG's priorities in 2008. The *National Partnership Agreement to Deliver a Seamless National Economy* (COAG 2008b) established a commitment by Australia's federal and state/territory governments to work together across 18 policy areas in order to deliver a consistent national approach in each area. Under this agreement, health workforce as a descriptor sits amongst such items as licensing of tradespeople, rail safety regulation, directors' liability and food regulation.

The need for reform of health workforce regulation had been effectively articulated and argued for by the Productivity Commission. It thus presented a 'policy alternative' (Kingdon 2011: 174) that could be pursued, given the right alignment of problems and policy highly placed on decision-makers' agendas and a conducive political environment, including COAG's drive towards efficiency and national consistency across a range of policy sectors. A crisis (or 'scandal', see Chapter 12) which captured the attention of governments and the community in 2005 might be seen a 'focusing event' (Kingdon 2011: 96). While there remains uncertainty about its role in shaping development of the Scheme, it adds additional complexity to the story of the Scheme's gestation, and possibly its ultimate design and manner of implementation.

The Jayant Patel Scandal in Bundaberg – a 'Focusing Event'?

Bundaberg is a small regional city in the north-eastern state of Queensland, located 380 kilometres (one hour by plane) north of the state capital, Brisbane. It has a population of around 100,000 people, and is 1,500 kilometres from Canberra (Australia's capital and location of the Australian Medical Council), and 2,000 kilometres from Melbourne, where the Royal Australasian College of Surgeons is based.[6] Like many other regional and rural communities around Australia, Bundaberg struggled to attract locally trained health practitioners and had become reliant on the efforts of overseas trained health practitioners for its health care delivery.

6 The Australian Medical Council was the body responsible for the primary assessment of medical qualifications obtained overseas, and the College of Surgeons is the body responsible for setting the standards of surgical education in Australia.

The case of Jayant Patel is a remarkable one, and was the focus of a formal Commission of Inquiry (Davies 2005). These commissions, undertaken by an eminent jurist, provide an ad hoc mechanism which governments can institute to investigate unusual, serious issues of alleged maladministration. In the Patel case, the Commission of Inquiry was conducted by the Hon Geoffrey Davies AO, a former judge in the Queensland Supreme Court. The report details the record of events concerning the Patel case and raised substantial concerns about not only that case, but also those of practitioners in other regional centres of Queensland – Harvey Bay, Rockhampton, Townsville and Charters Towers (Davies 2005). The sequence of events in the Patel case is listed below in Table 9.2.

Table 9.2 The Patel context: events and failures in regulatory control and clinical governance processes

11 Feb 2003	Jayant Patel registered under the 'Area of Need' scheme to work at Bundaberg Base Hospital by the Medical Board of Queensland. The Medical Board did not investigate a notation on his licensing documents from Oregon, USA, which was later found to reveal a restriction on his scope of practice. It also had not found that he had surrendered his licence in the state of New York. Assessment of qualifications and suitability against the position was not undertaken, in breach of the *Medical Practitioners Registration Act 2001(Qld)*.
Mar 2003	Jayant Patel registered and appointed as a Senior Medical Officer, subsequently appointed by the Acting Director of Medical Services as Director of Surgery. The initial appointment was undertaken without any assessment of clinical skill and competence. No credentialing or clinical privileging process was undertaken in contravention of a 2002 Queensland Health policy. The appointment to the Director of Surgery role was inconsistent with the conditions of Patel's registration.
Mar 2003–early 2005	Jayant Patel operated on patients. Toni Hoffman (Nurse Unit Manager of the Intensive Care Unit) first raises issues in June 2003 and provides a substantial record of concern to hospital management in October 2004. Over 20 complaints were made by staff and patients, with local management unresponsive and the complaints system inadequate. As Director of Surgery, Patel was unsupervised, also inconsistent with the conditions of his registration. The structural deficiencies of hospital budgeting were deemed to have contributed to local management inaction towards Patel.
Feb 2005	Queensland Health begins investigations.
Mar 2005	Concerns over Patel are raised in the Queensland Parliament.
Apr 2005	Jayant Patel resigns and returns to Oregon. Hedley Thomas, journalist with the Brisbane Courier Mail newspaper, breaks the story of previous registration restrictions.

Sources: Davies (2005), Flynn (2010)

The Davies Report was handed to the Queensland Government by the end of 2005, and within a year warrants were issued on 16 charges, including manslaughter, grievous bodily harm and fraud. After 18 months, Patel was extradited to Queensland and court proceedings commenced in June 2009. After a 15-week trial, he was found guilty of three counts of manslaughter and one of grievous bodily harm. And in one of those quirks of fate, the judge announced his sentencing of Patel to seven years in jail for three counts of manslaughter and one of grievous bodily harm on 1 July 2010 – the same day that the Scheme came into effect.

The circumstances that led to Patel's conviction provide a tangible demonstration of the implications of regulatory failure (Thomas 2007). The inherent inefficiencies of piecemeal and patchwork regulatory arrangements were brought into sharp focus in the small regional town of Bundaberg in Queensland, but might have occurred in towns or cities throughout Australia. Bundaberg was not the only location in Australia where instances of clinical governance failures in hospitals caused community concern during the early and mid 2000s (Masso and Eager 2009). These failures were complex and layered, with many resulting in significant inquiries of their own. The Patel case demonstrated failings in both the registration processes of the Queensland Medical Board and the clinical governance processes of Queensland Health (Davies 2005). Existing concerns over the assessment of standards expected of overseas trained health practitioners and support provided to them for integration into the workforce (McGrath 2004) found new relevance, with events at Bundaberg described as the 'catalyst for long overdue reform' in relation to overseas medical practitioners in the Australian health system (Harvey and Faunce 2005: 88).

The presence of 'crises' or 'focusing events' prior to the introduction of regulatory change is not a phenomenon unique to Australia. In the United Kingdom the cases of Harold Shipman (the general practitioner convicted in 2000 of the murder of 15 patients) and of the Bristol Infirmary (high death-rate of paediatric cardiac patients) likewise highlighted regulatory problems that led to substantive reform in medical practitioner regulation.[7]

The extensive preconditions for the reform that eventuated in the establishment of the Scheme existed prior to public awareness of events in Bundaberg. However, regardless of the fact that health workforce regulatory reform had already emerged through the 'policy primeval soup', the introduction of the Scheme has become identified with the series of events experienced by surgical patients within the Bundaberg community. Media coverage of the views of the Queensland Premier and Health Minister (Marszalek 2010) explicitly linked the introduction of the new scheme with the incidents in Bundaberg. Another commentator highlighted the influence of 'public outrage' about the case leading to a series of changes

7 See Allsop (2006) and Salter (2002) for detailed explorations of the relationship between these 'focusing events' and the timing and nature of medical practitioner regulatory reform in the United Kingdom.

including a single national medical board (Walton 2010). Others point to an association between the Patel case and the Scheme, but are less explicit as to whether the relationship was causal (for example, Flynn 2010, Jolly 2010).

The timing and consequences of the Patel case provide an apparent fit with Kingdon's framework. However, did it really function as a 'focusing event'? In our ongoing research on the development of the Scheme we will explore the manner and extent to which the case of Jayant Patel and response by decision-makers influenced the timing, structure and detail of the Scheme.

What's on the Other Side of the Policy Window?

Kingdon's framework recognizes that there are streams of activity in which policy alternatives and solutions are developed, identified and championed, and points to the role which focusing events can play in contributing to a policy decision. He also introduces the concept of a policy window (Kingdon 2011: 166), which is a convergence across and between streams that provides an opportunity to advance policy change. As outlined previously, there was an extensive set of conditions that led to the decision to embark upon a new national registration and accreditation scheme. These reflected both long-term challenges facing the structure of the health workforce and broader economic reforms. The parameters that had been set for the scheme reflected both these influences. We have also now examined the presence of a focusing event, the case of Patel in Bundaberg, and its perceived influence on the development of the scheme.

Given this background, it is clear that drawing the proposed arrangements into a coherent process that would achieve the proposed outcomes was a far from simple undertaking. The processes that moved the public deliberations of political leaders from their response to the Productivity Commission in 2006, to the presentation of an intergovernmental agreement in 2008 and the regulatory impact statement are yet to be extensively documented, explored, situated and understood within the context of this significant regulatory reform. These provide scope for important future research and analysis. We can nonetheless articulate the sequence of events that resulted in the launch of the Scheme in July 2010.

Once a formal commitment was made by the Prime Minister, state premiers and territory chief ministers, on 14 July 2006, events began to move quickly. A communiqué from the COAG meeting in April 2007 recorded progress of, and agreement towards, the parameters of the scheme and affirmed sources of influence. It noted that 'workforce responsiveness, flexibility, sustainability and innovation' would be explicitly supported (COAG 2007). The *Intergovernmental Agreement (IGA) for a National Registration and Accreditation Scheme for the Health Professions* was signed by the Prime Minister and the leaders of each state and territory in March 2008 (COAG 2008a). This document demonstrates the significant amount of work undertaken since COAG made its formal response to the Productivity Commission report in 2006.

In articulating the objectives of the Scheme, the IGA returns to the overarching rationales for government involvement pointing to: protection of the public; promotion of workforce mobility; and provision of mechanisms to ensure the high quality of local education and training and assess those practitioners who undertook training elsewhere. Arguably these objectives are the expected objectives of a Scheme designed to register practitioners and accredit their programmes of education and training. There had been legislated recognition of health practitioners in Australia, even prior to its formation as a single country, and to varying degrees, prior legislation articulated a public safety premise. The Australian community holds expectations that those individuals who represent themselves as health practitioners are going to provide them with diagnosis, treatment and care that is based on appropriate knowledge and skills (that is, competency) and that the manner in which it is provided is unencumbered by attributes that may compromise their safety or the outcomes of treatment. The conflict of these expectations in the Patel case is one factor that explains its prominence. The objectives of the scheme articulate this underlying premise prominently, 'to provide for the protection of the public by ensuring only practitioners who are suitably trained and qualified to practise in a competent and ethical manner are registered' (COAG 2008a: 3). Two additional objectives indicate that the service provision and workforce productivity issues discussed earlier are also pertinent, with the Scheme also being required to 'have regard' to issues of health service access, and workforce flexibility and innovation (COAG 2008a). It has also been argued that the right to health care (in countries like Australia) expressly imbues governments with the responsibility to provide regulatory frameworks that meet the expectations of the community (Salter 2002). The objectives of the Scheme reflect an appreciation of that responsibility.

Structurally, the Scheme is managed through two elements: the Australian Health Practitioner Regulation Agency (AHPRA) and profession-based boards. One of the key decisions for governments to make, reflecting the need and desire to address public safety concerns, was which professions would become regulated under the national scheme. Table 9.3 presents the outcomes of those deliberations, detailing which groups were regulated under the Scheme from 2010, and those joining the scheme in 2012. In line with this, from July 2010, there were boards for each of the first 10 professions regulated under the Scheme (*Health Practitioner Regulation National Law 2009*), with additional boards to be formed to oversee the professions that will join the Scheme in 2012 (McDonald 2010). The boards have also appointed accreditation authorities to make recommendations regarding accreditation standards and assess courses and providers (AHPRA 2011).

The 2006 COAG meeting envisaged that professions legislatively regulated in all states and territories would be brought into the Scheme. However, some variations and further decisions were required. A decision was taken to include podiatry as one of the initial groupings, even though it was not regulated in all jurisdictions, and the IGA recognized a 2007 decision by the Australian Health Ministers to prioritize work on the inclusion of Aboriginal and Torres Strait

Table 9.3 Professions regulated under the Health Practitioner Regulation National Law Act 2009

2010 entrants	2012 entrants
Chiropractors	Aboriginal and Torres Strait Islander Health practitioners
Dental practitioners†	Chinese Medicine practitioners
Medical practitioners	Medical Radiation practitioners
Nurses and Midwives	Occupational Therapists
Optometrists	
Osteopaths	
Pharmacists	
Physiotherapists	
Podiatrists	
Psychologists	

Note: † Includes dentists, dental therapists, dental hygienists, oral health therapists and dental prothesists

Islander Health Workers in the Scheme.[8] Under the auspices of the Australian Health Ministers' Advisory Council (AHMAC), a Regulatory Impact Statement (AHMAC 2009) was developed by the Governance Committee of the National Registration and Accreditation Implementation Project. This provided a mechanism for determining which partially regulated professions should join the scheme, and highlighted issues including costs, benefits and the principles contained in the IGA, affirming that the protection of the public interest was paramount and that no value was ascribed to protection of professional interests (AHMAC 2009). It also reviews existing regulatory arrangements and outlines the principles adopted to determine the basis for this significant legislative change.

As is indicated in Table 9.3, four professions are slated for inclusion in 2012, including Chinese medicine, which had previously only been regulated in Victoria. This has given rise to discussion from naturopaths and those who practise western herbal medicine in relation to the consequences of perceived inconsistent regulatory arrangements (Wardle 2010). Further, following the launch of the Scheme, AHMAC released draft guidelines seeking comment from stakeholders and the community on options for the regulation of health professions not registered under the Scheme, and in particular assessing the scope for involvement by health care complaints style bodies (AHMAC 2011).

We turn now to some other decisions required to introduce the Scheme. A detailed account of the process involved in turning the limited direction of chief and health ministers into an operational entity has recently been provided by the project director guiding the implementation of the scheme from May 2008 to December 2009 (Morauta 2011). This account provides an insight into the technical introduction of the scheme, and the complexities involved. In it, she

8 The only jurisdiction in which podiatry was not regulated was the Northern Territory (AHMAC 2009), which would be expected to have a very small workforce.

highlights another of its remarkable features. Earlier in the chapter, we recognized the potential challenges of developing political consensus across one federal and eight state and territory governments. The process of creating a single national entity, which required the powers previously vested through the state and territory parliaments to adhere to a new structure via a national law, was quite an undertaking. The adoption of a national law model saw three separate pieces of legislation initially passed in Queensland and then similar legislation passed in each of the states and territories.

The Commonwealth did not need to pass the same legislation as the states and territories, as it did not have powers to cede to a national body. However, there were nonetheless consequential legislative changes required, especially in relation to provisions for access to funding and insurance mechanisms under the remit of the Commonwealth (*Health Practitioner Regulation (Consequential Amendments) Bill 2010 (Cth)*). The process of Commonwealth legislation also enabled ventilation of concerns about detailed provisions of the legislation through inquiries conducted by the Senate (upper house) committees (Senate Community Affairs Committee 2010). These garnered some 1,000 submissions and 2,000 attendees at fora around Australia (Morauta 2011). Any shift in regulatory frameworks construed as reducing the influence of any or all of the professions would inevitably be closely examined and potentially resisted and stymied (De Voe and Short 2003, Palmer and Short 2010). In relation to previous experience in the state of Victoria, it has been noted that any 'reform is likely to generate considerable emotion within the professions because it challenges traditional hierarchies, the established division of labour, and the autonomy and control of the professions over their work' (Carlton 2005: 42). The importance and potential of the Scheme had certainly not been lost on those who were to be regulated, and on the regulatory entities that would disappear.

Conclusion

The Scheme has brought together and streamlined diversity from across eight states and territories and ten professions, and covers the major health professions within Australia. It drew together the registration of individual practitioners and the accreditation of the education and training required to ensure that practitioners have the appropriate knowledge and skills to undertake the roles they would be registered to undertake. As a paper exploring future reform of the health workforce contends, Australia has now made significant strides in terms of national consistency in comparison to other nations that operate in a federal structure (Health Workforce Australia 2011). The changes that have been made reflect a determination to: translate objectives of safety and protection of the public to regulation; enable improved workforce planning with consolidated national data (hence supporting access to health care); and facilitate improved practice with consistent registration requirements concerning recent practice and continuing professional education.

Health workforce governance reform is rarely achieved easily. It is generally undertaken not as a means to an end in itself, but to address problems that are shared across governments and the communities they serve. This was the case with the reform of health practitioner registration and accreditation, in which there was previously a confused diversity of regulatory regimes in place.

This chapter has described the problems that the national reform instituted in 2010 was designed to address, the wider political environment in which it was launched and the process by which the new regulatory system was developed and introduced, using the framework developed by Kingdon to analyse the evolution of the Scheme. There were both enduring policy problems and focusing events associated with this structural change to the governance of Australia's health workforce. It presents a complexity ripe for further analysis (Pacey, Short and Harley 2010), including a further assessment of the role of Patel and other cases as focusing events, and their influence in determining the details of the Scheme. The introduction of this Scheme marks a watershed in health workforce governance in Australia. With the passage of time, we will be more able to fully assess the effects of this change and determine the extent to which the Scheme, as operationalized, has delivered on the intention of providing best practice regulation to support the provision of safe health care to the Australian community.

References

Allsop, J. 2006. Regaining trust in medicine: professional and state strategies. *Current Sociology*, 54(4), 621–36.

ACCC (Australian Competition and Consumer Commission) and Australian Health Workforce Officials' Committee. 2005. *Review of Australian Specialist Medical Colleges: Report to Australian Health Ministers*. Canberra: Commonwealth of Australia.

AHMAC (Australian Health Ministers' Advisory Council). 2009. *Regulatory Impact Statement for the Decision to Implement the Health Practitioner Regulation National Law* Canberra.

AHMAC. 2011. *Options for Regulation of Unregistered Health Practitioners*. Adelaide.

AHMC (Australian Health Ministers' Conference). 2004a. *Australian Health Ministers Agree on Nationally Consistent Approach to Medical Registration: Joint Communiqué*.

AHMC. 2004b. *National Health Workforce Strategic Framework*.

AHPRA (Australian Health Practitioners Regulation Agency). 2011. *Accreditation Authorities*. [Online]. Available at: http://www.ahpra.gov.au/Education/Accreditation-Authorities.aspx [accessed: 30 August 2011].

AIHW (Australian Institute of Health and Welfare). 1992. *Australia's Health 1992: The Third Biennial Report of the Australian Institute of Health and Welfare*. Canberra: Commonwealth of Australia.

Australian Government. 2002. *Intergenerational Report 2002–2003*. Canberra: Commonwealth of Australia.

Australian Government. 2008. *Work as a Doctor in Australia: Area of Need*. [Online]. Available at: http://www.health.gov.au/Internet/otd/publishing.nsf/content/work-AON [accessed: 1 May 2011].

Australian Government. 2010. *2010–2011 Budget Overview*, Canberra: Commonwealth of Australia.

Bird, S. 2010. Mandatory reporting of health practitioners: notifiable conduct. *Australian Family Physician*, 39(8), 593–4.

Birkland, T.A. 1998. Focusing events, mobilization and agenda setting. *Journal of Public Policy*, 18(1), 53–74.

Carlton, A.-L. 2005. National models for regulation of the health professions. *Law in Context*, 23 (2), 21–51.

COAG (Council of Australian Governments). 2006a. *Health Workforce: National Professional Registration (Attachment B: COAG* Communiqué 14 July 2006). [Online]. Available at: http://www.coag.gov.au/coag_meeting_outcomes/2006–07–14/docs/attachment_b_health_workforce_registration.pdf [accessed: 1 May 2011].

COAG. 2006b. *Health Workforce: National Accreditation (Attachment C: COAG* Communiqué 14 July). [Online]. Available at: http://www.coag.gov.au/coag_meeting_outcomes/2006–07–14/docs/attachment_c_health_workforce_accreditation.pdf [accessed: 1 May 2011].

COAG. 2007. *Council of Australian Governments' Meeting 13 April 2007 Communiqué*. [Online]. Available at: http://www.coag.gov.au/coag_meeting_outcomes/2007–04–13/docs/coag130407.pdf [accessed: 1 May 2011].

COAG. 2008a. *Intergovernmental Agreement for a National Registration and Accreditation Scheme for the Health Professions*. [Online]. Available at: http://www.ahwo.gov.au/documents/National%20Registration%20and%20Accreditation/NATREG%20-%20Intergovernmental%20Agreement.pdf [accessed 1 May 2011]

COAG. 2008b. National Partnership Agreement to Delivery a Seamless Economy. [Online]. Available at: http://www.coag.gov.au/intergov_agreements/federal_financial_relations/docs/national_partnerships/seamless_national_economy_np.rtf [accessed: 1 May 2011].

Cohen, M.D., March, J.G. and Olsen, J.P. 1972. A garbage can model of organizational choice. *Administrative Science Quarterly*, 17(1), 1–25.

Commonwealth of Australia Constitution Act 1900 (Cth).

Davies, G. 2005. *Queensland Public Hospitals Commission of Inquiry*. Brisbane: Queensland Government.

De Voe, J.E. 2003. A policy transformed by politics: the case of the 1973 Australian Community Health Program. *Journal of Health Policy, Politics and the Law*, 28(1), 77–108.

De Voe, J.E. and Short, S.D. 2003. A shift in the historical trajectory of medical dominance: the case of Medibank and the Australian doctors' lobby. *Social Science and Medicine*, 57(2), 343–53.

Elks, S. 2010. Jayant Patel facing life in jail over patients' deaths. *The Australian*. [Online]. 30 June. Available at: http://www.theaustralian.com.au/news/nation/jayant-patel-facing-life-in-jail-over-patients-deaths/story-e6frg6nf-1225885927915 [accessed: 30 August 2011].

Flynn, J. 2010. *Lessons learned, changes made*. Paper to the 9th International Conference. International Association of Medical Regulatory Authorities (IAMRA), Philadelphia USA. 2010. Available at: http://www.iamra.com/pdf/conferece-2010-joanna-flynn.pdf (sic) [accessed: 1 May 2011].

Government of South Australia. 2010. *2010–2011 Budget Overview: Budget Paper 1*. [Online]. Available at: http://www.treasury.sa.gov.au/dtf/budget/publications_and_downloads/current_budget.jsp [accessed: 1 May 2011].

Harvey, K. and Faunce, T. 2005. A critical analysis of overseas-trained doctor (otd) factors in the Bundaberg Base Hospital Surgical Inquiry. *Law in Context*, 23(2), 73–91.

Health Practitioner Regulation Act 2009 (NSW).

Health Practitioner Regulation National Law Act 2009 (Qld).

Health Practitioner Regulation National Law (WA) Act 2010.

Health Workforce Australia 2011. *National Health Workforce Innovation and Reform Strategic Framework for Action: Background Paper*. Adelaide: Health Workforce Australia.

James, A. and Francis, K. 2011. Mandatory professional education: what is the prognosis? *Collegian – Journal of the Royal College of Nursing Australia*. 18(3), 131–6.

Jolly, R, 2010. Health Practitioner Regulation (Consequential Amendments) Bill 2010. *Bills Digest – Parliamentary Library*. [Online]. Available at: http://www.aph.gov.au/Library/pubs/bd/2009–10/10bd132.pdf [accessed: 12 September 2011].

Kingdon, J.W. 2011. *Agendas, Alternatives and Public Policies*. 2nd Edition. Boston: Longman.

Marszalek, J. 2010. Patel-type saga unlikely to occur: govt. *The Sydney Morning Herald*. [Online]. 30 June. Available at: http://news.smh.com.au/breaking-news-national/pateltype-saga-unlikely-to-occur-govt-20100630-zkeb.html [accessed: 1 May 2011].

Masso, M. and Eagar, K. 2009. Do public inquiries improve health care?, in *Patient Safety First: Responsive Regulation in Health Care*, edited by J. Healy and P. Dugdale. Sydney: Allen & Unwin, 318–40.

McDonald, F. 2010. The regulation of health professionals, in *Health Law in Australia*, edited by B. White, F. McDonald and L. Willmott. Sydney: Thomson Reuters (Professional) Australia, 509–55.

McGrath, B.P. 2004. Integration of overseas-training doctors into the Australian medical workforce. *Medical Journal of Australia*, 181(11/12), 640–42.

Morauta, L. 2011. Implementing a COAG reform using the national law model: Australia's national registration and accreditation scheme for health practitioners. *Australian Journal of Public Administration*, 70(1), 75–83.

Mutual Recognition Act 1992(Cwth)

Pacey, F., Short, S.D. and Harley, K. 2010. The Patel case and its consequences for health workforce governance in Australia: Rapid Response. *British Medical Journal*. [Online] Available at: http://www.bmj.com/content/341/bmj.c3646.extract/reply#bmj_el_244056 [accessed: 1 May 2011].

Palmer, G. and Short, S. 2010. *Health Care and Public Policy: An Australian Analysis*. 4th Edition. Melbourne: Palgrave Macmillian.

Productivity Commission Act 1998 (Cth).Productivity Commission. 2005a. *Economic Implications of an Ageing Australia.* Canberra: Productivity Commission.

Productivity Commission. 2005b. *Impacts of Advances in Medical Technology in Australia*. Canberra: Productivity Commission.

Productivity Commission. 2005c. *Australia's Health Workforce*. Canberra: Productivity Commission.

Queensland Government 2010. *State Budget 2010 2011, Budget Strategy and Outlook, Budget Paper No. 2*. [Online]. Available at: http://www.budget.qld.gov.au/budget-papers/2010–11/bp2–2010–11.pdf [accessed: 1 May 2011].

Reid, M.A. 2002. Reform of the Australian Health Care Agreements: progress or political ploy? *Medical Journal of Australia*, 177(6), 310–12.

Salter, B. 2002. Medical regulation: new politics and old power structures. *Politics*, 22(2), 59–67.

Senate Community Affairs Committee 2010. *Health Practitioner Regulation (Consequential Amendment) Bill 2010 [Provisions]*. Canberra: Commonwealth of Australia.

Thomas, H. 2007. *Sick to Death: A* Manipulative Surgeon and a Health System in Crisis – A Disaster Waiting to Happen. Sydney: Allen & Unwin.

United Kingdom Department of Health. 2007. *Trust, Assurance and Safety: The Regulation of Health Professionals* (White Paper). (Cm 7013) London: HMSO.

Walton, M. 2010. How the Patel case has changed the world of health care for ever. *Crikey*. [Online]. 5 July. Available at: http://www.crikey.com.au/2010/07/05/how-the-jayant-patel-case-has-changed-the-world-of-health-care-for-ever/ [accessed: 1 May 2011].

Wardle, J. 2010. The national registration and accreditation scheme: what would inclusion mean for Naturopathy and Western Herbal Medicine? Part I – the legislation. *Australian Journal of Medical Herbalism*, 22(4), 113–18.

Chapter 10
Governance Challenges for Primary Health Care

Paul Dugdale

Governance of the work done by health professionals in primary health care is complex and undergoing rapid transformation. It has an additional dimension of complexity compared to the governance of care based in large institutions because institution based health care workers do reach out from their institution into the community to provide primary care, and there interact with community based health care workers and many agencies outside the health sector altogether. To further complicate things, the primary health care workforce is being asked to shoulder some of the most complex challenges facing the health sector – this is why the World Health Report of 2008, devoted to primary health care, was titled 'Now, more than ever' (WHO 2008).

To help gain some insight into the challenges facing this complex field, the first half of this chapter gives a brief account of the context for health workforce regulation and a thumbnail sketch of the demographic and epidemiological challenges facing primary health care. It then shows how several strands of social and political theory can be brought to bear on the issue of health workforce governance. At a high level, the governmentality approach inspired by the work of Michel Foucault in the late 1970s (Foucault 2007) provides a way of focusing on the pervasive systems of thought and styles of rationality at work in contemporary governance. At a more practical level, political analyses of multilevel governance provide a range of empirical insights into how different layers of government collaborate in policy formation and implementation (Hooghe and Marks 2001).

The second half of the chapter moves to a more detailed level to examine the regional governance of primary health care. It draws upon the author's own practice and research work with Australian colleagues on health system culture topics such as inter-professional learning and the clinical logistics of chronic disease management. The conclusion proposes a multilevel governance challenge for transforming the culture of the health workforce toward better chronic disease management, through a three-part approach. This involves supporting the shift of health service providers to becoming more sophisticated knowledge workers, the provision of clinical units with monthly quality of care performance information, and support for improved patient health literacy.

The work of John Braithwaite and colleagues on responsive regulation and networked governance (Braithwaite et al. 2007) is helpful for understanding the way regulatory agencies must recognize and work with each other in order to govern something as diverse as the health workforce in any sort of coherent way. Governing the health workforce is of course related to governing a wide range of other things that affect the health of the population. However, if we were to analyse the statutes regulating the health system, those regulating the conduct of health professionals would stand out as certainly having the longest lineage, but perhaps as having the least direct reference to the myriad other statutes effective in the health sector . Later statutes dealing with health facility licensing, insurance regulation, benefit payment and the like, while far from cohesive, do essentially recognize the close connection between what can be done, where it can be done, and who is to pay for it. Yet clearly, everything in health is done by someone, most of it decided upon and carried out by health professionals, so the historical isolation of the statutes specifically regulating the professions has given way in practice to a network of governing agencies deploying closely interwoven strategies – often pulling in somewhat different directions, sometimes working in strategic harmony, sometimes tripping over each other.

In the modern world of international treaties, organized economic cooperation and increasing transnational flows of technology, expertise and forms of organization, the governance of the health workforce has become a global concern. The lateral connections between the health workforce and other parts of the economy are increasingly being considered in policy and industry strategy, most obviously the connections to education, welfare and community service provision. At the same time, the health workforce is increasingly mobile internationally. This is due to a series of trends including investment in education in developing countries (often driven by international aid strategies) leading to exporting of skilled workers and repatriation of earnings, facilitated by labour shortages around the globe in many professions including medicine and nursing.

These trends tend to tie up the health workforce, limiting their autonomy and prescribing how they are to practise, how they are to be trained, registered, supervised and so on. This book explores the proposition that these evolutions are creating a networked governance continuum that spans matters of access to services, matters of good health workforce education, and the provision of safe, high quality care by those services. Such a continuum makes it possible, and important, for analysts and policy makers to ask how health workforce regulation fits in relation to the broad sweep of government policy ambitions, as well as to the extensive suite of governance strategies at play in the health sector. How do globalisation and the increasing vogue for delegating tasks to multilevel governance arenas affect such ambitions and strategies? How coherent are the various components of the health system, and how does this coherence or lack of it affect access, management and safety? Governance, succinctly defined by Foucault as the conduct of conduct, is becoming increasingly concerned with the government of government. What direction can we give to this trend in order for it to better support the strivings of health professionals and to assure the health of the public they serve?

Emerging Challenges for Primary Care

This chapter is based primarily on the current situation in Australia. Australia has a certain uniqueness in its governmental structure and culture, in the history of its health system, and in the dynamics of its population and its burden of disease. On the other hand, it shares many features with other nations: it is a democratic federation; it has a public sector driven health system; and it has an aging population with the burden of disease tilting toward chronic, lifestyle-related conditions. But if we consider things only at the level of common features shared by several nations – and there are many that share several of the broad features just noted – then we will miss the rich particularities that drive the materiality and historicity of what is happening. All serious analysis has to be local to a significant extent. Hopefully the reader will forgive the Australia-centredness of this account, and be able to see the similarities or relevance to their country of interest.

Health systems are going through a period of reform in primary health and community care whereby community-based allied health and nursing services could become more integrated with general practice medicine. At the same time there is an increased pace of evolution in this broader primary care sector's relationship to specialist medical and hospital-based services. In Australia, this is the relationship that new regional bodies called 'Medicare Locals' are being created to govern. Current reforms in England's network of Primary Care Trusts are addressing similar concerns, although of course in a different historical and political context. The aims, mechanisms, and sensitivities of this new nexus of governing are important things to explore and speculate upon.

Many of the world's countries, including Australia, are also going through a transition on three fronts – demography, epidemiology and technology – that each contributes to a large rise in demand by older people for health services related to chronic disease. The argument here is that access to chronic disease management through primary health care and community services is looming as one of the biggest challenges facing the health system over the coming decade.

Demographically, the baby boomers of the western world (born 1946 to 1960, the decade and a half of high fertility that followed the end of World War Two) have started to retire. The bulk of working baby boomers will retire between 2011 and 2025. However, the leading edge of retired baby boomers (born 1946 to 1956, who in 2011 are aged 55–65) finished or will finish work prior to age 65 due to ill health or finding themselves unemployable due to structural change of the labour market. This largely male group is paralleled by a group of female boomers who have not worked since they had children in the 1960s and 70s. As they age, these demographics will create a big expansion of non-working, over 65 people with the usual rapid increase in chronic disease burden that this age group can expect.

Epidemiologically, there are important transitions occurring in diabetes, smoking and all-cause age-specific mortality (for detailed Australian statistics, see the Australian Institute of Health and Welfare reports drawn from the National Health survey). The incidence of diabetes type two is increasing, at least in part due to the increasing incidence of obesity. In due course, this will be reflected by increasing rates of the complications of diabetes: chronic heart diseases, chronic kidney disease and stroke. Baby boomers – particularly men – have a somewhat lower likelihood of having smoked 20 pack-years of tobacco cigarettes than their predecessors, but a considerably higher likelihood than the younger cohort of adults. With some lag, the declining prevalence of this risk factor will drive a reduction in the incidence of chronic lung disease, coronary artery disease, chronic kidney disease, peripheral vascular disease and stroke. Nevertheless, smoking related diseases will remain a large fraction of the total burden of disease amongst baby boomers in retirement, remembering that the lower rates of disease will be counteracted by the larger number of people in the cohort and increasing expectations of active treatment. It will be many years before the actual numbers of people in Australia with smoking related diseases being managed by health professionals shows any noticeable decline.

More broadly, baby boomer life expectancy will increase compared to the current generation of retirees due to the reduction in all causes mortality in post-retirement age groups. Some of this is driven by the healthier childhood and better nutrition experienced by the boomers (remembering that the previous cohort lived through World War Two during their childhood or early adulthood), the wider availability of vaccination, trauma care and antibiotics during their childhood and early adulthood, and perhaps to their higher levels of education and income. Some of it will arise from better access to the effective treatments now available for cardiovascular disease, diabetes and lung disease (the big three contributors to the ameliorable burden of disease), as well as a large number of diseases of lesser population impact.

Arranging access to effective treatments for increasing numbers of people with chronic disease is thus one of the most important known challenges looming upon the Australian health system. This is not a simple matter. To achieve it, the health workforce will need to grow, and will have to change the way it practises. For many people with chronic disease, effective care requires cooperation between a sizable multidisciplinary group of providers. Coordination of care and interdisciplinary practice are key skills the workforce requires to do this, not just because without it care is fragmented, but also because for many more complex patients, care providers without coordination tread on each other's toes, waste time in low-level conflicts, and make arguments to the patient for different prioritization of problems. The current spate of reforms in Australia's primary health and community care sector will be judged as successful or not to the extent that they respond to this challenge. And yet in Australia at least, the policy drivers for the reforms have been couched in terms of hospital cost efficiency, hospital waiting list reductions and health workforce shortages (COAG 2011). While these are of course important at the time of writing the challenge of improving chronic disease management has not been directly addressed by the national policy agenda. It will nevertheless loom as the crucial primary health care reform challenge from the population health perspective for the regional governance bodies – local hospital networks and Medicare Locals – that are currently being created. This is becoming abundantly clear to the health workforce, which is confronted by the rising tide of people with chronic diseases, and the increasing expectation for better care that these people have. The question then becomes, will the new governance bodies be relevant to the health workforce as it struggles to change the culture of chronic disease management within a large health system not renowned for being easy to change.

The Growth of Multilevel Governance

Medicare Locals and local hospital network boards have been created through the 2011 agreement between the national and state governments (COAG 2011). Governance of health in a federal nation like Australia is unavoidably multilevel, as neither national nor state level governments in the post-World War Two era are able to ignore healthcare without facing a backlash from their citizens. This need for multilevel governance is in itself important to understand as we untangle the way the health workforce is governed and seek to inform future policy development and system change.

At its core, multilevel governance moves functions and authority across jurisdictions After detailed study of multilevel governance in the European Union, a number of commentators have noted that such multilevel governance arenas are characterized by continual negotiation (Hooghe and Marks 2001). In multilevel governance arenas, objectives can rarely be made then taken for granted. Given the constantly shifting political agendas of the various governments that constitute such arenas, negotiation is continual, with even what is the subject of negotiation changing in unpredictable ways.

In Australia, multilevel governance has expanded at the same time as there has been a shift from cooperative to integrated federalism (Fenna 2009). The key proposition here is that from the mid 1980s onward, and symbolized by the renaming of the Premiers Conference as the Council of Australian Governments (COAG) in 1992, state and federal governments increased their interdependencies from some level of formal cooperation to one of a much more integrated pursuit of mutual policy objectives. This has been reflected in an intensification of things they worked on together, and numerous attempts at implementing more complex joint policies and programmes.

Multilevel governance is now indispensable in fields, such as education, natural resource management, taxation and corporate governance, where functions and authority overlap in Australia's federal system. In health, as in these other areas, intergovernmental bodies have become important operating parts of the government landscape. These include supra-national bodies established under the auspices of the United Nations or its subsidiary bodies (such as the World Health Assembly and the World Health Organization it governs) or between groups of nations, as well as sub-national bodies established between the national and provincial governments of a country. In Australia, COAG comprises the Prime Minister, the premiers of the states and the chief ministers of the territories. Below this are the ministerial councils of various portfolios, then a cascade of subordinate committees made up of bureaucrats from the two levels of government, often together with independent statutory office holders and non-government actors from various industry and consumer bodies at the table. We can take the word 'comitology' from the Eurocrats – the term is in common parlance in the corridors of the European Commission – to refer to the field of knowledge about the creation, structure and operation of these myriad committees that do so much of the work of government nowadays.

This has certainly been the case in the health sector since the introduction of the Medicare national health insurance scheme in the mid 1980s by the Federal Government, supported with more or less enthusiasm by the state governments that own and operate the network of public hospitals providing universal access and comprehensive hospital care, upon which Medicare relies. The governance of the health workforce has been at the very centre of a lot of the health matters that have been addressed in this evolving environment. At a summary level, we can say that the expansion of the national government's interest and activity in governing health financing has been followed closely by a comprehensive expansion of its interest in the governance of the health workforce (see Dugdale 2008 for a more elaborate version of this argument). This has included an expansion of nationally funded university training places, the creation of numerous national programmes to improve the quality and safety of care provided by the workforce (Healy and Dugdale 2009), and the transition of professional registration from the states to the national level (Healy, Maffi and Dugdale 2008).

The development of multilevel governance arenas in health over this period has coincided with an intensification of regionalism, with all Australian public sector health service delivery organizations having undergone an energetic arearization of their administrations over the last 30 years. This has also occurred in other sectors as well as in other parts of the world. Interestingly, in Europe, 'no policy area is more centralized at the national level in the year 2000 than in 1950, nor is there a single country in which regional governance has become weaker over the same period' (Hooghe and Marks 2001: xii).

A self-aware culture of multilevel governance has been able to emerge in Australia with some distinctiveness: an Australian comitology. This is evident not just in the number and style of intergovernmental bodies now in existence, but also by the way new policy development more often than not generates a vigorous imagining of yet more multilevel governance possibilities. The governance of the health workforce has been no exception.

With the election of the Howard government in Australia in 1996, the new health minister Dr Michael Wooldridge recognized a coming shortage of health workers in medicine, nursing and allied health. This shortage has since materialized as a worldwide problem. Wooldridge led the development of policy discussions between the national and state governments on health workforce education, which led fairly swiftly (over the following 15 years) to the establishment of 10 new medical schools and a doubling of medical graduates in Australia, as well as a large increase in medical immigration. There were similar expansions in nursing and allied health education. This university based educational effort was meshed to complementary expansions of undergraduate and postgraduate health service placements, which drove a spill over from their traditional location in teaching hospitals out into primary health care workplaces. This in turn has resulted in a growth of university health faculty members with a primary health care background. In addition to teaching, this faculty is driving a concomitant growth in clinical research into this sector. The central locus for coordinating this broad expansion has been the various incarnations of the Commonwealth state health workforce committee within the COAG committee structure under the health ministers, which eventually evolved into the Australian Health Workforce Agency, a statutory body created in 2008.

The Governance of Primary Health Care

Primary health care services include private general medical practices and allied health practices, state government operated community health services incorporating nursing and allied health professionals, and not for profit services that often receive public funding. Major players in the governance of these services in Australia include the Royal Australasian College of General Practitioners, large public regional health services, state health departments, and the Commonwealth Department of Health and Ageing.

Foucault has pointed out that national governments exhibit slow changing systems of thought, which he termed their 'governmentality' (Foucault 2007), meaning the mentality of government or governmental rationality (Burchell, Gordon and Miller 1991). Two historical governmental modes that concern us here are the liberal and the welfarist modes of governing (Barry, Osborne and Rose 1996). The liberal mode of governing is to support the various functional groupings that emerge in civil society to govern themselves in relation to their common interest (Burchell 1993). It has had many incarnations since its first description in political theory by John Locke in the late seventeenth century, and suffers from confusion with the many other meanings and uses of the term 'liberal' (from the Latin word for free).

The welfarist mode of direct government service provision that burgeoned in the 1960s and 1970s grew from the wartime command economies. As post-war welfare enterprises burgeoned, the distance grew between the administrators and those they administered for, and along with the divergence of perspectives on the actual purpose of welfare, welfarist programmes became unstable. The retreat from the welfare state in the 1980s (Graycar 1983) was driven as much by a radical disenchantment with the welfare state (Papadakis and Taylor-Gooby 1987, Offe 1984) as by the small government movement. Neoliberalism (Thatcherism,

Reagonomics, and Rogernomics in New Zealand) saw an expanded use of market-like mechanisms for state services. Extensive use was made of contracting to achieve government at a distance (Yeatman 1995, Rose 2000). Since then there has been considerable equivocation between welfarist direct service provision and neoliberal contracting out (Davis, Sullivan and Yeatman 1996), and there has also been the creation of spheres of mixed state and non-government actors working on governance together (Ericson and Stehr 2000).

This can be seen in the current Australian efforts to intensify the governance of primary health care. Regional Divisions of General Practice, established in the mid 1990s by grants from the Commonwealth government, will evolve into Primary Health Care Organisations: 'Medicare Locals' whose purpose is to coordinate and support the development of primary health care services in their region. The wholesale transfer of community health services from state government operated or funded health services to Commonwealth control, which was to be exercised by Medicare Locals, had been proposed by Prime Minister Rudd and agreed by COAG. However, following Rudd's replacement by Prime Minister Gillard this was dropped by COAG in February 2011. Of course, state governments may still contract Medicare Locals to provide or subcontract government funded community health services, and this is likely to occur in a piecemeal way.

Care shifting between primary and tertiary services is occurring in both directions. Because the states have responsibility for specialist medical and allied health services, but not for general practice, care shifting between primary and tertiary services can also amount to cost shifting between funders. This makes it central to the 'blame game' that featured heavily in the Rudd Labor Government's health rhetoric.

One of the tasks faced by Medicare Locals in the governance of primary health care is the reformation of the working relationships between general practitioners, medical specialists in various disciplines, allied health professionals and nurses. Two other major developments are also occurring in Australia in relation to specialist and allied health services, with less fanfare but possibly more importance for the transformation of primary health care. On the one hand, state government funded specialty health services (renal, cardiac, respiratory, endocrine) are increasing their community service offerings for people with their conditions of interest. On the other, the Commonwealth is gradually adding allied health benefits into the Medicare Benefits Schedule. This or related schemes now provides benefits for nursing, physiotherapy, dentistry, occupational therapy, psychology, and optometry services. While service volumes are small (except for optometry, which was included in the schedule from its inception in 1983), and rules surrounding these benefits are quite tight, volumes are growing steadily.

The increasing burden of chronic disease is changing the main game for primary health care and community services, and responding to this change will be a key objective for Medicare Locals. The World Health Report 2008 (WHO 2008), 'Primary health care, now more than ever', outlines the arguments for primary healthcare as the cornerstone of health systems, noting that while it may not be cheaper than the alternatives, it does provide better health outcomes.

Current Australian governance of primary health care is fragmented and lacks energy. Will Medicare Locals, creatures of COAG, end the blame game in primary health care? The tendering for Medicare Locals is perhaps the first time government has tendered out governance itself. However, neither statutory authority nor programme funds are being transferred to them at this stage. Medicare Locals will thus effectively be consultative bodies with strong lobbying credentials but little real power to govern the local workforce. Some may sizzle, many will fizzle. The remainder of this chapter considers the governance challenges facing local primary care governance bodies as they provide what steerage they can to the local health workforce engaged in primary health care provision. In some senses, primary health care may in fact be ungovernable (Stehr and Ericson 2000). Building trust into the system will be crucial, as it always is in multilevel governance arenas. The creation and availability of relevant, comparative data could drive transparency and invigorate reform. Based on wider experience with multilevel governance, we can expect to see Medicare Locals invest a fair bit of energy in the formation and reformation of objectives. This continual negotiation will foreclose on their ability to deliver through management by objectives. Corporate governance will loom large, with a heavy strategy and compliance burden falling on potentially ill-equipped boards. A key challenge for company boards and public sector advisory councils is to set the tone and direction of culture change among those they govern. This requires a wide view of the company or agency's place in the world, its business, and the ethics of how to conduct it.

Toward a Culture of Care-life Balance

In a sense, it is patients that govern what the health workforce does. By getting sick, by demanding treatment and care, they dictate the hour-by-hour work of the health professional. This is an important sense and, to open up a discussion of it, here is a brief digression about the birth of the modern novel. The novel is a fictionalized story based on our universally true inner self. The modern form of the English-language novel is often considered to have emerged in the mid eighteenth century, with Daniel Defoe's 'Robinson Crusoe' often cited as the first in the genre. An extraordinary tale of survival – based very loosely on an actual event of a shipwrecked mariner who was rescued to tell his story – the book gives a psychological account of living life that a wide range of readers could intimately relate to. Literary theorists have argued that the reader's capability and willingness to relate to the novel is at least as important as the telling of the tale in founding the success of the genre. Jonathan Franzen, the Pulitzer prize winning novelist, has summarized as follows:

> The great literary invention of the eighteenth century was, thus, not simply a genre but an attitude *toward* that genre. Our state of mind when we pick up a novel today – our knowledge that it's a work of imagination; our willing suspension of disbelief in it – is in fact one half of the novel's essence (Franzen 2011).

Franzen's insight is based on an understanding that cultural innovation requires the meshing of the activities of those producing culture and those consuming it, even though the author's task when writing a novel is vastly different from the public's task in reading it. Similarly, the production of health services by the health workforce is vastly different from their consumption by patients. The task facing those who would govern cultural innovation in health care is to understand these very different perspectives, and drive the effective meshing of the two worlds. More specifically, because of the demographic factors discussed above, the task facing those governing primary health care is to apply themselves to the clash of health system and life world in the field of chronic disease management.

The word 'chronic' comes from the Greek word '*chronos*', meaning time. Chronic disease lasts for a long time. It is often caused by risk factors playing out over a long time. Living with a chronic disease has a big impact on your time. Providing care to people with chronic disease is also quite time consuming. These temporal dimensions of chronic disease management greatly affect both people with chronic disease and the health professionals who care for them Shared understandings about the passing of time develop in any cultural setting. These understandings inform how people coordinate their activities. Such social constructions of time are historically derived and embedded in powerful structures of our society. The social construction of time in the life world of people with chronic illness varies from person to person, but is usually very different from the social construction of time in the complex systems and institutions in which health care providers operate.

The health system is a very intense place to work. It is busy and highly timetabled, with a lot of interacting parts. To make it all work, health services, like most large organizations, have developed intensive timetabling that governs the working lives of the health workforce. The sub-specialities of the health workforce need to be brought back together through multidisciplinary clinics. Bringing these together is a logistical feat of some complexity. Present arrangements in the health care system operate in historical ways that are based upon elaborate timetabling and systems that are attuned to providing acute care for specific episodes of ill health. The patient is relatively passive (and indeed needs to be patient) in these arrangements. The result is an unintentional mismatch between the ongoing health care needs of people with chronic disease and the care that the health system is geared to provide.

Many people with chronic disease are busy professionals who lead highly scheduled lives (perhaps like many readers of this chapter), who get updates to their diaries over the telecommunications network, and live their lives and work in a way which is pretty similar to the institutionalized systems world of the health sector. But a lot of people with chronic disease find themselves slowing down and find it more difficult to get around. Just as their disease progression means that they can do less things in a day, the demands of the health system upon them become greater and greater, compressing out the rest of their lives so that they need to spend a fair bit of time organizing their medications, healthcare and medically prescribed exercise and eating activities.

Patients with chronic diseases generally understand the impact of time use on their disease, and of the disease on their time use. This includes their ability to interact with the health system and to follow health advice about physical activity, food preparation and treatment regimens. Co-morbidities such as musculoskeletal disease and depression have a profound impact on physical mobility and motivation. For indigenous Australians, difficulties in envisioning their future can adversely affect health related actions in the present.

On the one hand, health professionals give detailed advice to patients with chronic disease about how to use their time, especially about exercising, preparing meals and maintaining their social activities. Often, they give advice to patients about their time use ('lifestyle') which is superficial, especially when co-morbidities are present. On the other hand, they also ask patients to attend a lot of consultations, including inconvenient appointments and referral run-arounds, they arrange many medical tests, and ask patients to obtain and consume many medicines. The health system is rife with service delays, and is notorious as an industry for inefficient handling of personal information requiring multiple retellings of complex histories. These problems are compounded by cultural issues and inadequate access for indigenous Australians to mainstream health services.

At best, these requirements for engagement with the health care system take away from the time the patient can follow the lifestyle advice. At worst, the health care system's expectations of patients with chronic disease are contradictory, unrealistic and impossible for even highly motivated patients to adopt.

Those concerned with primary health care policy and governance need to understand the social construction of time in chronic disease management, in a way that informs regional policy development and service reform. Chronic disease management can be improved through policies promoting care-life balance. These would aim to maximize patient quality of life in the present and future; and reorient the culture and day-to-day practices of the health workforce toward the achievement of this balance for their patients.

Australian chronic disease policy offers little to address the tensions that result between the time use patterns of patients and the internal time demands of the health system. Policies supporting patient centred care have some promise, but do not recognize the negative impact of health service culture on patient time use. Information technology developments such as clinical information exchange, online patient support and patient centred appointment scheduling are promising but are not sufficiently connected to the promotion of broader cultural change in health services. Chronic disease policy must recognize the value of rebuilding health system practices to improve patient control over their time use (requiring less patience), and promote more detailed engagement by health professionals in patients' restructuring their time use for increased physical activity, improved food preparation and better disease self-management.

It might be useful to look outside the health system to find strategies that can help us mesh the social construction of time in the system world of the health professional with time use in the life world of the patient. If we look at industry policy, work-life balance policy connects time use at work and at home to the negotiation of increased productivity at work and improved benefits relevant to life outside work. The work-life balance literature argues that work-life balance policy connects time use at work and home to the negotiation of increased productivity at work and improved benefits relevant to life outside work.

In the workforce over the last few decades, women's increased participation in higher education and in the workforce has led to changing dynamics in the work environment, and the phenomenal growth of part-time work since the 1970s can be directly attributed to the labour market meeting the demands of women in the workforce. Along with the development of information technology, this has resulted in more flexible work arrangements and a changing of the way in which time is used and structured to better meet the demands of the individual and the workplace. Surprisingly for some, this has in turn led to increased productivity by organizations that have accommodated a work-life balance for their workers, and the gains have been shared between better profits and higher wages (ILO 2007, Fagan et al forthcoming).

Can we open up a parallel analysis for chronic disease policy, showing how to connect the social construction of time use by patients, carers and health professionals to the improvement of health outcomes for people with chronic disease? Understanding the social construction of time and the significant changes that have occurred in the workplace due to the work-life balance agenda stands in stark contrast to the medical environment where production line thinking or military models of organization are still the dominant way of working. While work-life balance negotiations have occurred in the health sector between staff and management, no such negotiation has occurred between the health system and patient, and the system of rigid and inflexible use of time persists in nearly every area of medical activity. The result is that the systems world of the medical environment, without intention, dominates the world of the patient more and more, leading to much expense for the medical field and less time for patients to attend to their particular health needs.

Systems of Care and Clinical Logistics

Yet health care is not inherently more complicated than many other industries. Think about the hospitality and travel industries for a moment. The hospitality industry accommodates people overnight, pampers them, feeds them, and arranges varied recreational activities. The travel industry moves people around through airports (the only buildings that rival hospitals in complexity) and on airplanes, which are as technologically complex as anything in healthcare. They provide online scheduling, and are intensely client centred, or they go out of business. Imagine if you rang an airline and said 'I'd like to fly to Singapore', and they responded 'sure, how about on Tuesday afternoon in three months' time, we have a spare seat then'. That is unthinkable, yet that is how many parts of the health system deal with patients all the time.

The health sector can adopt some of the customer-focused scheduling technologies used by the hospitality and transport industries to coordinate their workforce. Already available technologies include online booking systems, recall and reminder systems, use of logistics software to schedule long chains of sequential services to optimize the time use of the patient as well as the health professionals, an electronic health record accessible wherever the patient is so they don't need to waste time going through their story over and over, radio-tracking of patients and health professionals so we can all find out where each other is at any point in time. This is particularly important for primary health care, given the way it involves people working across a variety of agencies and institutions.

'E-Health' is often used as a shorthand for this collection of reforms. While lack of adequate investment in information technology in the health sector has been a serious problem, it is important that we do not miss the wood for the trees. The real transformation is toward better cooperation for patient-centred care. Technology may facilitate this, but it is not patient-centred care itself. There is much else that needs to change in addition to the technology.

Systems of care are a series of interactions between health workers and patients. Interactions about care giving involve history taking, physical examination, diagnostic testing, education and advice given including prescriptions and arrangement of treatments. Depending on these components of care are put together, patients can get better or worse outcomes. A simple example is in diabetes. The system of care provided by clinicians should combine diagnosis according to the WHO standards, regular blood sugar monitoring including haemoglobin A1C testing, education for the patient so that they understand the physiology of diabetes, lifestyle change with their diet and exercise, along with regular blood pressure, eye and foot examination. All of those things are combined in a 'cycle of care' that produces better outcomes for patients. In many health care systems, including Australia, insurers tracks this care and if the full cycle is provided, they pay an incentive to the patient's doctor.

None of this was a new invention, it was a new system of care that was theorized as having better outcomes, but only by empirical study could it be proved that it resulted in better biological and health system outcomes. Governing health workforce activity through such pay for performance mechanisms is most effective when the financial incentive is in line with scientific evidence – in which health professionals place great store – and has the political support of the profession (see Chapter 4 in Dugdale 2008). It may be that there is more health gain to be got over the next 10 years from improved systems of care than there is in the entire current pharmaceutical pipeline of new drugs, particularly if research on systems of care and their translation into practice can gather pace. Making systems of care work requires the cooperation of the patients. To optimize this we need to minimize the clash of their life world with the health system. This is why a cultural understanding of how to engage the patient is absolutely central to systems of care research.

Many health systems, including Australia's, have a problem with scheduling. Australia's use of hospitals is at the upper end of OECD countries (OECD 2011). That may not be a good thing because hospitals are dangerous places. They should be the last resort for health care. Community based care, including home care, needs to be expanded, and better organized, if we are to bring our hospitalization rates down. There is little convincing evidence that this substitution will save money, and the WHO cautions against linking the expansion of primary health care to achieving savings (WHO 2008). But for many people, it is better care, with reduced risk of hospital based adverse events. As part of the shift to community based care we need to vigorously address the scheduling problems for chronic disease management, and tackle these with as much ingenuity (and infrastructure) as is currently applied to scheduling surgery.

Logistics, understood as the purposeful movement of people and things in space and time, is central to the provision of health care in large contemporary health systems. It is defined in the Macquarie Dictionary in relation to the military as 'the branch of military science concerned with the transportation and supply, and the movement of bodies of troops', and in relation to industry as 'the planning, implementation, and control of the details of an enterprise, especially the flow of goods, services, or information'.

We need to study the clinical logistics of chronic disease management. Clinical logistics is the logistics of patient-health service provider interactions and the associated flows of therapeutic goods and clinical information. The effective governance of health care requires the elucidation of the factors that optimize clinical logistics for high quality patient cares, in the domains of patient experience, health service culture and organization, and the community sector. A preliminary search of Google Scholar showed that while the term 'clinical logistics' does appear in the medical literature in relation to emergency medicine, procedural medicine, imaging, cancer treatment and rehabilitation, it is not in use in the chronic disease management literature. To open up a research agenda in clinical logistics for better chronic disease management, we need to think carefully about health service organization, including its history, institutions and incentive structures; health service provider culture, with its biases toward episodic care from specific services and disciplines; the distancing of patients and health service providers from the logistical arrangement of their interactions; and applications of information technology that do or promise to improve these arrangements. Concerning the community sector, we need to seek to learn lessons about current logistical difficulties from patient support and advocacy services, such as those provided by local politicians through their electoral officers. Essentially, the research should aim to identify a set of replicable strategies for achieving high quality clinical logistics and show how the achievement of such quality can be measured from our patients' perspective.

Toward Knowledge-based Governance of Culture Change

With institutions, much dispute is centred on the proper content of what Goffman has called 'frames', and within the health system what Strong has called 'role formats' (Strong 1979): what is or is not the correct way of doing this or that activity. This (together with personality conflicts) is what counts as the small 'p' politics within the institution. This type of disputation is typically resolved by the adoption of a policy or standard operating procedure. In that sense, policy is the outcome of politics. This may occur as a one-off fresh creation of a role or the much longer gestation of an oft-repeated moral, technical and politically astute way of solving things. Negotiation and exchange underlie role formats. The ceremonial order of the institution is essentially the sedimented layers of role formats that have built up over the years, including the policies reflecting a myriad of political compromises between participants (Nugus, Greenfield, Kljakovic et al. 2010, Nugus, Greenfield, Travaglia et al. 2010, Strong 1979).

Once something has been done a particular way for perhaps a decade it becomes not just the way we do things around here but the right way to do things, along with a moral overlay that makes it the proper way to do things. In World War Two (with its maximization of distrust between the antagonists), government directed command and control based enterprises invaded every aspect of civilian activity, let alone military life. Hospitals, including the governance of the health workforce within them, seem to have particularly suffered from and built upon this legacy. Creation of one new policy or role format on top of all this does not go very far in changing the culture. The weight of tradition leaves little room for optimism in the capacity of a new board or senior managers to drive major culture change through attention to policy detail. On the contrary, as Francis Fukuyama has pointed out, too many rules can be dysfunctional:

> Past a certain point, the proliferation of rules to regulate wider and wider sets of social relationships becomes not the hallmark of rational efficiency but a sign of social dysfunction. There is usually an inverse relationship between rules and trust: the more people depend on rules to regulate their interactions, the less they trust each other, and vice versa (Fukuyama 1995: 224).

This is one of the central cultural problems hospital management finds itself dealing with.

Against this general dilemma, there is a promising workforce governance strategy that may be transformative. This three part strategy involves promoting the evolution of health professionals as knowledge workers with discretion and judgement; the regular widespread distribution to local clinical units of quality of care performance information about the unit's patients (including patient identity); and promotion of greater patient health literacy, and capacity to take control of their own health care arrangements.

Hospitals have opened up in their alliance with community services, with outreach, and with network development in area health services. They are evolving into knowledge-based institutions. If role formats become knowledge based role formats, then information flows can transform how people perform within those role formats. This is particularly the case if there is scientific literacy amongst professionals, and can be amplified if there is growing health literacy amongst the clientele, because literacy is necessary for information flows to transform knowledge based role formats.

Increasing health literacy should promote inter-professional learning between health workers and patients. That alliance promotes cultural action, particularly if we get to the level of what Nutbeam has called 'critical health literacy' (Nutbeam 2009). Precisely though, what is cultural action? It is social interaction, and social interaction outside of the dominant culture is one of the most powerful forces for change. Community development work often tries to model this. As much of the chronic disease management workforce has discovered for themselves, talking with people with chronic disease in organized and highly literate way is something worth trying. At the whole of clinic level, the clinical audit work of getting more information flowing about the quality of patient care is a powerful form of cultural action. Health professionals like data, and if properly distributed to them they will not be able to avoid talking about it and hopefully that will produce change.

Consider the example of staff in a clinical service unit, primary or tertiary, who are given monthly glomerular filtration rate results for their patients that specifically identifies those patients with chronic kidney disease. In a knowledge-based industry, providing that information transforms staff attention on what needs to be done based on that information. It will help shift the workforce from their current episode based approach, toward better long-term monitoring and continuity of care. Hopefully such information flows will be transformative in a way that just producing new rules and new policies will not.

Ideally, such a governance strategy should be combined with support for changing attitudes of patients so that they become less patient. Could an alliance between patients and specialists, mediated by eHealth technology, actually govern continuing care by the primary health and community-based services sector? For example, could the coming bulge of retiring baby-boomer GPs form an alliance with specialist services, and demand more accessible, better coordinated community-based care for themselves and their age peers? Can health services provide them with better booking systems, online patient-access to results, key indicator tracking, regular patient-feedback tracking, self-management planning with full support, individualized 'textbooks' made up for each patient about their specific diseases, diagnostics, pharmaceuticals and lifestyle … These things will change the culture of health care, but they will need strong support to bring into reality.

We should remember that the next generation of the chronically ill will be better educated than previously, at the same time as their number grows. The retiring baby boomers are reputed to be more self-centred and more demanding of better services. Perhaps the central challenge for the governance of primary care is to feed the expectations of people with chronic disease, and lobby to create channels through which they can negotiate with health services to get what they want.

No one level of governance can run this sort of three-part strategy on its own. For clinical performance information to be aggregated so that benchmark performance can be ascertained, national statistical collection is required. Distribution of monthly quality information to units about their own patients must be governed by the local institution of association of community providers. Investment in the infrastructure to support this will be a matter for hospital owners – state government or private sector. Health workforce education to support the evolution toward more sophisticated knowledge based work, with local interpretation of information and more local discretion, will require close cooperation between universities and health services. Of course, coordinating the overall design of such systems will require discussion at length between the various levels of government. In summary, the whole network of multilevel governance will need to be brought to bear on each of the three parts of the proposed strategy. This is a noble challenge for the governance of primary health care indeed.

References

Barry, A., Osborne,T. and Rose, N. 1996. *Foucault and Political Reason: Liberalism, Neo-Liberalism, and Rationalities of Government*. Chicago: University of Chicago Press.

Boston, J., ed. 1995. *The State Under Contract*. Wellington: Bridgit Williams Books.

Braithwaite, J., Makkai, T. and Braithwaite, V.A. 2007. *Regulating Aged Care: Ritualism and the New Pyramid*. Cheltenham, UK: Edward Elgar.

Burchell, G. 1993. Liberal government and techniques of the self. *Economy and Society*, 22, 267–82.

Burchell, G., Gordon, C. and Miller, P. eds. 1991. *The Foucault effect: Studies in governmentality with two lectures and an interview with Michel Foucault*. London: Harvester Wheatsheaf.

COAG (Council of Australian Governments). 2011. *COAG Health Reform Agreement*. COAG. February.

Davis, G., Sullivan, B. and Yeatman, A. 1996. *A new contractualism?* Melbourne: Macmillan.

Dugdale, P. 2008. *Doing Health Policy in Australia*. Sydney: Allen & Unwin.

Ericson, R.V. and Stehr, N., eds. 2000. *Governing Modern Societies*. Toronto: University of Toronto Press.

Fagan, C. et al. Forthcoming. *The influence of working time arrangements on work–life integration or "balance": A review of the international evidence.* Geneva: International Labour Organization).

Fenna, A. 2009. Federalism, in *The Australian Study of Politics,* edited by R. A. W. Rhodes. Basingstoke, UK: Palgrave Macmillan, 146–59.

Foucault, M. 2007. *Lectures at the College de France, 1977–78: Security, Territory and Population*. New York: Palgrave Macmillan.

Franzen, J. 2011. Farther away: 'Robinson Crusoe', David Foster Wallace, and the island of solitude. *The New Yorker*, 18/4/11, 86–94.

Fukuyama, F. 1995. *Trust: The Social Virtues and the Creation of Prosperity*. New York: Free Press.

Goodin, R.E. 1996. *The Theory of Institutional Design*. Cambridge: Cambridge University Press.

Graycar, A. 1983. *Retreat from the welfare state*. Sydney: George Allen & Unwin.

Healy, J. and Dugdale, P., eds. 2009. *Patient Safety First: Responsive Regulation in Health Care*. Sydney: Allen & Unwin.

Healy, J. Maffi, C. and Dugdale, P. 2008. A national medical register for Australia. *Medical Journal of Australia*, 188(4), 247–9.

Hindess, B. 2000. Divide and govern, in *Governing Modern Societies*, edited by R. V. Ericson and N. Stehr. Toronto: University of Toronto Press, 118–40.

Hooghe L. and Marks, G. 2001. *Multi-Level Governance and European Integration*. Lanham MD: Rowman and Littlefield.

International Labour Office (ILO). 2007. *Decent working time: Balancing Workers' Needs with Business Requirements*. Geneva: ILO.

Miller, P. and Rose, N.1990. Governing economic life. *Economy and Society*, 19(1), 1–31.

Nutbeam, D. 2009. Building health literacy in Australia. *Medical Journal of Australia,* 191(10), 525-526.

Nugus, P., Greenfield, D., Kljakovic, M. and Dugdale, P. 2010. *Formal and enacted boundaries in health services*, in TASA 2010 Conference Proceedings: Social Causes, Private Lives, edited by S. Velayutham, N. Ebert and S. Watkins, The Australian Sociological Association, Sydney, 6–9 December 2010.

Nugus, P., Greenfield, D., Travaglia, J., Westbrook, J. and Braithwaite, J. 2010. How and where doctors exercise power: interprofessionalism, collaboration and leadership across a health system. *Social Science & Medicine*, 71, 898–909.

Offe, C. 1984. *Contradictions of the Welfare State*. London: Hutchinson.

Papadakis, E. and Taylor-Gooby, P. 1987. *The Private Provision of Public Welfare: State, Market and Community*. Sussex: Wheatsheaf Books.

Rose, N. 2000. Governing liberty, in *Governing Modern Societies*, edited by R.V. Ericson and N. Stehr. Toronto: University of Toronto Press, 141–76.

Stehr, N. and Ericson R.V. 2000. The ungovernability of modern societies: states, democracies, markets, participation, and citizens, in *Governing Modern Societies*, edited by R.V. Ericson and N. Stehr. Toronto: University of Toronto Press, 3–25.

Strong, P.M. 1979. *The Ceremonial Order of the Clinic: Parents, Doctors and Medical Bureaucracies*. London: RKP.

Williamson, O. 1996. *The Mechanisms of Governance*. Oxford: Oxford University Press.

WHO (World Health Organization). 2008. *World Health Report 2008: Primary health care: Now more than ever*. Geneva: WHO.

Yeatman, A. 1995. Interpreting contemporary contractualism, in *The State Under Contract*, edited by J. Boston. Wellington: Bridgit Williams Books, 124–39.

PART III
Safer Patients

Chapter 11

Regulating the Health Professions: Protecting Professionals or Protecting Patients?

Judith Healy

Introduction

Regulation of the health professions is undergoing reform in many countries: professionals are no longer trusted to regulate themselves free from external scrutiny but rather the state and the public are becoming more involved in regulatory decisions (Dubois et al. 2006). The rationale for current reforms is both to protect professionals and to protect patients. But the interests of these two groups are not always the same. This chapter explores the issue of *cui bono*. Who most benefits from regulatory reforms of the professions: professionals or patients? As Kieran Walshe points out, the '... dichotomy between the public and the professional interest – is central to the development of health professions regulation ...' (Walshe 2009: 144). This chapter examines recent changes to seven regulatory mechanisms and analyses the tensions between competing principles of transparency and confidentiality. A transparency strategy requires regulators to consider whether there is conflict or compatibility between the interests of professionals and the interests of the public.

The use of the term regulation needs some explanation. It is used here in the broad sense of steering the flow of events (Ayres and Braithwaite 1992), rather than the narrow view of enforcement of rules and regulations by the state or its agents. In other words, regulation is about steering and channelling as well as enforcement, and may be undertaken by state or non-state actors, whether external or internal to the field being regulated. Regulators steer through the use of supports (rewards) and sanctions (punishments). This approach is encapsulated in John Braithwaite's 'responsive regulation' model that urges regulators to be responsive to the context, culture and behaviour of those being regulated, to first try soft before hard regulation, but make clear that non-compliance will incur an escalation towards sterner sanctions (Ayres and Braithwaite 1992, Braithwaite et al. 2007). While applied to many sectors of the economy (Braithwaite 2008), the responsive regulation approach is particularly appropriate in the regulation of the health professions given their ethical culture and emphasis upon ongoing learning:

health professionals, after all, seek to do good not harm (Healy 2011, Healy and Braithwaite 2006).

The regulation of medical practitioners, and subsequently other health professionals, has its origins in the nineteenth century state-conferred mandate to practise as the medical profession. A professional mandate can be seen as a victory by an occupational group in protecting the public from charlatans (a good guys interpretation); alternatively, it can be seen as a profession protecting its monopoly by excluding others from its domain (a greedy guys interpretation) (Healy 2011: 97). Several health occupations (about 10 so far in Australia) have succeeded in achieving professional status through a legal mandate from the state. The lobby for legislation to protect professional territories, therefore, is motivated by self-interested professional monopoly as well as by community protection in the public interest (Irvine 2006). The over century-old professional regulation paradigm, however, is in the process of change: change that is strongly contested by some, such as the battle around medical autonomy. The period since the 1980s has seen an international regulatory trend away from mechanisms designed to protect professionals and towards mechanisms designed to protect patients (Walshe 2009: 163). This is accompanied by a shift to pluralist regulation involving multiple regulatory actors and multiple regulatory strategies (Allsop and Jones 2006). Health professionals now inhabit a complex work environment where their performance increasingly is scrutinized – a different world to the earlier more private world of the doctor-patient relationship.

Figure 11.1 depicts a pyramid that locates the regulatory mechanisms discussed in this chapter from a softer base to a sharper apex. While the two most

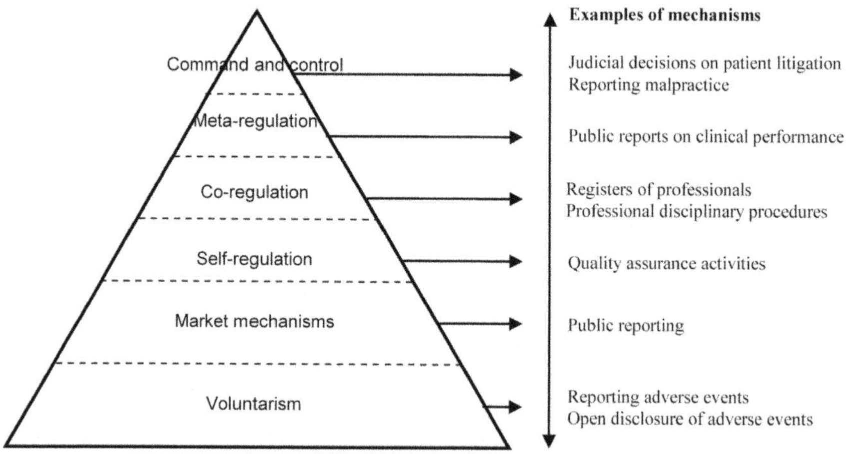

Figure 11.1 Pyramid of selected regulatory mechanisms

common regulatory strategies in the health sector remain voluntary regulation by individuals themselves and self-regulation by the professions, there is also a regulatory shift upwards towards stronger intervention by the state. For example, some previously voluntary mechanisms have been made mandatory, such as the recent requirement upon professionals in Australia to report malpractice by their peers. Stronger regulation involves strategies of co-regulation with the professions (such as accreditation of training programmes), meta-regulation by the state or its agents in ensuring that the professions better regulate themselves (such as public reporting on performance indicators), and enforcement strategies (command and control) at the apex of the pyramid (such as legislation and court orders).

Pluralist Regulation

The field of professional regulation has grown rapidly in the twenty-first century with new external regulatory bodies and mechanisms added to long-standing internal regulation by professional colleges and boards. For example, Australia established the Australian Commission on Health Care Safety and Quality in 2005 (from its precursor Council) and the Australian Health Practitioners Regulation Agency in 2010 (see Chapter 9). In the context of pluralist regulation by multiple regulators, the principle of harmonization has emerged as increasingly important. First, there is the problem of regulatory burden: to what extent can regulators harmonize their principles and practices (see discussion in Chapter 1) in order to avoid imposing too heavy a regulatory burden upon those being regulated? Health professionals have long complained about the mounting burden of 'paper work' and 'red tape'. Pluralist regulation in a complex field, such as a health sector, involves not only many regulators but also many regulatory mechanisms, which are necessary in order to offset the weaknesses inherent in single interventions. For example, exhorting practitioners to wash their hands before examining patients is seldom enough to change behaviour. Second, there is the problem of equity as a single regulatory mechanism can impact differentially on different groups. For example, overly narrow criteria for access to a profession can unfairly disadvantage people trained in other countries.

Regulators encounter many conflicts of principle and practice especially when multiple regulators and a multitude of regulatees (organizations and individuals) are involved (Braithwaite and Drahos 2000: chapters 21, 24). In order to avoid a heavy regulatory burden, an overall regulatory framework should be agreed. Such conversations involve negotiations between actors in order to sort out areas of compatibility and conflict and to clarify the expected impact of regulation (Black 2002). Changes to the regulation of the health professions in Australia thus are characterized by exhaustive consultations. This is necessary since the beliefs and values of actors have to be understood in order to respond to their concerns and to craft regulatory mechanisms that have more hope of being implemented. In a health sector, for example, should transparency to patients trump the principle of privacy for professionals?

Transparency as a Regulatory Principle and Instrument

Transparency can be conceptualized both as a principle and as an instrument for change. As a principle, it involves moral claims by democratic governments; as an instrument for change, it is a regulatory tool for promoting accountability (Florini 2007b: 2–3). Braithwaite and Drahos found, in studying regulation in the global economy, that transparency had become an overriding principle in regulatory discourse and practice (Braithwaite and Drahos 2000). A definition of regulatory transparency relevant to this discussion is 'the degree to which information is available to outsiders that enables them to have informed voice in decisions and/or to assess the decisions made by insiders' (Florini 2007b: 5).

Under a democratic model of society, citizens expect their government to disclose information on its policies and practices; under a market model of the economy, consumers need information if they are to make informed choices. Freedom of information is not an absolute principle, however, and must be weighed up against privacy and most laws define areas of exemption. Freedom of information type legislation, enacted in Australia and other nations, includes the right of people to access medical information that concerns them, but also protects their right to privacy so that others cannot access their personal medical information without express permission. The right to privacy is a key theme in health care, and confidentiality is deeply ingrained in health professionals, so that transparency can be a contentious principle (Healy 2011: 313–7). Health professionals are used to discussions 'behind closed doors', such as a patient's consultation with his/her medical practitioner, inter-professional discussions on patient cases, peer review meetings, and complaints about practitioners. The norm of patient confidentiality spills over to clinical and professional matters: transparency on professional performance thus requires a shift in thinking.

Greater transparency is enforced by informed consent legislation and promoted through cultural change; for example, doctors previously felt no obligation to provide full medical information to their patients, including a diagnosis on the fatal nature of their condition, or the potential risks associated with a procedure. But transparency involves some dilemmas. Will greater transparency regarding the clinical performance of professionals, including medical errors and malpractice, reinforce or undermine the trust of patients? Do patients prefer to place full trust in their doctor and not inquire further as to his/her actual competence: '… where ignorance is bliss, 'tis folly to be wise' (Gray 1742). Confidence in one's doctor is said to have therapeutic and psychological benefits. Atul Gawande has discussed the dilemma of knowing whether patients really want to know all the risks involved in their treatment. He points to the professional solidarity that makes surgeons reluctant to report the errors of others, when they know that surgery is an imperfect science, and that one day they too will make a mistake (Gawande 2003; 2008). Professional solidarity makes health professionals reluctant to report seriously substandard performance by their peers, which in effect means valuing loyalty to fellow professionals above loyalty to patients.

Transparency also is regarded as 'an administrative tool, a way of making increasingly large and complex government agencies work more efficiently and effectively, as well as with greater accountability to the citizenry' (Florini 2007a: 338). 'Regulation by revelation' or 'regulation by disclosure' is used as a tool to promote accountability in a wide range of areas (Florini 2007a, Hale 2008, Hamilton 2006). This strategy assumes that making information on performance public will result in changed behaviour by professionals. While disclosing information to the public on the performance of providers is a relatively new strategy for health care regulators, after long debate it is being adopted in many countries in order to promote improvements in quality and safety (Healy 2011: 314–7). Meta-regulators increasingly require internal regulators to report back on implementation, gather information on outcomes, and to publish this information.

How does regulation by disclosure work to alter the behaviour of disclosers and those disclosed to? Hale identifies three tools of enforcement that can bring about a change in behaviour in a 'transparency action cycle': market pressure, external discourse, and internal norms (Hale 2008: 73). The market pressure argument is that transparency reduces information asymmetry: it enables people (those disclosed to) to make informed choices and so prompts health care providers (the disclosers) to compete on quality and price. Market pressures have well-known limitations, however, in the case of health care. First, health care largely is a public good rather than a market commodity so that the production of health care is structured very differently to the production of other goods and services. Second, health care users typically lack the information necessary to make informed choices as to their doctor. Third, many patients are unable to exercise 'exit' or voice' because choices are not available, they are not well enough to go elsewhere, or are not confident enough to speak up. Fourth, health professionals (especially those in the public sector) have little incentive to compete to increase their market share of consumers since money does not always follow patients. Further, professionals in Australia have little incentive to change their behaviour as patient demand often outstrips service supply.

The external discourse (peer group and public opinion) may influence health professionals (the disclosers) to change their behaviour in order to maintain their good reputation. Reputations matter greatly to professionals so that public reports on performance (as discussed later) exert a reputational pressure to do better next time (Marshall et al. 2004). Public opinion is a powerful regulatory tool since a mandate from the state depends upon the state and the public having confidence in the trustworthiness of the health professions.

Norms within the health professions promote internal transparency and, in turn, improve performance, as in the well-established tradition of peer review. Further, it is difficult for a health professional, at least in a hospital, to hide substandard performance. Health care in large modern hospitals is undertaken by teams of professionals, not by single individuals able to cast a veil over their failures. Further, health departments are awash with data from public hospitals for internal monitoring purposes although this is mostly not shared with the public.

Who Benefits from Regulation by Revelation?

The shift in professional regulation from protecting professionals to protecting patients is evident in recent changes in Australia. Table 11.1 depicts the trend in recent regulatory reforms that mostly can be placed towards the 'protecting patients' end of the continuum. Each of these reforms involves some tension between transparency and confidentiality principles. These mechanisms are discussed in the remainder of this chapter within the framework of this book: access to the profession, good regulatory practice, and safer patients.

Table 11.1 Regulatory mechanisms: protecting professionals, protecting patients

Regulatory mechanisms	Protecting professionals ←	→ Protecting patients
Access to a profession		
Registers of professionals		▲
Professional disciplinary procedures		▲
Good practice		
Quality assurance activities	▲	
Public reporting on clinical performance		▲
Safer patients		
Adverse events reporting		▲
Open disclosure to patients of adverse events		▲
Litigation by patients		▲

Access to a profession traditionally has been controlled by a professional council, which decides who will be admitted to the profession, and undertakes disciplinary inquiries and determinations when complaints are made about members. Such decisions in many countries are no longer a matter for unfettered self-regulation by the professions, however, as the state now intervenes through strategies of co-regulation, meta-regulation and enforcement. *Good practice* initiatives aim to produce better professionals who achieve better health outcomes for their patients. For example, the avalanche of clinical guidelines offered to practitioners is an information strategy that relies upon voluntary compliance. But as the take-up of clinical guidelines by professionals tends to be low and slow, there is some pressure to set and enforce standards rather than just suggest good practice. *Safer patients* is the rubric for many regulatory mechanisms, ranging from urging staff to use a patient identification protocol to prevent mistakes, to public inquiries into malpractice. For example, public inquiries into 'medical scandals' attract considerable public attention and have resulted in major reforms (Healy 2011: 27–35, Masso and Eagar 2009; see also Chapter 12 in this volume). But as public inquiries often look for culprits and are not designed to protect professionals, they may have a negative impact on staff morale in the particular hospital, especially where the problems involve hospital management and/or health departments as much as individual practitioners.

Table 11.2 sets out the expected impact of the selected mechanisms upon six interest groups (six Ps). *Policy makers* include politicians, senior health department administrators, purchasers and funders, and regulators; *providers* include health service organizations and employers such as hospital directors; *professions* include professional associations, colleges and boards; *professionals* means individual professionals; the *public* means the general population; and *patients* means individual patients.

Access to a Profession

Registers of professionals Access to each of the state-sanctioned professions is controlled by a professional board that decides who will be admitted to its professional register. In Australia, 10 national boards (replacing the State boards for each of 10 professional groups) and an administrative oversight body, the Australian Health Practitioners Regulation Agency, were set up in 2010 under the *Health Practitioner Regulation (Administrative Arrangements) National Law Act 2008* and the *Health Practitioner Regulation National Law 2009*, after the enactment of national and parallel State legislation (see Chapter 9).

Professional boards (particularly medical boards) previously mostly had issued 'a licence for life' (if annual fees were paid). But from 2010 in Australia the national boards require health practitioners applying for re-registration to demonstrate that they have participated in a continuing professional development programme approved by their national board. This falls short of a 'fitness to practise' criterion, that is, some type of periodic assessment, as required in some countries, notably the United Kingdom for medical practitioners (Healy 2011: 111). International best practice now calls for 'life-long learning' by professionals, with most countries taking a learning model approach, although several European countries now apply an assessment model, whereby medical practitioners must regularly demonstrate that they remain up to date and fit to practise (Merkur et al. 2008). The new national registers in Australia offer more information to the public on the credentials of registered professionals. Previously, the State medical boards had offered varying and sparse information about the doctors listed on their medical registers (Healy et al. 2008). The public can now search the web-based registers for information on a particular practitioner that lists any endorsements, conditions, undertakings, notations or reprimands. The website also lists 'cancelled health practitioners' and links to a website of published disciplinary decisions by regulatory bodies. There is less transparency in relation to competence and disciplinary history, however, than in the United States (US) via the American Board of Medical Specialties and the Federation of State Medical Boards.

Stricter access to a profession and greater transparency impacts on all six interest groups (the six Ps). Policy makers demonstrate good governance, for

Table 11.2 Benefits of regulatory mechanisms to six groups

Regulatory mechanisms	Policy makers	Providers	Professions	Professionals	Public	Patients
Access						
Professional registers	Demonstrates co-regulation	Offers check on credentials	Protects reputation of a profession	Protects professional territory	Offers information	Offers check on practitioner
Professional disciplinary procedures	Demonstrate good governance	Reduce risk of substandard employees	Expand regulatory accountability	Impose sanctions on the few to protect the many	Enhance trust in professional standards	Reduce risk of experiencing malpractice
Good practice						
Quality assurance activities	Demonstrates good governance	Enhances trust in professionals	Enhances professional solidarity	Facilitates learning	Improves health care practice	Facilitates better health care but not necessarily better information
Public reporting on clinical performance	Strengthens account. for substandard performance	Increases risk of being 'shamed and blamed'	Adds reputational pressure	Adds reputational pressure	Enables consumer choice	Offers information
Safer patients						
Adverse events reporting	Increases risk of a 'medical scandal' and adds political pressure	Increases pressure to defend performance	Increases pressure to defend the profession	Must overcome reluctance to report	Enhances trust in regulation, reduces trust in professionals	Reminds patients to take more resp. for their own safety
Open disclosure to patients of adverse events	Raises risk of 'medical scandal' and adds political pressure	Disclosure procedure must be carefully managed	Calls for interpersonal skills training	Personally difficult to 'own up' to mistakes	Assurance of full information	Entitled to know but lessens trust?
Litigation by patients	Offers an integrity mechanism in a democratic society	Raises indemnity insurance	Wary of participation in quality assurance	Rising indemnity insurance, exaggerated perception of risk	Produces more defensive medicine	Traumatic for litigants, reduced scope for litigation

example, by appointing members from the public and the state to the national boards, so making them accountable to wider interests than just their profession, and by requiring professional registers to be more transparent. This is in the interests of providers because, as employers, they can more easily check the credentials of prospective employees including those who have moved from inter-State. The professions benefit from legislation that upholds standards and protects their reputation. Professionals can advertise their credentials on a register that is open to the public. While the public and patients need information in order to make informed choices about practitioners, the registers still offer basic information rather than any 'fitness to practise' assessment.

Professional disciplinary procedures In response to accountability criticisms of medical boards as 'soft on doctors', and in order to address the legal criticism of lack of separation of powers between the investigation of a complaint and its disciplinary determination, some countries have transferred disciplinary determinations in serious cases from internal professional panels to independent bodies. For example, after a series of medical scandals in the United Kingdom, such cases were taken away from the General Medical Council (Secretary of State for Health 2007). Australian governments have also now separated investigative and disciplinary decisions under the *Health Practitioner Regulation National Law 2009*. While most cases continue to be dealt with by internal professional panels, serious disciplinary matters are heard by an independent civil administration tribunal in each State, which usually comprise a legal practitioner chair and two health professionals from the relevant professional board. An independent 'public interest assessor' based in the Australian Health Practitioners Regulation Agency will ensure that the public interest is upheld in disciplinary decisions.

While most complaints about health professionals are made by members of the public, health professionals in Australia are now required to report colleagues whose performance poses a danger to their patients. Health professionals were not enthusiastic about this requirement, and while public opinion appears in favour, the press dubbed earlier legislation to this effect in New South Wales as 'dob in a doctor'. The *Health Practitioner Regulation National Law 2009* imposes a legal obligation on all registered health practitioners to report to the relevant board any registered health practitioner whose impaired health (physical, mental or affected by drugs or alcohol), or incompetent or unethical practice, places the public at serious risk of harm.

Reforms to disciplinary procedures followed long-standing criticisms, particularly of medical boards, as being too lenient. First, few complaints were deemed serious enough to proceed to a disciplinary tribunal, and second, very few doctors were struck off the medical register (Healy 2011: chapter 4). For example, between 2000 and 2009 (prior to the national legislation), of the 485 cases serious enough to be heard by disciplinary tribunals in Australia and New Zealand, only 43 per cent of these medical practitioners were removed from practice temporarily or permanently: nearly 18 per year in Australia (Elkin et al. 2011). Licences were revoked for a very small number of doctors, therefore, given that 66,700 medical practitioners were employed in the health sector in Australia in 2008 (Australian Institute of Health and Welfare 2010: 442). Further, the State medical boards preferred to deal confidentially with complaints and reasonably sought to rehabilitate rather than to punish doctors. Where the health of doctors was deemed to be impaired, whether physical, mental or affected by drugs or alcohol, they were directed to non-disciplinary programmes intended to remedy personal problems and to correct poor clinical performance (Freckelton 2009).

It is in the interest of policy makers to establish procedures that protect the public and maintain high professional standards. Disciplinary tribunals in recent years thus have begun to publish determinations in serious cases of malpractice that name the professional and set out the sanctions. Providers want the professions to take more responsibility for disciplining their members rather than leaving it to employers to detect and correct poor performance. It is in the interests of the professions to be seen to uphold standards rather than display excessive leniency to their professional colleagues. Transparency presents problems for individual professionals, however, as it is in their interests to invoke privacy in disciplinary matters that bear upon their reputation, career and earning capacity. Professionals also have a claim to privacy where their own health is involved, the proviso being that their medical practice should pose no risk to their patients. Patients may wish to know whether their doctor has seriously transgressed in his/her professional practice, however, and more problematically, whether he/she is being treated for alcoholism, drug addiction or a bi-polar disorder. It is in the public interest, however, if an impaired or poorly performing doctor can be rehabilitated and returned to good practice. It remains to be seen whether health professionals will comply with the mandatory requirement to report bad practice by their colleagues: that is, will they be more inclined to protect professionals than protect patients?

Good Practice

Quality assurance activities Confidentiality prevails over transparency in the case of quality improvement activities among professionals. Peer review discussions, such as mortality and morbidity (M&M) case reviews in surgery units of hospitals, remain confidential and not open to the public. The confidentiality of formal case discussions, when framed as a quality assurance activity, is now protected by legislation in Australia and in other countries. The rationale is that health professionals otherwise are reluctant to engage in such discussions for fear they would be punished for owning up to errors, and that patients and lawyers could use such information to sue them. The *Health Insurance (Quality Assurance Confidentiality) Amendment Act 1992* (Cth), followed by legislation in the Australian States, aims to ensure that the information given to quality assurance programmes is protected from disclosure to others, the intent being to promote learning by professionals from poor practice as well as good practice. In most States, a quality assurance committee must apply to a Minister for Health for privileged status and argue that confidential proceedings are 'in the public interest'.

Policy makers and providers support confidentiality for quality improvement activities in the belief that it produces safer and better health care and therefore is in the public interest. The professions expect to be trusted to regulate clinical performance among their members, while the functioning of effective peer review depends upon professional solidarity. The benefit for professionals is that confidentiality enables them to learn from both good and bad practice in a relatively supportive environment. One effect of the legislation, however, is to ensure such discussions remain 'secret doctors' business'. For example, the legislation does not allow a coroner access to investigation by a quality assurance committee on a serious adverse event that involved a patient's death. There is some disquiet, therefore, over whether qualified privilege protects doctors more than patients: in other words, whether privacy is claimed to let doctors off rather than to learn from mistakes.

Public reporting on clinical performance In contrast to confidential quality assurance, other programmes that also aim to make health care better and safer have adopted transparency as a regulatory instrument. Meta-regulators use public reporting on performance indicators as an instrument to make providers and professionals more accountable to the state, and to enable consumers to make informed choices. For example, England, Denmark, Germany and the US publish performance indicators that name and compare hospitals, and some US States publish 'report cards' on surgeons and their success rates. In England, the Care Quality Commission publishes annual 'health checks' on named hospitals (excellent, good, fair, weak), and publishes annual survival rates for hospital units and for surgeons for all cardiac surgery (Mayor 2006, Neil et al. 2004). But even advocates of public reporting regard it as a 'two edged sword whose effects can motivate and reward but also discourage and punish' (Leatherman and McCarthy 1999). While many methodological objections are raised about publishing performance indicators that identify providers and professionals, particularly in a 'league table' format, the selection of indicators and their measures is being progressively improved. The MyHospital website set up by the Australian Government in 2010 promises to 'shed a light' by enabling the public to compare the performance of hospitals, such as on type of services offered and waiting times for elective surgery. The intention is to expand this minimal information. The Australian Commission on Safety and Quality in Health Care has been tasked by the Health Ministers with developing clinical performance indicators. Such measures have long been discussed and some State health departments already publish performance measures although without identifying the hospitals.

Transparency does appear to be a regulatory mechanism for achieving improvements but not in the way expected. Systematic reviews have found that while public reporting had little impact upon patients (the potential users of the data), it did impact upon doctors and hospitals (the sources of the data) and thus did help improve the quality of health care (Fung et al. 2008, Hibbard et al. 2005, Marshall and Brook 2002). John Braithwaite and colleagues suggest that the power of public reports to improve quality might be enhanced by thinking of them less as a tool for strengthening markets and more as a tool for bolstering regulation via reputational threats (Braithwaite et al. 2007). The argument is that despite equivocal evidence on whether consumers and corporate purchasers make choices based on performance indicators, public reporting does change the behaviour of health providers for two reasons. First, providers and professionals care about the opinion of their peers and their public reputations. Second, health providers, particularly in the US, worry that accreditation agencies, indemnity insurers and medical malpractice lawyers may target them if they get a poor public report (Marshall et al. 2004).

Policy makers and purchasers as major funders of public hospitals, and the public as users of health services, want greater transparency on performance. Providers generally have to be forced by meta-regulators to adopt public reporting. For example, health departments in the Australian States, as the administrators of public hospitals, do not welcome public criticism and possible electoral punishment, hospitals as providers do not welcome comparisons with other hospitals, and the poor performers usually argue that their patients are sicker. There are three main arguments on the benefits of public reporting for policy makers, the public and patients. First, the personal autonomy argument is that people need reliable information in order to make informed decisions about health care treatment (Clarke and Oakley 2004). Second, the market argument is that public reporting enables purchasers and consumers to choose between providers so that demand will rise for high performers and drop for poor performers. Third, the quality argument is that as health providers and professionals care about their reputations, they will seek to do better and so standards will rise.

Safer Patients

Reporting adverse events Adverse event reporting systems have been established in many countries as a quality mechanism to enable providers and professionals to learn from and so prevent future adverse events. Despite the initial intention, reporting systems generally are not used as a measurement mechanism, given low compliance with reporting, and uncertainties about whether rising numbers of reports indicate more attention devoted to patient safety (by good reporters) or the actual occurrence of more adverse events (by poor performers). Countries vary on whether they have national or regional systems. Australia has reporting systems for public hospitals in each of the States and Territories that do not add up to a national database given different software and different incident classifications (Runciman 2002). While public hospitals in Australia must participate in their State system, reporting is voluntary on the part of staff (in legal terms, although hospitals urge staff to report), except in the case of serious adverse events where reports are required.

There is no rigorous research evidence, however, on whether adverse event reporting produces safer patient care. This is a major research gap given the effort and cost involved in setting up and maintaining reporting systems. Lucian Leape has concluded that although much of the evidence in the US on the positive impact of adverse event reporting is anecdotal, there are many success stories. For example, The Joint Commission (the US hospital accreditation non-government organization (NGO)) reporting system has provided evidence for sentinel event alerts, such as the removal of concentrated potassium chloride from hospital wards (Leape 2002).

In relation to transparency, reporting in most countries usually is voluntary and anonymous. Data from reporting systems mostly is used internally for quality improvement purposes, and where meta-regulators publish statistics, these are aggregated and de-identified in relation to hospitals and cases. The rationale is that reporting is intended as a learning opportunity, and that its use for monitoring and measuring is problematic given variable rates of reporting.

The international consensus is that good governance calls for policy makers to put in place some form of adverse event reporting. Providers maintain that internal reports present an important internal quality improvement opportunity, and considerable effort goes into training staff in the 'root cause analysis' of adverse events. While much effort goes into persuading professionals to report, most reports are lodged by nurses: 'physicians have been reluctant partners in reporting' (Leape 2002:1633). Adverse event reporting is more problematic for providers and professionals than other forms of performance reporting, since these reports are tied to particular cases and document 'things that go wrong'. Providers and professionals fear that transparency could incur punishment (some insurance funds in the US threaten not to pay for medical errors), and would enable patients and lawyers to sue. Adverse event reporting thus often is framed as a confidential quality assurance activity rather than as a transparent measure of performance.

Open disclosure to patients of adverse events A policy of open disclosure on adverse events aims to replace secrecy with transparency to the patients and family involved. While a doctor is legally required to obtain informed consent before a procedure, the law is less clear on whether a patient who suffers an adverse event is legally entitled to be told, although legislation was recently passed in two Canadian provinces (Gallagher et al. 2003, Levinson and Gallagher 2007). The anecdotal evidence is that people who receive an apology and a full explanation are less likely to sue their doctor or hospital (Kraman and Hamm 1999, Weeks and Bagian 2000). Australia does not yet have legislation that mandates open disclosure, although civil liability legislation protects against an apology being regarded in court as an admission of liability (Bennett and Freckelton 2006). Health departments in some Australian States recently have adopted an open disclosure policy based on a national standard, although it is unclear whether it has become standard practice in all public hospitals. Health providers and professionals are in the process of learning how best to explain and to apologize to patients and their families in the wake of an adverse event (Studdert 2009).

Policy makers in Australia do not yet unequivocally require open disclosure despite their endorsement of a national open disclosure standard; providers are cautious about possible legal repercussions; while the professions acknowledge an ethical obligation. Individual professionals find such disclosure personally very difficult, however, and remain worried whether disclosure will provoke litigation and increase their medical indemnity insurance. Patients say they want to be told when something goes wrong, but will such disclosures shake confidence in their health care providers?

Litigation by patients 'Regulation by litigation' is seen by some as a key mechanism for improving patient safety (Mello et al. 2005). Common law countries, including Australia, allow people to sue for compensation for medical injuries, mainly under the tort of negligence. Litigation by an aggrieved party moves alleged malpractice by a doctor into the public domain of a court, however, in practice most medical indemnity claims are settled out of court and thus are confidential documents. The effects of tort law reforms in all Australian States in the early 2000s were to reduce the opportunities for patients to sue doctors, to reduce the ambit of claims and the size of awards, and so to prevent doctors' medical indemnity premiums escalating further. But critics of these changes argue that the legislation went too far in restricting access to the courts by aggrieved patients. Who were the winners and losers from the tort law reforms in Australia?

From the perspective of policy makers, the option of litigation to redress grievances acts as a societal integrity mechanism, in that it calls someone to account for their action or lack of action. The main argument for litigation is that it is an important last resort for patients who claim to have suffered negligent health care (Hirsch 2009). But tort law systems have not produced significant improvements in patient safety (Ipp Report 2002). Countries with high rates of litigation, such as the US, have not produced better patient safety outcomes (Brennan and Berwick 1996), and countries with tort law systems do not have fewer adverse events than those with 'no fault' systems (Davis et al. 2003). McDonald argues that tort law is a weak regulatory instrument for achieving systemic change given its many barriers and tortuous procedures (McDonald 2008).

From the perspective of providers, the threat of malpractice litigation is said to prompt hospital managers to take patient safety measures more seriously (Brennan 1998). But managing the risk of litigation by patients is costly since hospitals must take out substantial indemnity cover. The medical profession argues that patient litigation leads to 'defensive medicine' rather than better health care. There is no clear evidence, however, that defensive doctors order unnecessary medical tests and so expose their patients to unnecessary risks (Brennan and Mello 2003: 269, Schoenbaum and Bovbjerg 2004). The legal profession, of course, is an advocate of patient litigation although the tort law reforms have somewhat reduced income-earning opportunities for lawyers. Doctors say that the fear of being sued deters them from reporting adverse events, and from participating in quality improvement activities, despite qualified privilege legislation. The largely anecdotal but influential argument is that the fear of patient litigation undermines learning from medical errors (Kachalia et al. 2008). Being sued is not a positive learning experience since the tort law system is adversarial and stressful for both doctors and patients (Vincent 2003, Vincent et al. 2006).

It is not in the public interest if the threat (or the perception of threat) of litigation deters health care professionals from participating in a safety culture where they can learn from their mistakes (Runciman et al. 2007: chapter 4). Further, most cases are settled out of court in confidential agreements so this lack of transparency blocks learning opportunities for the profession as a whole. For patients, the tort law system compensates only a very few who choose to litigate after suffering an adverse event.

Conclusions

The last decade has seen a dramatic increase in the number and variety of efforts by many actors to strengthen the regulation of the health professions in order to produce better and safer health care. Patients are expected to be the main beneficiaries of these reforms. Transparency has become a key instrument for producing greater accountability by the health professions to the state and greater accountability to the public. Policy makers use transparency as part of a meta-regulation strategy for monitoring whether the internal health sector regulators (professional groups and provider organizations) are doing a reasonable job in regulating their members and employees. The public wants more information, in principle, in order to make informed choices, although it is not clear to what extent they act on this information. Information should be made more accessible and more understandable to the public as citizens and as consumers. The health professions in Australia traditionally have left the public in the dark on regulatory decisions. The medical profession, in particular, has regarded such deliberations as 'secret doctors' business'.

Australia has been a laggard, in comparison to North America and European countries, in the information made available to the public on professional and clinical performance. This is changing, however, with the establishment of a new professional regulatory agency, more transparent regulatory decisions, and the beginnings of public reporting on clinical performance. The public is entitled to know how and why regulatory decisions are made and to be given more information on the competence of their health care professionals and providers. But 'for now we see through a glass, darkly' (1 Corinthians xiii:1).

References

Allsop, J. and Jones, K. 2006. *Quality Assurance in Medical Regulation in an International Context: Report for the Department of Health England.* London: University of Lincoln.

Australian Institute of Health and Welfare. 2010. *Australia's Health 2010.* Canberra: Australian Institute of Health and Welfare.

Ayres, I. and Braithwaite, J. 1992. *Responsive Regulation: Transcending the Regulation Debate.* New York. Oxford: Oxford University Press.

Bennett, B. and Freckelton, I. 2006. Life after the Ipp reforms: Medical negligence law, in *Disputes and Dilemmas in Health Law*, edited by I. Freckelton and K. Petersen. Leichhardt NSW: The Federation Press.

Black, J. 2002. Regulatory conversations. *Journal of Law and Society*, 29(1), 163–96.

Braithwaite, J. and Drahos, P. 2000. *Global Business Regulation.* Cambridge: Cambridge University Press.

Braithwaite, J. et al. 2007. *Regulating Aged Care: Ritualism and the New Pyramid.* Cheltenham. Northampton, MA: Edward Elgar.

Braithwaite, J. 2008. *Regulatory Capitalism: How it Works, Ideas for Making it Better.* Cheltenham. Northampton, MA: Edward Elgar.

Brennan, T. 1998. The role of regulation in quality improvement. *Milbank Quarterly*, 76, 709–31.

Brennan, T. and Berwick, D. 1996. *New Rules: Regulation, Markets and the Quality of American Health Care.* San Francisco, CA: Jossey-Bass.

Brennan, T. and Mello, M. 2003. Patient safety and medical malpractice: a case study. *Annals of Internal Medicine*, 139(4), 267–75.

Clarke, S. and Oakley, J. 2004. Informed consent and surgeons' performance. *Journal of Medicine and Philosophy*, 29(1), 11–35.

Davis, P. et al. 2003. Preventable in-hospital medical injury under the 'no fault' system in New Zealand. *Quality and Safety in Health Care*, 12(4), 240–1.

Dubois, C-A., et al. 2006. Reshaping the regulation of the workforce in European health care systems, in *Human Resources for Health in Europe*, edited by C-A. Dubois, M. McKee and E. Nolte. Maidenhead, Berkshire: Open University Press, 173–92.

Elkin, K. et al. 2011. Doctors disciplined for professional misconduct in Australia and New Zealand, 2000–2009. *Medical Journal of Australia*, 194(9), 452–6.

Florini, A. 2007a. Conclusion: whither transparency?, in *The Right to Know: Transparency for an Open World*, edited by A. Florini. New York: Columbia University Press, 337–48.

Florini, A. 2007b. Introduction: the battle over transparency, in *The Right to Know: Transparency for an Open World*, edited by A. Florini. New York: Columbia University Press, 1–6.

Freckelton, I. 2009. Non-disciplinary pathways in practitioner regulation, in *Patient Safety First: Strategies for Regulating Health Care*, edited by J. Healy and P. Dugdale. Crows Nest NSW: Allen & Unwin, 167–91.

Fung, C. et al. 2008. Evidence that publishing patient care performance data improves quality of care. *Annals of Internal Medicine*, 148, 111–23.

Gallagher, T.H. et al. 2003. Patients' and physicians' attitudes regarding the disclosure of medical errors. *Journal of the American Medical Association*, 289(8), 1001–1007.

Gawande, A. 2003. *Complications: A Surgeon's Notes on an Imperfect Science*. New York: Picador.

Gawande, A. 2008. *Better: A Surgeon's Notes on Performance*. New York: Picador.

Gray, T. 1742. *Ode on a distant prospect of Eton College*.

Hale, T.N. 2008. Transparency, accountability, and global governance. *Global Governance*, 14(1), 73–94.

Hamilton, J. 2006. *Regulation Through Revelation: The Origin, Politics, and Impacts of the Toxics Release Inventory Program*. Cambridge: Cambridge University Press.

Healy, J. 2011. *Improving Health Care Safety and Quality: Reluctant Regulators*. Farnham: Ashgate.

Healy, J. and Braithwaite, J. 2006. Designing safer health care through responsive regulation. *Medical Journal of Australia*, 184(10), S56–S59.

Healy, J. et al. 2008. A national medical register: balancing public transparency and professional privacy. *Medical Journal of Australia*, 188(4), 247–9.

Hibbard, J. et al. 2005. Hospital performance reports: impact on quality, market share, and reputation. Evidence from a controlled experiment shows the long-term effects of reporting hospitals' performance ratings to the public. *Health Affairs*, 24(4), 1150–60.

Hirsch, D. 2009. Does litigation against doctors and hospitals improve quality?, in *Patient Safety First: Strategies for Regulating Health Care*, edited by J. Healy and P. Dugdale. Crows Nest NSW: Allen & Unwin. 254–72.

Ipp Report. 2002. *Review of the Law of Negligence: Final Report*. Canberra: Commonwealth of Australia.

Irvine, D.H. 2006. New ideas about medical professionalism. *Medical Journal of Australia*, 184(5), 204–5.

Kachalia, A. et al. 2008. Beyond negligence: avoidability and medical injury compensation. *Social Science & Medicine*, 66(2), 387–402.

Kraman, S. and Hamm, G. 1999. Risk management: extreme honesty may be the best policy. *Annals of Internal Medicine*, 131(12), 963–7.

Leape, L. 2002. Reporting of adverse events. *New England Journal of Medicine*, 347(20), 1633–9.

Leatherman, S. and McCarthy, D. 1999. Public disclosure of health care performance reports: experience, evidence and issues of policy. *International Journal for Quality in Health Care*, 11(2), 93–8.

Levinson, W. and Gallagher, T.H. 2007. Disclosing medical errors to patients: a status report in 2007. *Canadian Medical Association Journal*, 177(3), 265–7.

Marshall, M. and Brook, R. 2002. Public reporting of comparative information about quality of healthcare (editorial). *Medical Journal of Australia*, 176, 205–6.

Marshall, M. et al. 2004. How do we maximise the impact of the public reporting of quality of care? *International Journal for Quality in Health Care*, 16(Supplement 1), i57–i63.

Masso, M. and Eagar, K. 2009. Do public inquiries improve health care?, in *Patient Safety First: Responsive Regulation in Health Care*, edited by J. Healy and P. Dugdale. Crows Nest NSW: Allen & Unwin, 318–40.

Mayor, S. 2006. UK website publishes cardiac surgery survival rates. *British Medical Journal*, 332(7549), 1049.

McDonald, F. 2008. Working to death: the regulation of working hours in health care. *Law & Policy*, 30(1), 108–40.

Mello, M. et al. 2005. Fostering rational regulation of patient safety. *Journal of Health Politics, Policy & Law*, 30(3), 375–426.

Merkur, S., Mossialos, E., Long, M. and McKee, M. 2008. Physician revalidation in Europe, *Clinical Medicine*, 8, 371–6.

Neil, D. et al. 2004. Public reporting of individual surgeon performance information: United Kingdom developments and Australian issues. *Medical Journal of Australia*, 181(5), 266–8.

Runciman, W. et al. 2007. *Safety and Ethics in Healthcare: A Guide to Getting it Right*. Aldershot: Ashgate.

Runciman, W.B. 2002. Lessons from the Australian Patient Safety Foundation: setting up a national patient safety surveillance system – is this the right model? *Quality and Safety in Health Care*, 11, 246–51.

Schoenbaum, S. and Bovbjerg, J. 2004. Malpractice reform must include steps to prevent medical injury. *Annals of Internal Medicine*, 140(1), 51–3.

Secretary of State for Health. 2007. *Trust, Assurance and Safety – The Regulation of Health Professionals in the 21st century*. London: The Stationery Office.

Studdert, D. 2009. Disclosure of medical injury, in *Patient Safety First: Responsive Regulation in Health Care*, edited by J. Healy and P. Dugdale. Crows Nest NSW: Allen & Unwin, 237–53.

Vincent, C. 2003. Compensation as a duty of care: the case for 'no fault'. *Quality in Australian Health Care*, 12, 240–241.

Vincent, C. et al. 2006. Learning from litigation: the role of claims analysis in patient safety, in *Patient Safety: Research into Practice*, edited by K. Walshe and R. Boaden. Maidenhead, Berkshire: Open University Press, 41–65.

Walshe, K. 2009. Regulating health professionals, in *Patient Safety First: Responsive Regulation in Health Care*, edited by J. Healy and P. Dugdale. Crows Nest NSW: Allen & Unwin, 144–66.

Weeks, W. and Bagian, J. 2000. Developing a culture of safety in the Veterans Affairs Administration. *Effective Clinical Practice*, 3, 270–276.

Chapter 12
Scandals, Public Inquiries and Health Professional Regulation

Fiona McDonald

Introduction

Since 1980 there has been an increasing incidence of the use of public inquiries as a process through which scandals raising patient safety and health care quality concerns can be subject to highly public scrutiny. The use of public inquiries and their impact on the governance of health or social systems, especially around issues of patient or client safety, has been examined by a number of commentators (Butler and Drakeford 2003, Masso and Eager 2009, Stanley and Manthorpe 2004, Walshe and Higgins 2002) but public inquiries into scandals in the health system also raise a question about the impact of these inquiries on public perceptions about the adequacy of the various mechanisms for health professional regulation.

This chapter examines public inquiries into scandals related to the professional practices of health professionals in two jurisdictions, Canada and Britain, between 1980 and 2005 to analyse the implications for health professional regulation. The focus on Canada and Britain is to enable a rich and detailed comparison. As Masso and Eager (2009: 318) note, public inquiries 'are typically the culmination of a "scandal" reported very widely in the media, and can be seen to represent a response to perceived regulatory failures'. Not every scandal results in a public inquiry (Masso and Eager 2009). Of those scandals that result in a public inquiry in the health context, not all raise concerns of regulatory failure by a health professions regulator or governance failure by health profession(s), although many do.

The public dissection of a scandal can drive change – the policy literature indicates that health-related scandals that resonate in the public consciousness can precipitate a cycle of regulatory shifts (Butler and Drakeford 2003, Stanley and Manthorpe 2004, Wells 1995). Scandals may lead to public inquiries, a public inquiry may result in new recommendations to enhance safety and manage risk and these recommendations may result in novel or increased regulation (Alaszewski and Coxon 2008). Fundamentally, regulation 'is the response to the now instinctive reaction that "something should be done about it"' (Moran 2003: 26).

If the public comes to believe that regulatory agencies are not sufficiently responsive to scandals, before or after the scandal emerges into the public spotlight, regulators may lose the public's trust. Without trust, regulatory actors may lose legitimacy (Wells 1995). The impetus to legitimize the health system and regulators within that system is an integral objective of any responses to inquiries in this context.

This chapter will argue that public inquiries may raise the public's perception of the risks associated with the mechanisms for regulating the health professions, provide a narrative of why the public's trust in established regulatory actors could be questioned, and raise concerns about the adequacy of existing prospective and retrospective forms of accountability. This cycle could place the acceptability of existing regulatory norms in question and create a demand for greater controls to be imposed on the health professions by the state or by the profession. The first section of this paper will discuss the role and purpose of public inquiries. The second section will outline the author's understanding of health professional regulation. The third section outlines an analytic framework from social theory centred on the factors of risk, trust, accountability and control. The final section applies this framework to analyse the impact of health related public inquiries in Britain and Canada on health professional regulation.

Public Inquiries

In general, governments most commonly constitute public inquiries during periods of crisis, change, growth, or adjustment (McDonald 2010a). While some are convened as a form of social inquiry into a pressing policy problem, this chapter will focus on investigatory inquiries, convened as a response to an issue of grave public concern and often arising from scandal or tragedy. Investigatory inquiries ask what happened, why, and what lessons can be learned for the future (Bradley 2003). In common-law countries public inquiries have long been an important tool to ensure accountability, particularly of government and government actors, but also of private actors (Manson and Mullen 2003). Investigatory inquiries have been described as mechanisms to put the state on trial (Salter 1989).

It is important to note there are a variety of ways such investigatory inquiries can be constituted. For example, in Britain a Royal Commission of Inquiry can be convened under the *Tribunals of Inquiry (Evidence) Act 1921*, a public inquiry may be convened under specific statutory powers, for example, pursuant to s. 84 of the *National Health Service Act 1977*, or government may commission a public inquiry without recourse to statutory powers. There are also other forms of public or quasi-public inquiry, for example, Parliamentary inquiries and coronial inquests. Inquiries may also be commissioned by regulatory actors or in rare cases may be commissioned privately. It is not perhaps the form of the inquiry that is important but the degree of scrutiny inherent in an independent review of a particular event. In the health context, many of these inquiries directly or indirectly place the spotlight on the activities of health professionals, health professions and health professions regulators.

Regulation of the Health Professions

It has long been recognized that the provision of health services to patients is not without risk, and that individuals who provide such services should be regulated (McDonald 2010b). Traditionally, regulatory frameworks endeavouring to ensure that services were provided safely focus either on individuals (that is, regulation by litigation) (see discussion in Chapter 11) or the professional guilds – the health professions in this context. Government sanctioned self-regulation occurs when government, through legislation, delegates regulatory powers to a profession(s) to self-govern. Underpinning government sanctioned self-regulation is 'an unparalleled faith in the ability of medical professionals [and other health professionals] to regulate themselves' (Mello, Kelly and Brennan 2005: 375).

In part, the relationship between the state and the professions has been characterized as a form of social contract. The British Committee of Inquiry into the Regulation of the Medical Profession (1975: 3) described the relationship as:

> A contract between the public and the profession, by which the public go to the profession for medical treatment because the profession has made sure it will provide satisfactory treatment. Such a contract has the characteristic of all freely made contracts – mutual advantage.

As Stacey (1989) noted, there is a form of public accountability inherent in this characterization of the relationship – a collective accountability of the profession to the public, oftentimes through government, for ensuring professionals practise appropriately. But the fact that accountability is an inherent characteristic of the social contract between the profession and the public/state does not necessarily mean that formal accountability mechanisms are clear.

Larkin (1988: 118) has described this conferral of powers to the health professions as creating almost a '"state within the modern state" with either acquired or invested sovereignty'. There are, of course, limits to that sovereignty, as government also can, if it chooses to, constrain what Larkin (1988: 120) refers to as the 'character and extent' of the powers devolved to the professions. However, traditionally government sanctioned self-regulation is premised on faith that the health professionals and health professions are 'responsible political actors' (Kagan and Scholz 1984) or 'virtuous' actors (Braithwaite 2002). As McDonald (2008) notes, given the ethical commitments of health professionals and the health professions to do no harm and act in the best interests of their patients and the public, governments have tended to assume responsibility and virtuosity on the part of the professions and left considerable discretionary leeway to the professions as to how they exercised their functions. Effective self-regulation is not, however, simply a function of the imposition of rules and standards from above (from the regulatory bodies to the regulated) but involves regulation from below or within. In other words, the regulated must also accept responsibility for internal self-governance to foster what Paul (2000) refers to as the internal morality of the professions. The reports of public inquiries provide a narrative that informs public perceptions about whether self-regulation is effective or not.

Risk, Trust, Accountability and Control

Social theorists increasingly suggest western societies are in a state of transition where new social structures and norms are superseding the old, previously dominant structures of power and authority (McDonald 2010a). Drawing on social theory, this section will suggest that the following four factors are of central concern when considering health professional regulation (1) the degree of risk associated with how health professionals are regulated; (2) the levels of distrust or mistrust associated with the current institutional and structural regulatory arrangements; (3) whether accountability measures are (in)effective; and (4) the desired level of control over these matters by the state (McDonald 2010a). This author maintains that these factors contribute to the decision-making process about whether reform to regulatory processes for health professionals is required.

Beck, Giddens and Lash (1994) suggest that we increasingly live in a 'risk society' where society is preoccupied with regulating risks to the public. As Lupton (1999: 25) describes it, risk has 'become an increasingly pervasive concept of human existence in western societies' and organizes, monitors and regulates the conduct of societal actors. Some also suggest the emergence of a 'post-trust society' (Lofstedt 2005) at least insofar as societies are increasingly expressing mistrust of traditional and established institutions of social order that were traditionally trusted to regulate risks – in this context the health professions. If the public or key policy-actors begin to mistrust, or at least to feel ambivalent about, key institutions, the regulatory frameworks surrounding those key institutions may be reformed in an attempt to restore or bolster trust. Others postulate a blame society where someone or something must always be blamed and therefore be held responsible and accountable (Douglas 1992). As Lupton (1999: 45) puts it, 'in contemporary western cultures, every death, every accident and every misfortune is "chargeable to someone's account" – someone must be found to be blamed'.

At a more applied level, social theorists and empirical researchers alike consider that the interrelationships between trust/distrust and risk perception are key determinants of the acceptability of policy or, for the purposes of this chapter, regulation. What remains contentious is the causality of the relationships between risk and trust. Some posit a causal explanation: trust influences risk perception which influences perceptions as to the acceptability of policies (Poortinga and Pidgeon 2005). Others posit an associationist model of trust: trust influences and is influenced by perceptions of policy acceptability which in turn influences and is influenced by risk (Poortinga and Pidgeon 2005). There is empirical evidence to support both interpretations of the relationship between risk and trust, although the evidence to date more strongly supports the associationist model (Poortinga and Pidgeon 2005).

Setting aside empiricism for the present, this chapter will argue on a normative level that both the causal and the associationist models apply, at least in relation to the regulation of the health professions, but that these models must expand to include the interrelated concepts of accountability and control. Perceptions that mechanisms both exist and are adequate to ensure that institutions are accountable for their actions are an important determinant as to whether current controls on specific activities or practices are sufficient and, accordingly, whether changes in the levels and mechanisms of control are required. Trust is a determining factor of the perception and acceptability of risk, which is in turn a determining factor as to the degree of accountability required of policy-actors. This then determines policy or regulatory acceptability, which in turn influences perceptions of how much control is required, which affects trust, and so on. This cycle, trust-risk-accountability-acceptability (control), provides a basis upon which to assess public inquiries. The following section applies this cycle to analyse the impact of public inquiries into the actions of health professionals.

The Impact of Public Inquiries

Risk

Aggregation An aggregation of public inquiries may raise perceptions about the level of risk associated with the way in which health professionals are regulated and promote a fundamental reappraisal of the established regulatory framework. Fourteen public inquiries were commissioned within Britain's National Health Service (NHS) between 1980 and 2005, raising issues that touched upon professional regulation. Table 12.1 sets out the details of those inquiries, including the year, location and a brief description of the events that led to the inquiries.

There was a fairly constant barrage of negative publicity about the health system and the health professions. Public inquiry processes can be prime news fodder in which the faces and voices of patients and/or families could be heard.

In Canada, the picture is different. During the period 1980–2005, this author identified only three scandals relating to health professionals, and these scandals are described in Table 12.2. This table again presents the location, date and a brief description of the event.

These scandals were few in number and dispersed in time. The relative infrequency of these events suggests that there was unlikely to be any aggregate affect.

Table 12.1 Scandals in the British National Health Service leading to inquiries 1980–2005

Year	Event	Inquiry
1979–80	Rampton Special Hospital: Allegations of large-scale ill-treatment and brutality against patients in a forensic psychiatric facility	(1980)
1991	Ashworth Special Hospital: Allegations that patients in a forensic psychiatric hospital were mistreated, including that a patient died after a beating, and other patients were sexually or physically assaulted	(1992)
1991	Beverly Allitt: A nurse, Beverly Allitt, was convicted of murdering four children, attempting to murder three others, and the grievous bodily harm of six others in the children's ward at Grantham and Kesteven Hospital.	(1994)
1993	Richard Neale: Dr Neale, gynaecologist, was struck off the medical register in Ontario, Canada, after a patient died, but gained registration in Britain and continued to practise. There were allegations that he was incompetent.	(2004)
1996	Kent and Canterbury Hospitals Trust: Allegations that cervical screening practices were inadequate, which resulted in 90,000 cervical smears being re-examined.	(1997)
1996	Rodney Ledward: Allegations that Dr Ledward, obstetrician/gynaecologist, provided inadequate treatment over a 16-year period.	(2000)
1996	Bristol Royal Infirmary: Allegations that the treatment provided to children undergoing paediatric cardiac surgery at the Bristol Royal Infirmary between 1984 and 1995 was inadequate.	(2001)
1997	Ashworth Special Hospital: Allegations that patients misused drugs and alcohol, had access to pornography, and one patient was an active paedophile within the Personality Disorder Unit.	(1997)
1997	Royal Devon and Exeter Hospital: Allegations that breast cancer screening practices were inadequate	(1997)
1998	Dr Peter Green: Dr Green, GP, was convicted of nine counts of indecent assault against patients.	(2001)
1998	Dr Clifford Ayling: Dr Ayling, GP, was convicted of 12 charges of indecent assault relating to ten patients.	(2004)
1998	Dr Harold Shipman: Dr Shipman, GP, was convicted of the murder of 15 patients. The public inquiry concluded he murdered a total of 200 patients and suspected he murdered a minimum of 45 others.	(2005)
1999	Royal Liverpool Children's Inquiry: Allegations that organs from deceased children were retained without the knowledge or consent of their families	(2001)
1999	Drs Kerr and Haslam: Dr Kerr, psychiatrist, was convicted of indecent assault of a female patient, and Dr Haslam, psychiatrist, was convicted of indecent assault on four female patients.	(2005)

Table 12.2 Scandals in Canadian Health Systems leading to inquiries 1980–2005

Years	Event	Inquiry
1981	Hospital for Sick Children (HSC), Ontario: 35 babies/children die at the HSC from suspected digoxin poisoning. A nurse is arrested but discharged for lack of evidence at a preliminary hearing	(1983 and 1984)
1990	Sexual abuse: Allegations of inadequate complaint-handling by the College of Physicians and Surgeons of Ontario (CPSO) in respect of allegations of sexual abuse by physicians	(1991)
1994	Manitoba paediatric cardiac surgery: 12 children die during or after paediatric cardiac surgery at the Winnipeg Health Sciences Centre (WHSC), Manitoba	(2000)

Scale of scandal The numbers of victims, and therefore the scale of the events reviewed by a public inquiry, generally affects the impact upon the public because inquiries bring risk to life. One life lost unnecessarily is bad, but the loss of multiple lives graphically illustrates the degree of risk.

In Canada, the scale of the scandals that related to health professional regulation varied. The two public inquiries relating to Canadian Hospitals (Hospital for Sick Children (HSC) (Dubin Inquiry 1983, Grange Inquiry 1984)) involved 35 patients and Winnipeg Health Sciences Centre (WHSC) (Sinclair Inquest 1998) involved less than 15 patients. The allegations that the College of Physicians and Surgeons of Ontario (CPSO) had ineffectively dealt with sexual abuse complaints involved multiple patients: the Taskforce on Sexual Abuse of Patients by Physicians (TSAPP) heard 303 detailed reports of sexual abuse of patients by doctors and other health professionals (TSAPP 1991). Although these events all had multiple victims, the intervals between these cases probably limited their aggregate effect on risk perception.

Many of the public inquiries in Britain had far-reaching effects upon large patient populations. Ninety thousand cervical-screening tests were re-read at Kent and Canterbury, affecting many thousands of patients (Wells Inquiry 1997). Dr Harold Shipman is suspected of killing around 245 of his patients (Shipman Inquiry 2002). Possibly hundreds of children and families were affected by a decade of paediatric heart surgery procedures, with morbidity and mortality rates for some procedures outside the norm (Bristol Inquiry 2000). Many thousands of families across Britain discovered that some health professionals and hospitals had retained organs or tissue from the bodies of deceased children and adults without the knowledge or consent of families (an audit disclosed 54,000 retained organs across the NHS (Department of Health 2000)). Eight hundred allegations of brutality exposed at Rampton Hospital were said to have involved 100 nurses (Rampton Inquiry 1980). Thirteen children were murdered or harmed at Grantham and Kesteven Hospital by Nurse Beverly Allitt (Allitt Inquiry 1994). Upwards of 40 patients were thought to have been affected by the actions of Dr Ayling (Ayling

Inquiry 2004) – and the list goes on. Scale reinforces risk perception – the more victims, the greater the perception that there are risks to everyone associated with health professionals and that those risks must be managed.

Again, aggregation plays a role in amplifying the perceived risks. Regardless of differences in population size between Britain (50,431,700 in 2005) and Canada (32,107,043 in 2005), the numbers of people affected by the scandals were exponentially higher in Britain than in Canada on aggregate – potentially creating a perception that the risks to patients were more widespread in Britain.

Locations of risk It has been suggested that Canada's constitutional structure may have contributed to public inquiries having highly localized impacts (Davies 2001, Gillies 2003). With 13 health systems within Canada, each governed by different regulatory frameworks, it is easy to see how events occurring in one jurisdiction can be discounted by others as being a problem peculiar to that jurisdiction. One commentator noted in respect of the WHSC scandal: 'If it had happened in Toronto then it would have had a much bigger impact, but people outside Manitoba just said "well that's Winnipeg for you"' (cited in Gillies 2003). Conversely, the concerns about the operations of the CPSO, and especially the recommendations made by the TSAPP, which one would have thought to be highly localized, in fact had a national impact (Robinson 1999). Other provinces, such as British Columbia, Alberta, Québec, Prince Edward Island, Saskatchewan, and New Brunswick, established committees to review the issue (Robinson 1999) and as a result there were changes to the regulatory frameworks or development of policy statements or guidelines. The picture is different in Britain. Most of the public inquiries during this period related to health professionals practising in the kinds of ordinary sites of care accessed by millions each year. Therefore risks were more likely to be regarded as not isolated or not restricted to one 'bad' hospital or 'bad' doctor, but universal and inherent in the system.

The narrative of scandals Considering the narratives of scandal as illustrated by the public inquiries is vital. Narratives of events tell chronological stories about the impact of scandals on people's lives. Hence narratives enable the public to identify and empathize with the individuals caught up in the scandal and feel more concern about the issues disclosed by the scandal. Such narratives may have the impact of raising perceptions of the level and degree of risks faced by the public from poor regulation (Butler and Drakeford 2003, McDonald 2010a, Poumadère and Mays 2003).

In 1990, the Ontario public focused on the perceived failures of the CPSO to adequately address complaints and impose appropriate penalties on doctors who acted in a sexually inappropriate manner towards their patients (TSAPP 1991). The TSAPP concluded that the CPSO had done a poor job of managing complaints of sexual misconduct and often imposed penalties on doctors that the public perceived as being too lenient. This reflected an over-identification by the regulator with those it regulated (Rogers 2007). The risks highlighted by this inquiry were twofold: that patients might be at risk of sexual abuse by doctors; and that the regulatory body responsible for managing complaints might be ineffectual in protecting the public.

At the WHSC 12 children died and other children experienced serious complications during or after paediatric cardiac heart surgery in 1994 (Sinclair Inquest 1998). Given the context – a newly appointed and inexperienced surgeon performing delicate, highly specialized surgery – it was possible to characterize the scandal as a one-off failure of effective governance by the WHSC and thus localize public perception of any risks.

The level of the risk associated with public inquiries in Britain was quite different. Seven of the British public inquiries investigated allegations that health professionals had committed serious criminal offences against their patients: everything from physical abuse and mistreatment to sexual abuse and assaults, and serial murder. Through the processes of criminal prosecution and a commission of inquiry (Shipman Inquiry 2002), it was established that Dr Harold Shipman was one of the world's worst serial killers. The scope and scale of his criminal offending against patients was unprecedented. Nurse Beverly Allitt was convicted of the murder of four of her child patients, attempting to murder three others, and six instances of causing grievous bodily harm (Allitt Inquiry 1994). Dr Ayling, a general practitioner, was convicted of 12 counts of indecent assault against 10 patients (Ayling Inquiry 2004). Dr Kerr, psychiatrist, was convicted of one count of indecent assault against a patient (Kerr/Haslam Inquiry 2005). Sixty-seven other patients gave evidence to the Kerr/Haslam Inquiry (2005) alleging Dr Kerr committed sexual misconduct during the 23 years he was in practice at York. Dr Haslam, a psychiatrist who worked with Dr Kerr, was convicted of four counts of indecent assault. Dr Green, a general practitioner, was found guilty of nine counts of indecent assault against five patients, including one teenage patient. It subsequently emerged that there were 21 other allegations that Dr Green committed sexual misconduct against patients (Green Inquiry 2001). There were also two scandals where endemic abuse of patients by staff was alleged inside forensic psychiatric facilities (Ashworth Inquiry 1992, Rampton Inquiry 1980). In aggregate, these scandals create a highly troubling picture of rampant and serial criminal conduct by health professionals against patients on a level hitherto unimagined and unchecked by regulation.

Most of the other public inquiries in Britain involved substantiated allegations of inadequate clinical performance and/or conduct. For example, concerns were raised and substantiated about surgical procedures performed by two paediatric cardiac surgeons, Mr Wishart and Mr Dhasmana, who had unacceptably high mortality and/or morbidity rates over a 10-year period (Bristol Inquiry 2001). Dr Richard Neale, an obstetrician and gynaecologist, faced allegations in relation to his conduct and competence (Neale Inquiry 2004). Dr Ledward was another obstetrician and gynaecologist who faced allegations that he had provided consistently inadequate treatment over a 16-year period (Ledward Inquiry 2000). There were also narratives of misread slides and scans at hospitals across Britain resulting in the potential misdiagnosis of hundreds and perhaps thousands of women (Royal Devon Inquiry 1997). The Royal Liverpool Children's Hospital (RLCH) Inquiry (2001) determined that Dr van Velzen at the Royal Liverpool Children's Hospital (RLCH) had retained 2,080 children's hearts, other organs from more than 800 children, and 400 foetuses, some of which were used for research, but most of which were simply stored, all without the knowledge and consent of parents. The aggregate effect of these British scandals was to suggest that many doctors had conduct and/or competence issues and posed a risk to patients, risks it appeared existent regulatory structures were unable to manage.

Responses to scandal Some suggest that '*responses* to the risk event actually *define* the risk itself' (Poumadère and Mays 2003: 209). The highly public interaction between the risk(s) and resultant legal processes may heighten public perceptions of the seriousness of the risk (Wells 1995). Put another way, if a specific event results in a death or deaths, the choice of the mechanism(s) used to address the acts or omissions that contributed to that death sends a message to the public about how they should perceive the seriousness and significance of the act and what the level of risk associated with that act is. Characterizing many of the scandals examined within this chapter is the multiplicity of official responses to their emergence. For example, Dr Shipman's conduct saw a police investigation, General Medical Council (GMC) processes, and a public inquiry. The conduct of Drs Neale, Haslam and Kerr resulted in internal NHS inquiries, GMC processes, police investigations, and public inquiries. A multiplicity of internal and external inquiry processes may further reinforce the sense that there was a risk and the risk may continue and therefore need management.

The criminal law is the penultimate symbol of societal condemnation of an act or practice. It generally comprises offences that are *mala in se* ('evil in itself') and therefore incorporates moral denunciation of the act and punishment of the offender. It speaks volumes if criminal charges are laid against health professionals. That so many British cases saw a police investigation and/or successful criminal prosecution sent a message to the public about how they should perceive risk.

The use of a coronial inquest, seen in Winnipeg, has a different, more muted, symbolic effect. An inquest is, after all, a relatively routine inquiry into the cause of a particular individual's death and any factors that contributed to that death. On the other hand, the establishment of a commission of inquiry, seen in most scandals in Britain, and in two out of the three scandals in Canada, confirms that an event is out of the ordinary and of sufficient importance that ordinary mechanisms of inquiry/investigation, such as inquests, are not sufficient (Butler and Drakeford 2003). In general, an independent inquiry is commissioned because, justified or not, there is a perception that there has been some failure to act or there were deficiencies in the actions that were taken. Thus, to commission a public inquiry sends a signal to the public about the level of the risk associated with existing institutional structures. As such, an independent inquiry is both a response to a scandal and a confirmation of a scandal's wider importance (McDonald 2010a).

The incidence, scale, scope, and nature of the risks regarding health professional regulation apparent from the British public inquiries were different separately, and in aggregate, from those of the Canadian public inquiries. Taken together, the British public inquiries arguably provide grounds for a higher perception of the extent of the risks associated with the existent regulatory framework for health professionals. Conversely, in Canada, the incidence, scale, scope and nature of the risks associated with health professional regulation were smaller.

Trust

As discussed at the beginning of this chapter, trust in key actors influences public perceptions of the level of risk and ultimately of the acceptability of existent regulatory frameworks. Trust is multifaceted and is manifested by examinations of conduct.

Duration of the scandal The duration of scandals may be an important factor in reinforcing trust or creating mistrust. Public inquiries often raise many questions: Why did systems not identify problems? Why did systems and/or individuals not respond effectively to problems? Was there a cover-up? They often illustrate a series of missed opportunities, where systems and individuals could have intervened but, for whatever reason, did not, or where interventions were unsuccessful (Stanley and Manthorpe 2004). Generally, it seems, then, that the longer the duration of the event and the more missed opportunities to intervene that are exposed, the greater the perception that actors and systems failed, creating conditions for mistrust. It may contribute to a perception that actors responsible for regulation put professional or self-interest ahead of the public interest, and thus are not worthy of the trust vested in them.

Two of the three Canadian scandals examined by public inquiries were of a relatively limited duration – under one year – before some form of definitive intervention occurred. Many of the scandals examined by public inquiries in Britain were of long duration, and identified a number of missed opportunities for intervention. At the extreme, public inquiries in Britain established that Dr Shipman had been murdering his patients for a 27-year period; and Drs Ayling, Kerr, Haslam, and Green had been involved in sexualized conduct with patients, including sexual assaults, for respectively 27, 24, 23, and 13 years. Higher than normal rates of surgical complications from paediatric cardiac surgery in Bristol occurred for approximately 11 years; by contrast only 11 months was to pass at WHSC in Canada before paediatric cardiac surgery was suspended due to safety concerns. The relatively short duration of most Canadian scandals may illustrate more effective governance systems – systems worthy, then, of the trust reposed in them by the public. That so many problems could go on for so long in Britain indicates, among many other things, a failure in regulatory systems such that trust in those systems can be undermined.

The narrative of scandals The narratives of scandals are also important in influencing trust because they can graphically illustrate reasons why the public should mistrust certain actors in the health system. In Britain, the narrative of scandals, separately and in aggregate, was sufficient to create a rationale for the public to mistrust key actors, in particular the ability of the medical profession to self-regulate. Scandals may illustrate governance failures by individual health professionals (professional self-regulation) and/or by the regulators (government sanctioned self-regulation).

In relation to professional self-regulation, a significant divergence may be seen between the two jurisdictions. In Britain, the many public inquiries illustrated a deficit in the practices and mechanisms of professional self-regulation both in respect of what Paul terms 'the internal morality of the profession' (2000) and the profession's responsibilities as a regulator. In Canada, the public inquiries illustrated professions that, on the whole, were responsive and acted appropriately to concerns. A key facet of the internal morality of the professions, especially in terms of the social contract, is the will to act as self-regulatory actors – all individual members of the profession must be active in regulating their profession. The narratives of scandal illustrate much about how members of professions internalize their responsibilities and whether they maintain the trust of the public in their capacity to self-regulate.

In Canada, there were few illustrations of lapses in the internal morality of the profession, and those that did occur were markedly different from scandals in Britain. At the HSC, the Dubin Inquiry (1983) identified some systemic problems that contributed to a delay in determining that the deaths could have been murders, but the internal morality of the professions was never questioned. At the WHSC, from the beginning of Dr Odim's tenure nurses and anaesthetists expressed concern about the practices of the surgeon and the high death rates within the programme. Ultimately, the anaesthetists withdrew their services from the programme, citing high death rates. These actors continued to raise concerns until the programme was shut down, although the Inquest noted that many were reluctant to explicitly specify that they believed the surgeon was not competent (1998). Although the Inquest criticized the timeliness and effectiveness of the WHSC's response, it took only 11 months after Dr Odim had commenced practice for paediatric cardiac surgery to be halted. Contrast this with the Bristol case, where it took 11 years before the paediatric cardiac surgery programme was suspended. Professional self-regulation at WHSC was perhaps not optimal, but it certainly did not wholly fail either. In contrast in Ontario, the TSAPP (1991) commissioned research that found that many doctors who suspected colleagues of sexually abusing patients did not report this to the CPSO.

In Britain, the inquiries concluded there had been many missed opportunities for intervention. Some of these were due to the systemic issues within the NHS, some with the processes of regulatory actors, specifically the GMC, discussed below, but often they were because health professionals failed to recognize concerns, failed to act upon those concerns, or failed to act effectively. The retained organs scandals in Britain illustrated problems with the internal morality of medicine. Inquiries established that organ retention after autopsy, often without the knowledge or consent of families, was a standard professional practice (Bristol Inquiry 2000, RLCH 2001). This illustrated a disjunction in perspectives about retaining organs for medical research between parents and the public and the medical profession. For many medical professionals, the retention of body parts and tissues was essential for education and research (Bristol Inquiry 2000). Doctors noted that families were not informed in detail about post-mortem and organ retention practices out of a 'simple and understandable wish to spare them further anguish and distress at the time of bereavement' (Department of Health 2001). This paternalistic position, at odds with the development of the law of consent, was adversely commented upon in both the RLCH Inquiry (2001) and the interim report of the Bristol Inquiry (2000). In contrast, parents used such terms as 'grave-robbing', 'body-snatching', and 'desecrated' to describe what had happened to the bodies of their children (RLCH 2001). As McDonald (2010a: 242) noted 'the organ retention inquiries prompted calls for immediate law reform, given the profession had evidently proved incapable of self-regulating the practices of its members in accordance with public sentiment and robust medical ethics'. A representative from the advocacy group, Parents Who Interred their Child Twice, was quoted as stating: 'Guidelines are not enough. It has been proven that they have been ignored. Self-regulation by the medical profession has been shown to be inadequate. We must have changes in the law' (Department of Health 2001: 3). This statement is significant in that it emphasizes a marked distrust of the accepted regulatory paradigm of self-regulation and it points to the need for implementation of more control mechanisms to ensure good practice from the profession.

The Green Inquiry (2001) found that over the course of a 13-year period, 23 individuals or organizations had knowledge of concerns about Dr Green's sexualized professional conduct. The Bristol Inquiry (2001) too showed that many health professionals, including senior medical administrators, were aware of concerns about high death rates in some procedures, and yet little action was taken for a number of years, despite the valiant efforts of a whistle-blower.

The Shipman Inquiry determined that Dr Shipman had been murdering his patients with relative impunity since 1971, accelerating in numbers and incidence since 1992. As the court hearing the criminal proceedings noted, 'the fact that deaths occurred over a long period without detection is suggestive of a breakdown in those checks and controls which should operate to prevent such a tragedy' (cited in *R v Secretary of State for Health, ex parte Wagstaff and others* 2001). The Shipman Inquiry also noted that professional colleagues either did not identify or did not respond to concerns about a colleague's professional conduct or performance. Although eventually (after 27 years) a doctor did report concerns about Dr Shipman to the coroner, the Shipman Inquiry (2004) noted several instances where it believed health professionals had failed to do this. In one case Dr Shipman injected a patient with a large bolus dose (that is, direct injection) of diamorphine, a drug that was contra-indicated for her as she had asthma. Doctors and nursing staff at the hospital believed Dr Shipman had made a mistake in giving her the drug, in an excessive dose, and had administered it incorrectly, yet no one reported their concerns. One of the doctors proffered three excuses: that he did not know how to report concerns about a general practitioner within the NHS; he believed that the GMC required more information before it would take action; and he considered it unprofessional to disparage colleagues. The Shipman Inquiry (2004) also focused on a period in 1993 when, on 14 occasions, Dr Shipman prescribed 30 mg ampoules of morphine for patients. This dose was too large to treat heart attack victims and too small to treat cancer patients. Despite pharmacists' legal and ethical obligations to patients to raise concerns about doctors' prescriptions or prescribing practices, in these cases the pharmacist concerned did not identify problems with Dr Shipman's prescribing practices. Nor did she question the fact that he routinely picked up prescriptions of controlled drugs for his patients. The Shipman Inquiry concluded that the pharmacist's professional judgement had been compromised by her trust in Dr Shipman. A co-self-regulatory process reliant on the professionalism of doctors and pharmacists failed – and failed over a long period of time.

The Inquiry into Dr Ayling also illustrated a multiplicity of failings by health professions to effectively self-regulate. The neighbouring general practice kept records of patient transfers from Dr Ayling's practice, including the patients' reasons for transferring. Between 1985 and 1998, there were 44 patients on their records whose reasons for transferring, in the opinion of the Ayling Inquiry, warranted further examination or investigation (Ayling Inquiry 2004). Health professionals knew that Dr Ayling's conduct towards patients was sexualized yet took no action or took insufficient action. A witness before the Inquiry commented:

> … I felt that the procedures were more heavily weighted in favour of the doctor rather than the patient. This was rooted in the predominant culture of the time of 'doctor knows best', the presumption of the effectiveness of self-regulation and an inherent professional defensiveness when challenged (Ayling Inquiry 2004: 114).

The Kerr/Haslam Inquiry also noted concerns about professional self-regulation. Dr Kerr practised for 24 years before his retirement, and Dr Haslam for 23 years. The Kerr/Haslam Inquiry (2005: 5) noted:

> The story that has emerged is not one of a deliberate conspiracy by healthcare professionals knowingly acting to conceal sexual misdemeanours (or worse) of two of their consultant colleagues … But, for a complex of reasons … many nonetheless ignored warning bells or dismissed rumours and some chose to remain silent when they should have been raising their voices.

The British cases illustrated a medical profession that was reluctant to self-regulate even when the conduct or performance of colleagues placed patients at risk

– behaviour that created mistrust of the profession's willingness to self-regulate without compulsion and oversight by other actors. These other actors included regulatory bodies established by legislation with the purpose of regulating the health professions. An examination of the performance of regulatory bodies in Canada and Britain shows a divergence in the performance of these bodies with implications for the level of trust that could or should be given to these regulatory actors.

In two Canadian inquiries the performance of the regulatory actors was an issue, but these paled into insignificance compared to what the British inquiries illustrated about the GMC. In Winnipeg, the inquest report directed a mild rebuke towards the College of Physicians and Surgeons of Manitoba (CPSM). Despite the highly public nature of the concerns about the competence of Dr Odim, no investigation of his competence was initiated by the CPSM until a number of years had passed. Justice Sinclair (1998) recommended that the CPSM review its practices so it could initiate an investigation without a complaint.

There was significant public disquiet in 1990 about the perceived failures of the CPSO to impose appropriate penalties on doctors who acted in a sexually inappropriate manner towards their patients. In that year, the disciplinary committee of the CPSO exonerated a doctor of sexual abuse after he used a so-called psychotherapy technique called 'pelvic bonding' on a patient.[1] At that time, the CPSO was still applying a variant of the common-law Bolam test in its disciplinary procedures. Thus if 'a responsible body of medical men' gave evidence that a particular practice was appropriate, even if it was a body of one, the doctor would not be found to have fallen below the expected standard of practice. The CPSO deferred to the opinion of a few laypersons (because no doctors could be found to defend the use of this 'treatment') that the 'treatment' was reputable. The CPSO's decision, unsurprisingly, resulted in a 'public uproar' and gave rise to a perception that the CPSO placed the interests of the profession above the public's safety (Robinson 1999). The formation of the TSAPP by the CPSO was associational self-regulation in action – a self-regulatory body was compelled by public pressure to recognize a possible problem and take action to both confirm it and devise solutions. As a consequence of the TSAPP's report, the CPSO sought and gained amendments to the *Regulated Health Professions Act* (S.O. 1991 c. 8 as amended by S.O. 1993 c. 37) – the umbrella legislation that governs the regulation of health professions in Ontario. These changes instituted a zero-tolerance policy for sexual abuse, introduced mandatory reporting by doctors of suspected sexual abuse committed by other doctors, and imposed a mandatory penalty of deregistration for particularly serious cases.

The work of the TSAPP and associated publicity had an impact across the country, with other provinces, such as British Columbia, Alberta, Québec, Prince

1 Where a patient is required to place their face in their therapist's genital area ostensibly to remind the patient of the security experienced as a child while hugging his/her parent.

Edward Island, Saskatchewan, and New Brunswick, establishing committees to review the issue. In some provinces there were changes to the legal frameworks; in others, policy statements or guidelines were issued. Regulatory bodies in Canada arguably retained public trust and respect by acting quickly, even if this was under pressure and in the face of public scrutiny.[2] When self-regulatory actors act promptly on evidence of public disquiet, self-regulation is seen to work. By instituting these changes to the regulatory framework, along with education for the profession and the public, it can be argued that Canadian regulatory authorities created an environment where sexual abuse was less likely to be overlooked. They also rebuilt trust in the self-regulatory process by affirming that regulatory agencies would make substantive changes to the legal framework within which they, and their registrants, operated and to place the public interest ahead of the interests of the profession. In short, Canadian regulatory bodies demonstrated that they were accountable to the public – that they were responsive, responsible, and virtuous regulators.

This may have been reflective of a change in professional culture where Canadian health professions were less dominated by a so-called 'old guard' and more attuned to changing societal norms. Contrast this with the position in Britain, where professional bodies sent mixed messages about what conduct constituted sexual abuse, and where there was therefore a lack of clarity surrounding the issue at least until the late 1990s. Dr Haslam (later convicted of four counts of indecent assault against patients) wrote an open letter on behalf of the Society of Clinical Psychiatrists to the British Medical Journal in 1992 arguing that sexual relations with a patient are not always harmful (cited in Kennedy 2006). The GMC and the health professions in Britain were aware of developments in Canada and elsewhere, but took no action to address sexual misconduct. There was a perception that key actors within the GMC were resistant to changes to protect the public when those changes would be unpopular with the profession (McDonald 2010a). The GMC was considered by some commentators to be dominated by an entrenched group of the 'old guard', whereas in Canada the medical profession was seen as progressive, certainly in comparison (McDonald 2010a). For example, the Canadian Medical Association set up a Gender Issues Committee in 1990, indicating awareness by and within the profession of the importance of gender issues (Anonymous 1993). It also appears that attitudes of deference to doctors lingered in Britain until the late 1990s, whereas significant changes to the doctor-patient relationship were occurring in Canada from the late 1980s and early 1990s, as well as in the way in which the community regarded sexual abuse (McDonald 2010a).

This arguably more-effective, regulatory self-governance in Canada may also be seen in respect of two episodes connected with two prominent British scandals. Dr van Velzen, the infamous pathologist criticized in the RLCH Inquiry, moved to a position in a Canadian hospital in 1995. Dr van Velzen was fired from that

2 Rogers (2007) has critiqued the long-term effect of the changes on practices within the CPSO.

position in 1998, not because of concerns about organ retention, but because of concerns about clinical competency. Dr van Velzen was issued a written reprimand from the College of Physicians and Surgeons of Nova Scotia for falling below acceptable standards of clinical practice (RLCH Inquiry 2001).

Similarly, Dr Richard Neale fell afoul of Canadian regulatory processes before he commenced his career in Britain. In 1977, Dr Neale performed a high-risk surgery on a patient, against the advice of a senior colleague. The patient died. A subsequent investigation by the College of Physicians and Surgeons of British Columbia said that Dr Neale should withdraw from practice or undergo further training. Dr Neale chose the latter option and completed further training in Ontario. In 1980, another patient died after receiving an elective induction of pregnancy from Dr Neale. In 1982 the CPSO commenced an investigation into Dr Neale's management of this case. In late 1984, Dr Neale sought voluntary deregistration and returned to Britain. Despite this, the CPSO proceeded with its disciplinary proceedings and concluded that his lack of competence, and his subsequent alteration of medical records, amounted to serious professional misconduct. His name was erased from the medical register. The Canadian systems recognized that Dr Neale's conduct placed patients at risk, and disciplinary measures were instituted to ensure public safety.

In contrast to the responsive regulatory response in Canada, the GMC's operations attracted much ongoing criticism. Its many perceived failures resulted '... in calls for the GMC, a self-regulating body, to be scrapped' (Syal 2000). The scandals disclosed a raft of failures by the GMC, both prospective and reactive. Davies (2007: 237) notes that 'in simple terms, the GMC ... made no effort to look for it [misconduct]. They simply waited passively for complaints to be brought to them and ... even then they were often unwilling to act'. After the fact that Dr Neale had been deregistered in Canada in the 1980s became public, there were questions about why he was permitted to practise in Britain when the GMC was aware of his deregistration? The media concluded that this '... again calls into question the ability of the GMC to police the medical profession effectively' (Anonymous 2000). In Britain, the Kerr/Haslam scandal also created conditions for the mistrust of the GMC's commitment to policing the profession and acting in the public interest. From 1996, the GMC received multiple complaints from doctors, the York NHS Trust and patients about Dr Haslam's alleged sexual abuse of patients, but took little action. When Dr Haslam voluntarily withdrew his name from the register in 1999 the GMC's proceedings ceased. The Kerr/Haslam Inquiry (2005: 407) concluded that 'when patients and the NHS are speaking with the same voice, it is to be hoped and expected that the GMC will heed criticisms and put their house in order. If not, their house must be put in order for them'.

Criticisms also emerged about the GMCs slow response to very serious allegations of sexual misconduct against Dr Ayling and Dr Green. The Bristol Inquiry (2001: chap 25) did not directly consider the role of the GMC, but it noted:

> All professional bodies charged with responsibility for disciplining their members must constantly keep in mind that they do so on behalf of the wider public. The trust granted to them is that they act in the public interest to preserve and maintain the safety and quality of healthcare provided to patients. ... But the pace of change is not fast enough and the public's patience is running out (Bristol Inquiry 2011: 74).

The Shipman Inquiry (2004) concluded that the GMC as regulator of the medical profession had not in the past been successful in its primary purpose of protecting patients and 'disclosed a raft of flaws in professional governance' (Richards 2006).

The extent of the loss of trust in the GMC as a regulator was evident by some of the submissions received by the Shipman Inquiry (2004) that suggested that the GMC should no longer be permitted to regulate the profession. That lack of trust could not have been remedied by the Inquiry's somewhat tepid endorsement of the GMC as a regulator. While the inquiry did not recommend that the GMC lose its regulatory powers to govern the profession, it reached some fairly damning conclusions about the GMC – that it had failed to act in the interests of patients, instead acting in the interests of doctors, and that this failure was due to the culture within the GMC, a culture that had not radically changed since the GMC was formed in the mid 1800s. Smith (2005: 1) summed this up by saying that the GMC 'is reactive rather than proactive, prefers that doctors should be trusted rather than held accountable, places consensus before leadership, is driven by expediency and compromise, and in the last analysis will put fairness to doctors ahead of patient protection'. The Shipman Inquiry (2004) also concluded that, although the GMC may take action when the need to do so was pointed out to it, on the whole the GMC had not been able to identify and act upon its shortcomings.

What the narratives of scandals illustrate about government-sanctioned self-regulation is that its execution in Britain was profoundly inefficient, ineffective, ineffectual, and self-interested. In Canada, the few scandals illustrated that professional self-regulation was not a perfect instrument but that many health professionals subscribed to a form of internal morality. It also demonstrated that regulators were sufficiently responsive to public concerns, in tune with public sentiment, and concerned about public safety and professional integrity that self-regulation remained a viable artefact. The actions of regulators had generally maintained public trust.

Accountability

Rowe and Calnan (2006: 379) note that 'changes in trust are driven by the dialectical relationship between trust, power, governance and accountability, so that each affects the other in a continuing iterative process' (379). Accountability may be retrospective or prospective in nature. Much of the focus of attention on accountability is on mechanisms that retrospectively attempt to assign responsibility or, as Douglas (1992) would have it, blame after the fact. However, accountability also has an important prospective role. Mechanisms for accountability, by specifying the obligations of actors within that sphere, may orient everyone towards compliance and, optimally, towards a culture of improvement in practices and processes (Sharpe 2004). Although the relationship between the state and the health professions appears, as Tuohy (2003) notes, hedged around with formal accountability mechanisms, at its essence it has traditionally been based on collegiality and trust. If accountability mechanisms are perceived as ineffective or unresponsive, then there are grounds to call for a review of the existing regulatory framework so as to make actors more accountable. Sorrell (2007: 55) argues that 'it is not the *publication* of the standards but the *enforcement* of the standards that matters to whether trust is well placed'.

In the Ontario sexual abuse scandal, concerns expressed about the CPSO arose because the CPSO's ineffective policies and processes denied patients and the public accountability (TSAPP 1991). In taking immediate steps to institute a review of its practices, CPSO showed that it perceived that it was, at least to some extent, accountable to the public for its actions. The measures taken by other medical regulators across Canada to institute changes to policies and practices also demonstrated an acceptance that they were accountable to the public.

In Britain, much of the concern expressed about the GMC was because its processes failed to ensure that patients could hold doctors accountable, and there was no real mechanism through which the public could, in turn, hold the GMC accountable for that failing. An example of failures to ensure accountability could be seen in the Kerr/Haslam (2005) scandal. There the GMC appeared to put the interests of Dr Haslam – and perhaps also its own convenience in regard to the investigations and disciplinary proceedings it would have otherwise had to undertake – ahead of the interests of complainants when it allowed him to voluntarily withdraw his name from the register. Arguably, the GMC also sacrificed the public interest in failing to ensure that those given public privileges are also held accountable for any violations of public trust. Although it kept no records of its decision-making processes, the GMC explained its decision by suggesting that voluntary withdrawal was a speedy way to remove a doctor from practice – an action ultimately, in its view, in the public interest. While it may have been expedient, such action understandably undermined trust in the regulator as its practices appeared to undermine mechanisms to hold doctors accountable to individuals and to the public.

Control

Increased perception of risks, accompanied by a mistrust of health regulators and perceptions that current accountability mechanisms are ineffective, may result in increasing demands for greater control. Barber (1983: 132) describes this phenomenon as 'the increasing desire of the less powerful of all kinds to have a little more control over those whose greater power vitally affects them'.

This control is generally obtained through the revision of existing regulatory instruments and the use of other regulatory or quasi-regulatory instruments in parallel to the regulation of health professionals.

The combined effect of the events in Britain was to create public and political demands for greater control over the actions of health professionals and oversight of health professional regulators. The 1990s and 2000s saw the beginning of reform to the existing framework for the regulation of health professionals, the implementation of independent oversight mechanisms reviewing the operations of government-sanctioned self-regulatory actors and more broadly a strengthening of other forms of regulation that affect how health professionals practice (Allsop and Jones 2008, McDonald 2010a, Walshe 2009; see also Chapter 6 in this volume).

The converse – a largely unchanged perception of risk, sustained trust, and effective accountability mechanisms – may result in much more limited demands for greater regulatory control, as can be seen in the Canadian systems. In these systems, there have been some changes to the 'character and extent' of the powers devolved to the professions, in that greater formalized accountability requirements are required (McDonald 2010a), but many of these changes have been proactively driven by the regulators, not as a response to scandal.

Conclusion

Scandals may create perceptions about levels of risk to the public, whether trust in actors is or should be maintained, and whether actors are appropriately accountable. If the public perceives any inadequacies in the existing regulatory framework there may be demands for greater external control over the practices of the health professions. A close examination of the scandals in Canada and Britain that raise issues in respect of health professional practices allows analysis of the effect of scandals on public perceptions of the acceptability of the existing regulatory frameworks. It appears in Canada that a lesser manifestation of risks, coupled with responsive regulators and effective accountability mechanisms resulted in the maintenance of government-sanctioned self-regulation as the primary mode of regulation. In Britain the number and incidence of scandals, apparently ineffectual regulators, and limited opportunities for accountability resulted in public demands for changes to the existent structures for government-sanctioned self-regulation.

Greater external control, whether through amendments to the legislative framework to reduce the discretion of the regulators, through the creation of meta-regulatory frameworks to regulate the regulators, or through the employment or creation of parallel regulatory processes to be used in the health sector, almost inevitably results in a renegotiation of professional autonomy. A greater emphasis on what Paul (2000) terms external morality sees the standards and norms of the profession being determined, at least to some extent, by external actors, with the profession's self-regulatory autonomy to determine what Paul (2000) terms internal morality being, at least somewhat, constrained. The erosion of professional autonomy changes, to an extent to be determined, the nature of professionalism.

Whilst scandals and resultant inquiries play a role on in shaping public opinion, which to a greater or lesser extent also drives political opinion and shapes political priorities, considering these events is isolation from the broader context may be to overstate the influence of public inquiries. Governments also have their own broader regulatory goals or policy priorities related either to the health sector or to the public sector in general and this broader context may be as influential or even more pivotal in shaping regulatory change. Public inquiries may provide fuel to a fire that is already burning and make it easier to justify wide-ranging change that the government of the day had planned to or would have liked to institute.

Acknowledgements

This research was part of a doctoral research project supported by the Nova Scotia Health Research Foundation, the Canadian Institutes of Health Research and the Alberta Heritage Foundation for Medical Research.

References

Alaszewski, A. and Coxon, K. 2008. Restructuring health care: developing systems to identify risk and prevent harm, in *Health Risk and Vulnerability,* edited by A. Petersen and I. Wilkinson. London and New York: Routledge, 66–84.

[Allitt Inquiry] Department of Health. 1994. *The Allitt Inquiry: Independent Inquiry Relating to Deaths and Injuries on the Children's Ward at Grantham and Kesteven General Hospital*. London: HMSO.

Allsop, J. and Jones, K. 2008. Protecting patients: international trends in medical governance, in *Rethinking Professional Governance: International Directions in Healthcare*, edited by E. Kuhlmann and M. Saks. Bristol: Policy Press, 15–27.

Anonymous. 1993. Several issues dominate agenda of meeting of CMA's Gender Issues Committee. *Canadian Medical Association Journal*, 148(1), 69.

Anonymous. 2000. Surgeon 'mistreated women'. *BBC* News [Online, 12 June]. Available at: http://news.bbc.co.uk/2/hi/health/787709.stm [accessed: 15 July 2011].

[Ashworth Inquiry] Committee of Inquiry. 1992. *Report of the Committee of Inquiry into Complaints about Ashworth Hospital*. London: HMSO.

[Ayling Inquiry] Committee of Inquiry. 2004. *Committee of Inquiry to Investigate how the NHS* Handled Allegations about the Performance and Conduct of Clifford *Ayling*. London: HMSO.

Barber, B. 1983. *The Logic and Limits of Trust*. New Jersey: Rutgers University Press.

Beck, U., Giddens, A. and Lash, S., eds. 1994. *Reflexive Modernization: Politics, Tradition and Aesthetics in the Modern Social Order*. Cambridge: Polity Press.

Bradley, A.W. 2003. Commissions of inquiry and governmental accountability: recent British experience, in *Commissions of Inquiry: Praise or Reappraise?* edited by A. Manson and D. Mullan. Toronto: Irwin Law, 31–78.

Braithwaite, J. 2002. Rewards and Regulation. *Journal of Law and Society*, 29: 12–26.

[Bristol Inquiry] The Bristol Royal Infirmary Inquiry. 2000. *The Inquiry into the Management of Care of Children Receiving Complex Heart Surgery at The Bristol Royal Infirmary – Interim Report: Removal and Retention of Human Material*. Norwich: The Stationery Office Limited.

[Bristol Inquiry] The Bristol Royal Infirmary Inquiry. 2001. *The Report of the Public Inquiry into Children's Heart Surgery at the Bristol Royal Infirmary 1984–1995: Learning from Bristol*. Norwich: The Stationery Office Limited.

Butler, I. and Drakeford, M. 2003. *Social Policy, Social Welfare and Scandal: How British Public Policy is Made*. Basingstoke and New York: Palgrave Macmillan.

Carter, H. 2005. Former Alder Hey pathologist struck off. *The Guardian* [Online, 21 June]. Available at: http://www.guardian.co.uk/uk/2005/jun/21/alderhey.helencarter [accessed: 15 July 2011].

Committee of Inquiry. 1999. *Ashworth Special Hospital: Report of the Committee of Inquiry*. London: HMSO.

Davies, J. 2001. Painful inquiries: lessons from Winnipeg. *Canadian Medical Association Journal*, 65(11), 1503–4.

Davies, M. 2007. *Medical Self-Regulation: Crisis and Change*. Farnham: Ashgate.

Department of Health. 2000. *Report of a Census of Organs and Tissues Retained by Pathology Services in England*. London: Stationary Office.

Department of Health. 2001. Royal College of Pathologists Ref 101 in *Chief Medical Officer's Summit on Organ Retention: Evidence Documentation*, London: Department of Health.

Douglas, M. 1992. *Risk and Blame: Essays in Cultural Theory*. London: Routledge.

[Dubin Inquiry] Hospital for Sick Children Review Committee. 1983. *Report of the Hospital for Sick Children Review Committee*. Toronto: The Committee.

Gillies, A. 2003. *What Makes a Good Healthcare System? Comparisons, Values, Drivers*. Abingdon: Radcliffe Medical Press.

[Grange Inquiry] Royal Commission of Inquiry. 1984. *Report of the Royal Commission of Inquiry Into Certain Deaths at the Hospital for Sick Children and Related Matters*. Toronto: Ministry of the Attorney General.

[Green Inquiry] Commission for Health Improvement. 2001. *Investigation into Issues Arising from the case of Loughborough GP Peter Green*. London: Stationery Office.

Kagan, R. and Scholz, J. 1984. The 'Criminology of the Corporation' and regulatory enforcement strategies, in *Enforcing Regulation*, edited by K. Hawkins and J.M. Thomas. Boston: Kluwer-Nijhoff, 67–96.

Kennedy, P. 2006. Kerr/Haslam Inquiry into Sexual Abuse of Patients by Psychiatrists. *Psychiatric Bulletin*, 30, 204–6.

[Kerr/Haslam Inquiry] Committee of Inquiry. 2005. *The Kerr/Haslam Inquiry: Final Report*. London: HMSO.

[Krever Inquiry] Commission of Inquiry on the Blood System in Canada. 1997. *Final Report*. Ottawa: Public Works and Government Services Canada.

Larkin, G. 1988. Medical dominance in Britain: image and historical reality. *Milbank Quarterly*, 66(Suppl 2), 117–32.

[Ledward Inquiry] Committee of Inquiry. 2000. *An Inquiry into Quality & Practice Within the National Health Service Arising from the Actions of Rodney Ledward*. London: Department of Health.

Lofstedt, R.E. 2005. *Risk Management in Post-Trust Societies*. Basingstoke: Palgrave Macmillan.

Lupton, D. 1999. *Risk*. London and New York: Routledge.

Manson, A. and Mullan, D., eds. 2003. *Commissions of Inquiry: Praise or Reappraise?* Toronto: Irwin Law.

Masso, M. and Eager, K. 2009. Do public inquiries improve health care?, in *Patient Safety First: Responsive Regulation in Health Care*. Edited by J. Healy and P. Dugdale. Sydney: Allen & Unwin, 318–40.

McDonald, F. 2008. Working to death: the regulation of working hours in healthcare. *Law & Policy*, 30(1), 108–40.

McDonald, F. 2010a. *Patient Safety Law: Regulatory Change in Britain and Canada* JSD thesis. Halifax: Dalhousie University.

McDonald, F. 2010b. The regulation of health professionals, in *Health Law in Australia*, edited by B. White, et al. Sydney: Thomson, 509–55.

Mello, M., Kelly, C. and Brennan, T. 2005. Fostering rational regulation of patient safety. *Journal of Health Politics, Policy and Law*, 30(3), 375–426.

Moran, M. 2003. *The British Regulatory State: High Modernism and Hyper-Innovation*. Oxford: Oxford University Press.

National Health Service Act 1977.

[Neale Inquiry] Committee of Inquiry. 2004. *Committee of Inquiry to Investigate How the NHS* Handled Allegations about the Performance and Conduct of Richard Neale. London: HMSO.

Paul, C. 2000. The internal and external morality of medicine: lessons from New Zealand. *British Medical Journal*, 320(7233), 499–503.

Poumadère, M. and Mays, C. 2003. The dynamics of risk amplification and attenuation in context: a French case study, in *The Social Amplification of Risk*, edited by N. Pidgeon, et al. Cambridge: Cambridge University Press, 209–42.

Poortinga, W. and Pidgeon, N. 2005. Trust in risk regulation: cause or consequence of the acceptability of GM food? *Risk Analysis*, 25(1), 199–209.

R v Secretary of State for Health, ex parte Wagstaff and others [*Wagstaff*]; *R v. Secretary of State for Health, ex parte Associated Newspapers Ltd and others* [2001] 1 WLR 292, 56 BMLR 199.

[Rampton Inquiry] Committee of Inquiry. 1980. *Report of the Review of Rampton Hospital*. London: HMSO.

Regulated Health Professions Act S.O. 1991 c. 8 as amended by S.O. 1993 c. 37.

Report of the Committee of Inquiry into the Regulation of the Medical Profession. 1975. (Cmnd. 6018), London: HMSO.

Richards, T. 2006. Chairwoman of Shipman Inquiry protests at lack of action. *British Medical Journal*, 332(7550), 1111.

[RLCH Inquiry] The Royal Liverpool Children's Inquiry, 2001. *Report of the Royal Liverpool Children's Inquiry*. London: Stationery Office.

Robinson, C. 1999. Sexual misconduct: the Canadian experience, in *Physician Sexual Misconduct*, edited by J. Bloom et al. London and Washington D.C.: American Psychiatric Publications, 127–49.

Rogers, S. 2007. Zero tolerance some of the time: doctors, discipline and sexual abuse in Ontario. *Health Law Journal*, 15, 335–99.

Rowe, R. and Calnan, M. 2006. Trust relations in health care: developing a theoretical framework for the 'new' NHS. *Journal of Health, Organisation and Management*, 20(5), 376–96.

[Royal Devon Inquiry] Calman, K. and Department of Health. 1997. *Breast Cancer Services in Exeter and Quality Assurance for Breast Screening: Report to the Secretary of State*. London: HMSO.

Salter, L. 1989. Two contradictions in public inquiries. *Dalhousie Law Journal*, 12, 173.

Sharpe, V. 2004. Introduction: accountability and justice in patient safety reform, in *Accountability: Patient Safety and Policy Reform*, edited by V. Sharpe. Washington D.C.: Georgetown University Press, 1–26.

The Shipman Inquiry. 2002. *Death Disguised*. London: HMSO.

The Shipman Inquiry. 2004. *Safeguarding Patients: Lessons from the Past – Proposals for the Future*, London: HMSO.

[Sinclair Inquest] Sinclair, M. 1998. *The Report of the Manitoba Paediatric Cardiac Surgery Inquest: An Inquiry Into Twelve Deaths at the Winnipeg Health Sciences Centre in 1994*. Winnipeg: Provincial Court of Manitoba.

Smith, R. 2005. The GMC: expediency before principle. *British Medical Journal*, 330(7481), 1–2.

Sorrell, T. 2007. Safety, accountability, and 'choice' after the Bristol Inquiry, in *Informed Consent and Clinician Accountability: The Ethics of Report Cards on Surgeon Performance*, edited by S. Clarke and J. Oakley. Cambridge: Cambridge University Press, 52–64.

Stacey, M. 1989. The General Medical Council and professional accountability. *Public Policy and Administration*, 4(1), 12–27.

Stanley, N. and Manthorpe, J. 2004. *The Age of the Inquiry: Learning and Blaming in Health and Social Care*. London and New York: Routledge.

Syal, R. 2000. GMC 'hit squad' to speed rulings on misconduct. *Daily Telegraph* [Online, 16 July]. Available at: http://www.telegraph.co.uk/health/1348739/

GMC-hit-squad-to-speed-rulings-on-misconduct.html [accessed: 15 July 2011].

Tribunals of Inquiry (Evidence) Act 1921.

[TSAPP] Taskforce on the Sexual Abuse of Patients by Physicians. 1991. *The Final Report of the Taskforce on the Sexual Abuse of Patients by Physicians.* Toronto: College of Physicians and Surgeons of Ontario.

Tuohy, C. 2003. Agency, contract and governance: shifting shapes of accountability in the health care arena. *Journal of Health Politics, Policy and Law*, 28(2–3), 195–215.

Walshe, K. 2009. Regulating health professionals, in *Patient Safety First: Responsive Regulation in Health Care*, edited by J. Healy and P. Dugdale. Crows Nest, NSW: Allen & Unwin, 144–66.

Walshe, K. and Higgins, J. 2002. The use and impact of inquiries in the NHS. *British Medical Journal*, 325(7369), 895–900.

Wells, C. 1995. *Negotiating Tragedy: Law and Disasters.* London: Sweet & Maxwell.

[Wells Inquiry] Wells, W. 1997. *Review of Cervical Screening Services at Kent and Canterbury Hospitals NHS* Trust. London: NHS Executive.

Chapter 13

The Perfect Storm: a Case of Wrong-sided Surgery

Helen Turnbull

> The file is under my bed and every now and then I drag it out from under the bed to have a look. If I could say just one word it's guilt. It's a big black scar that never seems to go away. I don't know why I keep looking at the file. I should let it go. No one teaches you on how to come to terms with your own mistakes (Author's interview with surgeon, 20 May 2011).

Medical practitioners are trained to work diligently, operate precisely and, in the words of the Hippocratic Oath, to 'do no harm' (Edelstein 1943: 56). However, over the course of a practitioner's career, errors can and will occur. In many cases the errors will be small and may result only in 'near misses'. In some cases though, the errors will have catastrophic consequences for the patient and, as the quote illustrates, the practitioner.

Ensuring patient safety is one of the most significant challenges facing health care professionals and the health care system today. Although this challenge is met with a variety of approaches, many of these share a common basis – that of (professional) self-regulation. Many forms of self-regulation exist. These include the development of clinical standards, guidelines and checklists endorsed by professional organizations as well as self-regulation that focuses on the maintenance of personal professional standards by an individual practitioner working within not only the context of the health system but also the legal system.

The following chapter highlights the intersection of these forms of self-regulation using the example of an Australian surgeon who performed a mastectomy on the wrong breast. The case illustrates how major clinical errors can occur and discusses the role of professional standards and checklists in identifying errors and preventing harm. This case is a good example of the complexities of professionalism and highlights the importance of different forms of self-regulation operating in combination to avert such events.

The Surgeon's Story

In the Surgeon's Rooms

> I saw this elderly 78 year old lady with dementia, for the first time in my rooms. She spoke with a poor grasp of English and was accompanied by her daughter. As well as her dementia, she was physically disabled and walked with extreme difficulty. During the consultation she was excitable, screeching and fidgeting constantly. She was unable to provide a history and her daughter served as interpreter.
>
> It is my practice to arrange for patients with breast cancer to be seen on the last appointment of the day in order to allow for an uninterrupted session and to enable a full discussion of their condition.
>
> It is my rule to see patients with cancer on two separate consultations. During the first consultation, patients are generally distraught and apprehensive and may not fully absorb what is explained to them. At this first consultation I discuss the diagnosis, potential types of treatment and the risks involved and at the second consultation I answer the patient's questions, organize the consent forms and arrange the patient's hospitalization. Patients are asked to bring a relative or support person with them to both consultations.
>
> On the first visit I took a history and examined the patient. Her daughter provided most of the information. The physical examination was performed with some difficulty due to her uncooperative nature. I was of the opinion, both clinically and mammographically, that the left breast lump was highly suspicious of malignancy. I advised confirmation of malignancy by fine needle aspiration biopsy (FNAB) and if this was proven to be the case, I explained to the daughter that there were two surgical treatment options for her mother – conservative (lumpectomy) followed by radiotherapy or alternatively radical surgery (mastectomy and clearance of her axilla). We also discussed the pros and cons of both options, including the likelihood of complications.
>
> My patients are provided with a publication on breast cancer and its treatment and they are encouraged to read this between the first and second consultations. This manual provides them with more information to assist them in making an informed decision. Following the consultation, the patient's daughter was asked to telephone me for the result of the biopsy, and to inform me of her decision regarding the treatment options for her mother. Neither the consent form for surgery nor the request for admission form was signed at that first visit.
>
> A few days later, the patient's daughter rang and was told that the FNAB results had confirmed malignancy. She told me that she had opted for her mother to

have a mastectomy, as she did not feel that her mother would be able to tolerate the rigours of adjuvant radiotherapy over a six-week period.

Despite her age and her mental condition, the patient was otherwise healthy. I felt the decision was reasonable and proper. The daughter was asked to return to my office to complete a consent form and to arrange for her hospitalization.

Normally, a consent form is completed in the presence of the patient at the second consultation, the lesion checked and form signed. In view of the patient's physical and mental disabilities I did not think it appropriate to ask her to suffer more distress coming back to the rooms. Instead I suggested to the daughter, who held the power of attorney, that she collect the form from the surgery herself.

On the following morning, I had a busy session in my rooms during which I saw a total of 22 patients commencing at 8.10 am. As it happened, the daughter's husband arrived to collect the form mid morning. I completed both consent and admission request forms at the receptionist's desk in between patient appointments. On both forms I mistakenly wrote R total mastectomy. The son-in-law was asked to have the form signed by the daughter and to lodge it at the hospital where she was to be admitted.

The Operation

On the day of admission, poignantly, Friday 13, I had three operations listed: a Laparoscopic Cholecystectomy, Excision of Hydrocele and a Mastectomy and axillary dissection. The patient was the third on the operating list commencing at 11.20 am. Prior to starting, I was informed that my regular surgical registrar was not able to attend my operating list and that another registrar would stand in for him

My first contact with the patient on the day of the operation would have been in the anaesthetic bay (adjoining the operating theatre) where I would have gone through the notes and checked the consent form. I would normally greet and examine the patient and ask if there were any questions. In this particular instance the patient was neither able to communicate with me nor allow me to examine her without becoming quite distressed. She shrieked loudly on my approach. At the time, I had not realized that she had not been formally clerked in by a resident doctor when she presented to the hospital the night before, nor did her notes and X-rays arrive from the nursing home, nor was she accompanied by a relative or carer to the operating room. Furthermore, she had not attended the pre-admission clinic, as was routine, where a pre-operative assessment and identification of the procedure would have taken place.

> The patient had been draped and prepared for surgery prior to my entry into the operating theatre. The registrar was the primary surgeon and I was his assistant. The patient underwent a right total mastectomy and axillary dissection with no problems encountered during the operation. The procedure lasted one hour and twenty minutes.

Post-operative

> That afternoon I operated at another hospital beginning at about 2.00 pm with a list of eight patients. At the end of the day, about 6.00 pm, I received a telephone call from my registrar, who informed me of the development of a haematoma in the patient's right axilla, and indicated that the wrong side operation had been performed. I was stunned and distraught. In 28 years of practice nothing like this had ever happened to me. I hurriedly returned to the hospital where I arranged to meet the patient's daughter and son-in-law in the annex of the operating theatre. Also present was the registrar who carried out the surgery and at least two of the operating theatre nurses. I spent some considerable time speaking frankly to the patient's relatives describing what had occurred. I remember feeling incredibly stressed and devastated by the event. I sincerely apologized for my error and accepted full responsibility for what had happened.
>
> I explained that it was necessary for the patient to be returned to the operating theatre for evacuation of the haematoma in her right axilla. That being the case, I offered the patient's daughter my intention to operate on the correct breast at the same time, thus obviating the need for her to have a third operation later. I provided her with the opportunity to involve a different surgeon to carry out both procedures. I was overtaken with surprise when the daughter expressed continuing confidence in me and agreed and consented to have the second procedure performed by me. The operation proceeded uneventfully.
>
> The patient remained in my care for the remainder of her stay in hospital and continued to return to see me for her post-operative care. During these visits, she was always accompanied by her daughter, who remained very sympathetic and understanding of the situation. Moreover, I never felt any antagonism by her towards me in the ensuing months or since. On my part, I have taken steps to ensure this kind of incident never happens again but will remain mentally scarred for the rest of my life (Surgeon's commentary provided to author, May 2011).

This case is an illustration of a 'wrong-site mastectomy (the right breast was removed instead of the left breast) and whilst, superficially, the error might appear simple, further scrutiny uncovered a multitude of errors which led to the incorrect breast being removed. Some errors were small, while others, according to the Medical Tribunal of New South Wales, indicated a standard of practice significantly below that expected of a specialist breast surgeon (Health Care Complaints Commission v Dr A 2006). The surgeon was subsequently found guilty of unsatisfactory professional conduct and was reprimanded.

Wrong-site Surgery: How Common is the Problem?

From both a public and professional perspective, wrong-site (including wrong-sided) surgery is a highly unacceptable outcome which should never happen, hence its description as a 'never' event (Michaels and Makary 2007). Despite this, however, in the US the incidence has been estimated to be around 1 in every 112,000 (non-spinal) operations (Kwaan et al. 2006) and a review of the American Association of Orthopaedic Surgeons litigation data suggested that an orthopaedic surgeon had a 25 per cent chance of performing wrong-site surgery during his or her career (Canale 2005). In Australia, a national report on sentinel events in public hospitals for 2004–05 found that wrong patient or body-part procedures were the largest category, 53 out of 130 (41 per cent) sentinel events (Australian Institute of Health and Welfare and the Australian Commission on Safety and Quality in Health Care 2007: 14). However, because of the nature of reporting schemes, these estimates may not reliably reflect the true incidence of wrong- site surgery.

The Role of Checklists in Preventing or Minimizing Error

Standard checklists are designed for use in the operating room and represent one form of self-regulation to minimize errors and to promote safety. There is reasonable evidence that the use of such checklists may assist surgeons in preventing a range of errors in surgery (Stahel et al. 2010), including wrong site surgery. A wide range of checklists, including the US Universal Protocol (Joint Commission on Accreditation of Healthcare Organizations 2003) and the World Health Organization's (WHO) Surgical Safety Checklist (World Alliance for Patient Safety 2008) are in current use.

The WHO Surgical Safety Checklist creates divisions in the surgical timeline. These divisions isolate specific stages in one surgical process. There are three critical time phases marked by different events:

1. Before induction of anaesthesia (sign-in)
2. Before skin incision (time-out)
3. Before patient leaves the operating room (sign-out)

Sign-in Sign-in occurs before the induction of anaesthesia. During this phase the patient's identity, the site and type of procedure and consent are confirmed. During the sign-in process a check takes place to see that the site has been marked, that the anaesthesia safety check has been completed, and the pulse oximeter is functioning. There is also a check on the patient's allergies, airway/aspiration risks and potential blood loss.

Time-out Time-out occurs before the skin incision when all team members introduce themselves by name and role. The surgeon, anaesthetist and nurse then need to verbally confirm the identity of the patient, and the site and nature of the procedure. In time-out, the checklist is orientated towards anticipated critical events. The surgeon is expected to review the possible unexpected or critical steps, the operative duration of the surgery and anticipated blood loss. The anaesthesia team reviews any patient-specific concerns. The nursing team reviews the existing sterility and whether there are any equipment issues or other concerns. Two further steps are checking whether antibiotic prophylaxis has been given within the last 60 minutes and whether essential imaging has been displayed.

Sign-out Sign-out occurs before the patient leaves the operating room. The nurse verbally confirms with the team that the name of the procedure has been recorded and the counts are correct, the specimen has been labelled appropriately and whether there are any equipment problems to be addressed. The final element of sign-out is where the surgical team reviews any key concerns for recovery and management of the particular patient.

Studies suggest that wrong-site occurrences are primarily related to errors in judgement (85 per cent) and the lack of performing a 'time-out' (72 per cent) (Stahel et al. 2010). The Checklist has been adapted for use in various settings. For example, the England and Wales five-step version includes an additional briefing and debriefing (NHS 2009). The Australian and New Zealand three-step version of the Surgical Safety Checklist includes added checks for prosthesis/special equipment (sign-in) and thromboprophylaxis (time-out) (Gough 2010).

The common purpose of all surgical safety checklists is to preserve patient safety and to:

> help ensure that teams consistently follow a few critical safety steps and thereby minimise the most common and avoidable risks endangering the lives and wellbeing of surgical patients. The Checklist guides a verbal team-based interaction as a means of confirming that appropriate standards of care are ensured for every patient (WHO 2009: 100).

The effectiveness of this WHO checklist has been evaluated in a large before-after study of over 7,000 patients admitted for non-cardiac surgery to hospitals in eight different countries over a one-year period between 2007 and 2008. The study, reported in the *New England Journal of Medicine*, compared the 30-day complication rates of patients admitted before and after the introduction of the WHO. Checklist (Haynes et al. 2009). The findings showed that the implementation of the checklist was associated with significant reductions in post-operative complication and mortality rates, in the order of 36 per cent.

The case illustration of a wrong-sided mastectomy, discussed earlier in the chapter, occurred in the early 2000s. It preceded the existence of the WHO Checklist, and nothing comparable was otherwise widely available in Australia. Nor were there any formal guidelines, procedures and/or policies to address wrong patient and wrong site surgery at this time. However, an important question remains: would the use of a checklist, such as the Australian and New Zealand edition, in the same set of circumstances have prevented such an event?

Would the Use of a Surgical Safety Checklist Have Prevented the Wrong-site Mastectomy?

Figure 13.1 illustrates the application of the Australian and New Zealand edition of the Surgical Safety Checklist to this case.

Left Mastectomy Operation - Sign-in (before induction of anaesthesia)

Check

Patient's identity confirmed → ward nurse handover to theatre nurse

→ identification bracelet

Should the proposed operation stop at this stage?

A dementia patient and no relative / support person present

Check

Site - Right breast → consent form

Procedure - Right side mastectomy → hospital admission form

Consent - Right side mastectomy → hospital medical records

Should the proposed operation stop at this stage?

Surgeon did not have his room's medical records present

(not universal practice at that time)

Missing documents in hospital records – test / x-ray results

Figure 13.1 Application of a checklist to this case

In the event that the surgeon had adhered to the surgical checklist process, if available, would the error still have occurred? As can be seen in Figure 13.1, if the surgeon had followed the surgical safety checklist the error would have been identified before skin incision because the team would have been alerted to the absence of essential imaging to confirm the correct site.

The WHO implementation manual describes the process in relation to essential imaging. It explains that:

> During the 'Time-Out', the coordinator should ask the surgeon if imaging is needed for the case. If so, the coordinator should verbally confirm that the essential imaging is in the room and prominently displayed for use during the operation. Only then should the box be checked. If imaging is needed but not available, it should be obtained. The surgeon will decide whether to proceed without the imaging if it is necessary but unavailable. In such a circumstances, however, the box should be left unchecked (World Alliance for Patient Safety, 2008: 17).

The Royal Australasian College of Surgeons (2009) guidelines on ensuring correct side surgery emphasize the importance of having the appropriate images available before the team confirms the site and side of the proposed surgery. Additionally, the nature of the checklist would have drawn the surgeon's attention to the critical requirement of having independent verification of the correct side. At the very least, the checklist coordinator would have been required to question the availability of alternative independent verification of the proposed surgery site if X-ray films were not available.

Beyond Surgical Checklists: the Role of Individual-level and System-level Factors

According to the checklist criteria, error identification would have occurred when the surgical team checked that the essential imaging was on display in the theatre. However, on retrospective analysis of the case, the absence of a standard checklist accounted for only part of the adverse outcome. Two other factors are likely to have played an important role; the first is the sheer multiplicity of errors – both individual and systemic – and the second, rather counterintuitive, factor is the surgeon's kind and empathetic nature.

The vast majority of medical accidents occur as a result of both human (or individual) and systemic errors (Kohn, Corrigan and Donaldson 2000).

Human Error

Human error in health care can fall into three types – cognitive, skills-based and rule-based (Rasmussen 1990). Cognitive error relates to an incorrect interpretation,

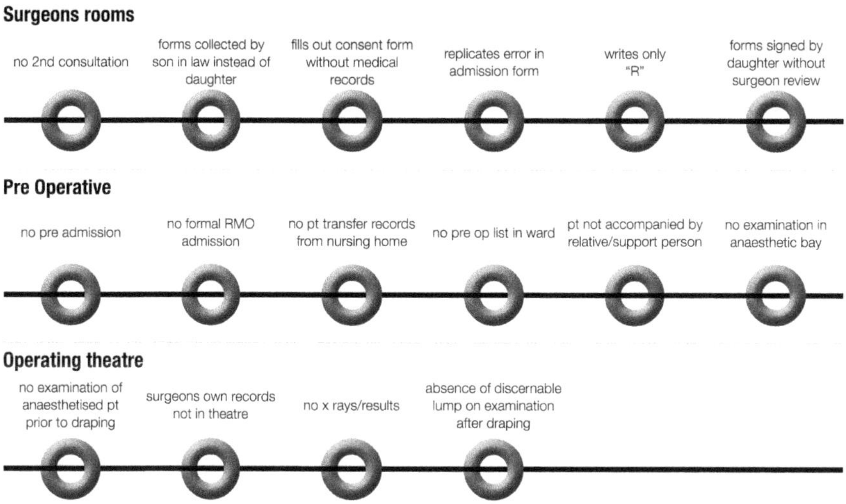

Figure 13.2 The multiplicity of errors

skills-based error arises from inadvertently omitting to do something and rules-based error comes from deliberately not doing something.

In this case, the surgeon writing 'R' instead of 'L' on the admission form and then replicating that error in the consent form was a 'cognitive' error. The subsequent errors committed by the surgeon were 'rule-based' errors. There were no examples of 'skill-based' errors in this case. Specific rule-based errors were:

1. The omission of a formal second consultation.
2. Substituting a discussion for the second consultation.
3. Completing the consent form/admission without referring to his own medical records.
4. Using only the initial 'R' rather than writing 'right' or 'left' in full.
5. Forms were signed by the family without the surgeon being present.
6. No examination in the anaesthetic bay.
7. Proceeding without independent verification in the theatre.

These errors were the result of the surgeon departing from his normal practice in an attempt to assist the patient with her specific needs and to expedite the surgical procedure.

Systemic Error

Medical errors can also be attributed to the systems in which individuals operate and as a result, there is increasing acknowledgement of the need to analyse accidents 'in context'. Systemic errors are more likely to occur in systems that are complex and tightly coupled, such as operating theatres. However, errors may result from the complete absence of a system or because the system is intrinsically weak. Intrinsic system failures pose the greatest threat to safety as they can lead to a deviation from acceptable standards or procedures which results in human error (Kohn, Corrigan and Donaldson 2000).

In this case, the system-level errors were significant. Fundamental hospital procedures were not followed. There was no pre-admission and no formal admission to hospital by a resident doctor. Nursing home records and X-rays were not available in the operating theatre. A pre-operation list was not written up in the ward and a final pre-operative handover check between the ward nurse and the operating theatre nurse did not occur. Furthermore, there was a public view that this hospital was poorly resourced and understaffed. These are all examples of intrinsic failures within a system which contributed to the ultimate human error – removal of the wrong breast (Health Care Complaints Commission v Dr A 2006).

The Tribunal accepted the surgeon's evidence that he wrongly assumed that the usual hospital protocols had been implemented (Health Care Complaints Commission v Dr A 2006).

Empathetic and Kind Surgeon: the Risk of Being too Nice

The surgeon who undertook the wrong site mastectomy was described by the Medical Tribunal as:

> universally held in very high regard by health professionals and patients alike. He is regarded as an extremely competent, responsible, and caring surgeon. His reputation, in the district in which he has practised both as a surgeon and an individual, has been described as 'second to none'. The qualities that have contributed to that reputation include a high level of surgical skill and professionalism, sound clinical judgment, high ethical and moral standards, dedication to his work and patients, and a high standard of mentoring and teaching of other health professionals (Health Care Complaints Commission v Dr A 2006: 44).

The Medical Tribunal noted that character evidence received from 'eminent medical practitioners, many of whom have known the [surgeon] for a very long period of time, can only be described as of the highest quality and overwhelmingly compelling and favourable' (Health Care Complaints Commission v Dr A 2006: 44).

The surgeon was not only regarded as a highly skilled professional by both his peers and his patients, but also as a fundamentally caring practitioner. In this case, the surgeon deviated from his normal practice to accommodate the frailties of this particular patient. The surgeon's normal practice was to have two consultations – one to explain the alternatives and the other to answer the patient's questions, organize the consent forms and arrange the patient's hospitalization. In view of the patient's physical and mental disabilities, and having ascertained that the patient's daughter had the appropriate power of attorney, the surgeon did not think it was appropriate to ask the patient to return to the rooms. He had noted that the patient found attendance at the first consultation very distressing. The surgeon departed from his standard procedure by suggesting that the daughter simply pick up the consent and admission forms. When the son-in-law arrived without notice to pick up the forms, the surgeon had not wanted to keep the son-in-law waiting or to interrupt the morning's busy schedule causing delay for his patients, so he omitted his usual procedure of sitting down with the son-in-law to go through the consent process. Kindness and compassion are desirable qualities in a practitioner and make an important contribution to medical professionalism and to improved quality care and patient safety. However, it was the surgeon's kindness, in this case, that contributed to his departure from standard professional practice and the human errors that led to the procedure being performed on the wrong breast. This highlights the need to balance compassion for patients with maintaining appropriate clinical standards, another element of medical professionalism.

Medical Professionalism

The Royal College of Physicians of London (2005: 8) (the College) has said that 'professionalism lies at the heart of being a good doctor'. Moreover, the College considers that 'medical professionalism signifies a set of values, behaviours, and relationships that underpins the trust the public has in doctors' (2005: 14). They further comment that the 'behaviours that strengthen trust are recognisable to everybody. They include courtesy, kindness, understanding, humility, honesty and confidentiality. These behaviours create an environment of safety around the patient. A deficit in these behaviours will undermine trust. They are essential to being a good doctor' (2005: 15).

The surgeon, in this case, displayed these desired behaviours. He demonstrated kindness and understanding in dealing with his patient who had dementia. He acted humbly and honestly in admitting his error and accepting full responsibility. The surgeon's behaviour following this adverse event clearly reinforced the trust relationship between the patient's family and himself, demonstrated by the family's preference for having the surgeon carry out the corrective surgery rather than someone else.

By exhibiting the qualities of a good medical professional, the surgeon was able to manage the adverse consequences and reassure the parties involved. He concentrated on ongoing patient safety and not on an individual surgical result. He did not turn inwards to protect himself but turned outwards to lead the team and, in doing so, demonstrated strong leadership.

Leadership is essential in the health workforce due to the ever-changing nature of medicine and society's health care expectations. 'The regulatory system must provide a framework that encourages doctors to maintain a strong sense of patient-related commitment throughout their careers, and to improve continuously what they do. That can only be achieved by engaging with doctors so that they take ownership of the values and principles of good practice' (Catto 2006: 3). Taking ownership of values and principles of good practice in order to maintain patient safety reflects true leadership.

The surgeon made immediate changes to his practice. He ensures that (1) the procedure/s recorded on the admission request and consent forms are verified by him from the outset; (2) the consent form is signed by the patient in his presence (or, if necessary, by the person responsible for the patient if the patient is not competent to give consent); and (3) prior to commencing surgery, there is independent verification of the correct procedure available in theatre (and beforehand) from a number of different sources, including his own clinical records, imaging and other investigations and transfer records (Health Care Complaints Commission v Dr A 2006: 46). He states: 'I am a little paranoid now. I check and re-check. I talk to the patient more often than I used to. I have cancelled the operation because the particular patient's X-rays were not there. I have delayed an operation because the medical records from my rooms were not in my briefcase' (Author's interview with surgeon, 20 May 2011).

In giving a character reference to the Tribunal, one of the surgeon's colleagues commented, 'There was no question that his experience in this case has made a difference to our routine procedures ... He showed leadership to bring about changes and has remained committed to them since'.

The surgeon's colleague makes an important point. Application of a checklist can prevent errors, but the profession has to own the checklist for it to be effective. Learning from mistakes, and improving practice as a result, reflects professionalism and good leadership.

Legal Regulation

Professionalism, however, is not enough. There is a vulnerability in human behaviour that leads us to make mistakes. In this surgeon's case, the Medical Tribunal had a clear view of the events, suggesting that 'wrong-side surgery.... is totally avoidable if proper care is taken' (Health Care Complaints Commission v Dr A 2006: 47).

The Medical Tribunal is a protective jurisdiction. Its primary focus is the protection of the public. In the exercise of its protective jurisdiction the Tribunal is 'required to take into account the maintenance of the standards of the medical profession, the maintenance of public confidence in the medical profession and the protection of the community' (Health Care Complaints Commission v Dr A 2006: 43).

The Tribunal's role is to send a clear message to both the community and the profession that medical practitioners are to be accountable in the practice of medicine. Medical practitioners practising standards significantly below what is reasonably expected by peers will not be tolerated. Legal regulation is there for the protection of the public.

Conclusion

The safety and quality of care provided to patients is at the heart of good medical practice. Checklists are tools that facilitate adherence to best practice, with some arguing that their true value lies in 'encouraging communication among teams and stimulating further reform to bring about a culture of safety to the very centre of patients' care' (Anon. 2008). However, checklists alone will not eliminate the possibility of error. In particular, they do not replace the medical practitioner's professional responsibility to the patient. In this case, the combination of systemic and human errors, and a departure from professional standards paradoxically resulting from professional concern to accommodate the patient's needs, created the 'perfect storm'. The result was an event which not only resulted in harm to the patient but has had major personal and professional ramifications for the surgeon involved. However, many lessons can be learnt from this case: in particular, that prevention of error and patient safety requires a combination of forms of self-regulation, including the development and application of checklists, maintenance of professional standards and the wide adoption of systems that support the delivery of quality care.

There are two challenges: to communicate these lessons throughout the health system and for medical educators, colleges and health organizations to instil in medical practitioners the importance of creating a culture of risk management. Perhaps the best means of achieving this is for medical practitioners (like the surgeon in this case) to speak out about their experiences; experiences which can be most harrowing. Indeed, as the surgeon explains:

> I often ask the question, who teaches you on how to cope with this type of event? I suppose it reflects on your upbringing, what you have learnt from your mentors and the nature of your personality. It is a bit like a grieving process. I really needed support in that grieving process so that I could understand what was happening to me (Author's interview with surgeon, 20 May 2011).

Acknowledgement

The author gratefully acknowledges the support of Avant Mutual Group Ltd and of the surgeon, without whose willingness to share his story this chapter would not have been possible.

References

Anon. 2008. WHO's patient-safety checklist for surgery (editorial). *Lancet* 372: 1.

Australian Institute of Health and Welfare and Australian Commission on Safety and Quality in Health Care. 2007. *Sentinel Events in Australian Public Hospitals 2004–05*. Cat. no. HSE. 51. Canberra.

Canale, S.T. 2005. Wrong-site surgery: a preventable complication. *Clin Orth Rel Res*, 443, 26–9.

Catto, G. 2006. Good doctors, safer patients. *General Medical Council News, 9, 3.*

Edelstein, L. 1943. *The Hippocratic Oath: Text, Translation and Interpretation.* Baltimore: Johns Hopkins Press.

Gough, I. 2010. A surgical safety checklist for Australia and New Zealand (editorial). *ANZ* J *Surg*, 80, 1–2.

Haynes, A.B., Weiser, T.G., Berry, W.R., Lipsitz, S.R., Breizat, A-H.S., Dellinger, E.P., Herbosa, T., Joseph, S., Kibatala, P.L., Lapitan, M.C.M., Merry, A.F., Moorthy, K., Reznick, R.K., Taylor, B. and Gawande, A.A. for the Safe Surgery Saves Lives Study Group. 2009. A surgical safety checklist to reduce morbidity and mortality in a global population. *N Engl J* Med, 360, 491–9.

Health Care Complaints Commission v Dr A [2006] NSWMT1.

Joint Commission on Accreditation of Healthcare Organizations (JCAHO). 2003. *Universal Protocol for Preventing Wrong Site, Wrong Procedure, Wrong Person Surgery*. US: JCAHO.

Kohn, L.T., Corrigan, J.M., Donaldson, M.S., eds. 2000. *To Err is Human: Building a Safer Health System*. Washington, DC: National Academy Press.

Kwaan, M.R., Studdert, D.M., Zinner, M.J., Gawande, A.A. 2006. Incidence, patterns, and prevention of wrong-site surgery. *Arch Surg.*, 141(4), 353–7.

Makary, M.A. 2010. The hazard of more reporting in quality measurement: invited critique on wrong-site and wrong-patient procedures in the universal protocol era. *Arch Surg*, 145, 984.

Michaels, R.M. and Makary, M.A. 2007. Achieving the National Quality Forum's 'never events': prevention of wrong site, wrong procedure, and wrong patient operations. *Ann Surg*, 245(4), 526–32.

Rasmussen, J. 1990. The role of error in organizing behaviour. *Ergonomics*, 33, 1185–99.

Royal Australasian College of Surgeons. 2009. *Royal Australasian College of Surgeons Guidelines for Ensuring Correct Patient, Correct Procedure, Correct Side and Correct Site Surgery*. Melbourne.

Royal College of Physicians 2005. *Doctors in Society: Medical Professionalism in a Changing World.* Report of a working party of the Royal College of Physicians of London. London: RCP.

Stahel, P.F., Sabel, A.L., Victoroff, M.S., Varnell, J., Lembitz, A., Boyle, D.J., Clarke, T.J., Smith, W.R. and Mehler, P.S. 2010. Wrong-site and wrong-patient procedures in the universal protocol era: analysis of a prospective database of physician self-reported occurrences. *Arch Surg*, 14, 978–84.

World Alliance for Patient Safety. 2008. *Implementation Manual Surgical Safety Checklist* (first edition). *Safe Surgery Saves Lives*. Geneva: World Health Organization.

World Health Organization. 2009. *WHO* Guidelines for Safe Surgery: Safe Surgery Saves Lives. Geneva. NLM classification: W0178.

Index

For Product Safety Concerns and Information please contact our EU representative GPSR@taylorandfrancis.com
Taylor & Francis Verlag GmbH, Kaufingerstraße 24, 80331 München, Germany

www.ingramcontent.com/pod-product-compliance
Ingram Content Group UK Ltd.
Pitfield, Milton Keynes, MK11 3LW, UK
UKHW022013180926
475701UK00003B/349
* 9 7 8 1 1 3 8 2 7 3 7 0 2 *